BTS

ICONS OF K-POP

This paperback edition first published in 2023
First published in Great Britain in 2018 by
Michael O'Mara Books Limited
9 Lion Yard
Tremadoc Road
London SW4 7NQ

A CIP catalogue record for this book is available from the British Library.

Papers used by Michael O'Mara Books Limited are natural, recyclable products made from wood grown in sustainable forests. The manufacturing processes conform to the environmental regulations of the country of origin.

ISBN: 978-1-78929-547-4 in paperback print format
ISBN: 978-1-78243-970-7 in ebook format

1 2 3 4 5 6 7 8 9 10

Designed and typeset by Claire Cater

Cover design by Natasha Le Coultre

Front cover photography: Adam Schultz / White House Photo / Alamy Live News
Back cover photography: Johnny Nunez / Getty Images for The Recording Academy
Design elements: Shutterstock

Printed and bound by CPI Group (UK) Ltd, Croydon, CR0 4YY

www.mombooks.com

ICONS OF K-POP

FULLY REVISED AND UPDATED

THE UNOFFICIAL BIOGRAPHY

ADRIAN BESLEY

Michael O'Mara Books Limited

CONTENTS

INTRODUCTION

BANGTAN WORLD

In the summer of 2022, BTS released a 3-disc, 48-track album called *Proof*. It contained a collection of songs that followed their nine year journey to success. The album topped charts around the world, from Germany to Japan and from Australia to Canada, and was their sixth number one album on the US Billboard charts. They were truly sitting on top of the world.

Their achievements are phenomenal. BTS hold over 20 world records; not just from record sales and streams, but from awards and concerts and across YouTube, Instagram, Twitter and TikTok. The first Korean artists to receive Grammy nominations, the fastest group since The Beatles to have six number one singles on the US Billboard chart – and they have performed sold-out shows across the world, spoken at the UN General Assembly and met with President Biden.

Just a few days after the release of *Proof*, BTS announced that they would be taking a break to concentrate on solo activities for the next few years. Their rise from no-hopers to the biggest group in the world had been achieved through the determination to endure hard times, the serendipity of seven incredible personalities coming together, an astonishing array of musical and dance skills and years of tireless, exhausting work.

BTS are one of many K-pop groups, but what's remarkable about them is that they're a K-pop group unlike any other in the history of Korean entertainment culture. BTS are unique because they succeeded without the backing of a major music company, the members of the group are heavily involved with the writing and production of their own songs and, most notably, they're not afraid to talk about their aspirations and their anxieties, and to be the voice of their generation.

This book charts the rise of BTS. From seven boys with seven dreams to one superstar group of young men who achieved a shared vision of global success, *BTS: Icons of K-Pop* demonstrates just how they reached such remarkable heights, all while singing and rapping in a language many people don't understand. The songs are an irresistible combination of catchy and emotional, and the dances are simply awe-inspiring. The book also looks at the background to BTS's music, details exactly what it's like to see BTS live and which big names BTS have met along the way. And then, of course, there are the haircuts and the clothes. Welcome to the world of Bangtan!

The book also looks at the band's incredible fan base. ARMY are one of the most – if not *the* most – informed, dedicated and unified fandoms in the world. Not only are they vociferous about their love for the group, but they translate lyrics and interviews, have helped BTS win awards and have created an online community that reflects the ideals of the group themselves. Their story is part of BTS's story, and neither would be the same without the other.

BTS are also known for their huge online presence, one of the highlights being their Bangtan Bombs. These short YouTube videos are full of shared jokes or offer brilliant insights into the life and times of BTS, and a number of these are recorded in these pages. At the end of the book you'll also find a glossary that explains some useful Korean words and K-pop terms.

The group's journey hasn't been easy, and each and every member has had to work incredibly hard. As teenage trainees from ordinary backgrounds they rehearsed until they were note- and step-perfect. That determination and dedication is still evident today and this book is also about their individual personalities, their friendships, their moments of self-doubt and their elation at their achievements.

This book's first edition told the story of BTS's incredible rise to global popularity. However, since it was first published, they have gone on to achieve so much more. It was revised in early 2020 and has now been fully updated for a second time to include their astonishing achievements over the last few years. The fascinating story of BTS is not over yet and they seem certain to continue setting new records and standards. Whatever the future holds, the story of how they became icons of not just K-pop but the world remains a fascinating one. I hope you enjoy reliving the details of that incredible journey.

ADRIAN BESLEY

ONE

BEGINNINGS

BTS have helped put South Korean pop music on the map. Thanks to the interest they have generated, many are now familiar with the slick choreography, the blend of rappers and singers, groups living and training together for years before debuting and the appearances on TV shows full of crazy challenges and fun games. These and other aspects make K-pop unique and special – and the story of BTS is entwined with its culture and traditions.

While they are now an international phenomenon, they were once a group of boys just happy to make music; recording their first song and performing on Korean television felt like the ultimate achievement. They had grown up with K-pop and understood the particular expectations, hardships and trials of the idol life. That they attempted this, succeeded against all the odds and pushed the boundaries of K-pop is just one aspect of the amazing nature of this group.

What we call K-pop began in 1992. It can be dated to the appearance of Seo Taiji and Boys on a TV talent show where they performed their single 'Nan Arayo' ('I Know'). They came last in the talent show, but their song, an innovative fusion of American and Korean pop, soon topped the country's charts – for seventeen weeks. Seo Taiji and Boys (who years later invited BTS to appear at their reunion concert) would inspire a host of new groups eager to create Korean music influenced by US rock, pop, R&B and especially 1990s hip-hop. Despite the US influence, Korean pop music would establish its own distinct characteristics. The conservative moral code of Korean society holds sway, ensuring that songs with references to sex, drugs and alcohol are banned from radio and television, and there is almost no tradition of questioning society or raising political issues in music. Artists are expected to remain charming and innocent at all times.

Then there is Korean television, which is watched by millions and vital to the success of K-pop acts. Music shows proliferate, with *Inkigayo*, *Show! Music Core*, *Music Bank*, *M Countdown*, *Show Champion* and *The Show Choice* ensuring there is a pop programme on TV most days of the week. The fact that the shows usually feature 'live' acts instead of music videos ensures that performance is a prized aspect of K-pop. On-point choreography, stage presence, stunning outfits and good looks are essential.

Acts will try to feature their 'debut' (first) or 'comeback' (new) songs on these shows, and each awards a weekly trophy based on various permutations of chart position, downloads and viewers' votes. These trophies are fiercely contested, with the ultimate achievement being a clean sweep of victories across all shows; BTS's 'DNA', 'Blood Sweat & Tears', 'Butter' and 'Dynamite' have all done this.

K-pop artists are also expected to take their place, as a group or individually, alongside comedians, actors and other celebrities on the nation's incredibly popular variety shows. These sometimes involve interviews and performances, but more often focus on amusing challenges that highlight artists' characters, skills and humour. BTS made a great early impression with appearances on *Knowing Bros* and *Weekly Idol*, and went on to have their own variety shows in *Rookie King*, *Run BTS!* and *BTS Gayo*. There are even regular televised Idol Games, a mini-Olympics in which K-pop artists compete against each other in various sports, BTS being particularly strong in the 4 × 400-metre relay.

Having established themselves, K-pop artists eagerly await the awards season that spans the New Year period. There are many ceremonies, but the most prestigious are the Golden Disc Awards, the Melon Music Awards

(MMAs), Mnet Asian Music Awards (MAMAs) and the Seoul Music Awards. These offer *bonsangs* (prizes) given to a number of high-achieving acts, but every artist ultimately craves a *daesang*, the top prize given for the artist of the year and, depending on the ceremony, sometimes for the song and album of the year, too. With such exposure, K-pop artists are expected to be singers and dancers, look great and show their personality. This takes a lot of hard work. Remember the pioneering Seo Taiji and Boys? When they split in 1996, Yang Hyun-suk, one of the 'Boys', set up YG Entertainment to create, produce and manage K-pop groups. Around the same time and with the same aims, SM Entertainment and JYP Entertainment were formed. The 'Big Three', as they came to be known, would end up dominating K-pop as they managed to produce a succession of successful artists and groups who are known as idols.

The process begins with the companies hosting fiercely competitive auditions and scouring talent shows in search of potential idols. The successful young artists, often in their early teens or even younger, are contracted as trainees and live in dormitories with other hopefuls. Together they face a gruelling boot camp of dancing, singing, exercise, diet regimes, and English and Japanese lessons (or Korean lessons if they came from another country), as well as tuition on how to perform on TV and conduct themselves in public. On top of all that, they still have to do their schoolwork!

The companies will put their trainees into groups or select them as solo artists, sometimes swapping them around or terminating their contracts if they don't make the grade or fit the particular requirements. K-pop groups often have more members than their Western equivalents, because they try to offer fans a complete package of skills. They have specialist rappers, vocalists, dancers and even 'visuals' – members included for their looks and stage presence. The company provides the name, image, choreography and songs, often with little input from the group.

Common to nearly every K-pop group is a leader, who is often the eldest, although that isn't the case with BTS's RM. When the group appears in public or collects awards, the leader acts as the spokesperson and is also the go-between, taking instructions from the company and passing them on to the other members. The group will also have a *maknae*, the name given to the youngest member. In BTS that's Jung Kook. The *maknae* is like the baby of the family, cute and adorable. Often extremely talented and beautiful, they are very much the pride of each group.

The launch of the act, usually on one of the weekly music shows, is known as their 'debut stage'. This is a massive moment for new groups. The company will have been preparing the ground for months, releasing teaser photographs of members, setting up social media accounts, posting preview performances and even starting a fan club. The passion of K-pop fans is an essential element in sustaining a successful act. Interaction with fans through social media and fan meets can quickly garner the most dedicated and loyal support. These fans are often given an official name by the group, have their own forums and create an incredible atmosphere at concerts. The group Twice named their fan club Once, Seventeen have Carat and, of course, BTS have ARMY.

K-pop fans have devised ingenious ways of interacting with their idols. Not content with simple screaming and wild applause (although that happens), they hold up light sticks in the group's colour, sometimes in coordinated waves, produce massive banners of support and perform fan chants over the intros and breaks or as a reply to choruses.

If a new group can negotiate a successful debut and build a fan base, they will have a chance of a 'comeback'. This doesn't mean they remain dormant for a time or even necessarily have a break; it's just the term used for the launch of a new single or album and its promotion on the weekly shows. Once again previewed and teased beforehand, the comeback often has a new 'concept': a subtle or even a major change in image or sound.

Once established, the K-pop act is perfectly placed to ride a wave – the Korean wave known as *hallyu*. Korean culture has been growing in global prominence over the past decade or two. From television drama to cosmetics and pop music, South Korean exports have become fashionable and popular from Japan to the USA. Psy's hit 'Gangnam Style' is an early example, but since BTS's astronomical success, the once-rare phenomenon of K-pop songs appearing on the US Billboard charts is now a regular sight.

To get this far requires a lot of investment, influence and know-how from the entertainment company. Success breeds success and the Big Three have come to dominate and even control the K-pop industry. Some groups had proved it is possible to get a small foothold in the business, but to make it as international idols? That's surely a dream too far. It would take someone with great experience, a little luck and a willingness to stretch K-pop's rules and traditions. Enter Bang Si-hyuk. Bang Si-hyuk was a successful composer and producer with Big Three company JYP. He had established a reputation as a hit-maker with groups such as g.o.d and Wonder Girls, earning his nickname 'Hitman'. In 2005, he left JYP to set up his own entertainment company, named Big Hit. He had some success with mixed-gender group 8Eight, and with 2AM (co-managed with JYP), and then in 2010 he came up with a plan to launch a rap act. This plan was the seed that would grow into a K-pop colossus: BTS. Kim Namjoon, soon to be named Rap Monster (later shortened to RM), had joined Big Hit as a solo rapper in 2010. He had been rapping in the underground hip-hop scene, a more rebellious arena than idol K-pop, where artists can act independently but perform to comparatively small crowds. As the idea of a rap act took root in the mind of Bang Si-hyuk, he moved RM into an embryonic group with other underground rappers, including Kidoh (who ended up in idol group Topp Dogg, now known as Xeno-T), Iron and Supreme Boi, which was further expanded with the arrival of Min Yoongi, aka Suga.

Around the end of 2011, Hitman Bang changed the direction of the group to pursue a less rap-focused, more mainstream sound with vocalists and dancers as well as rappers. Dance prodigy Jung Hoseok (J-Hope), who had joined the company the previous year, was one possible new member. Some of the original rappers left, unhappy with this new direction. Supreme Boi stayed at Big Hit; he would join the songwriting and production team, along with Slow Rabbit. Pdogg, a Big Hit producer (and still an important member of the BTS production team), was charged with putting this group together. He had around thirty trainees at Big Hit and he would watch, record and assess them, put them into teams and give them assignments. By early 2012, Seokjin (Jin), Jungkook and Taehyung (V) had auditioned and joined the Big Hit team. However, the line-up was still not fixed. Other trainees in the mix included Jeong In-seong and Park Seo-ham, who now line up with idol group KNK, and Boys Republic member Suwoong. For all these guys, undergoing the arduous trainee hardships and homesickness, the future was still uncertain: they might not be selected for the group and even then they might have a long wait before they debuted.

In the early summer of 2012, Jimin, the last member of the group to join, signed with Big Hit. BTS was finally taking shape, with four making up what K-pop fans call the 'rap line' (Kidoh would leave later in the year) and four on the 'vocal line'. This proposed idol group even had a name. Big Kids and Young Nation were among those considered, but Bangtan Sonyeondan, which translates to Bulletproof Boy Scouts, was the preferred option – at least by the Big Hit supremo, whose opinion counted most.

Bang had now assembled and selected his group. He had a leader in Rap Monster, the first of them to join Big Hit, who was intelligent and articulate, with the bonus of being fluent in English; a main dancer, J-Hope, who was a national dance competition-winner; and a *maknae* in Jung Kook, who could have signed with any of the Big Three. The others had shown they were prepared to put in the necessary hours of hard work and showed real promise. Most of all, they were a completely charming group of boys, who seemed to bring out the best in each other.

Bang had a vision for his new group. He had given them a name that showed they would fight the prejudices and hardships experienced by their generation. They would speak out for teens and twenty-somethings. In order for this to work, he loosened some of the shackles of K-pop. In a 2019 interview with *Time* magazine, he said, 'I promised them they would be able to pursue the music they wanted [including hip-hop]. Because it was hip-hop, they could express their thoughts and we wouldn't touch that [...] I kept that promise, and believe that had an impact.'

The task for Bangtan Sonyeondan (many would soon be calling them BTS) appeared enormous. Their company had very little money with which to back them and break the supremacy of SM's EXO and Girls' Generation or YG's 2NE1. Their songs were based around 1990s-style US rap that was losing popularity in Korea and the rebellious attitude of their songs was already raising eyebrows. The group had a mountain to climb before they even got started. As 2013 approached, they prepared to take their first steps up that mountain.

TWO

WE ARE BULLETPROOF

Do you remember where you were on 13 June 2013? It was a Thursday and you were probably tucked up in bed dreaming but, as you slept, on the other side of the world, in Seoul, South Korea, seven guys were hitting the stage on a TV music show. BTS was happening.

One day, 13 June will be an international holiday, but let's rewind a little … Out in Korea, intriguing teasers had been emerging for some time about a fresh new group. With his extensive experience in the K-pop business, Big Hit Entertainment CEO Bang Si-hyuk knew just how to build excitement for a new act. Back in 2012, Big Hit had launched a blog that announced the impending arrival of Bangtan Sonyeondan, introduced the band members and showcased their photos to those early followers. The word was out: Big Hit had an idol group in the making.

On 17 December 2012, a YouTube account was created as the first bit of BTS content was aired: a video of original member Rap Monster's version of Kanye West's 'Power'. This was soon followed by another RM rap, 'Let's Introduce BANGTAN ROOM'. These first two videos are still up on YouTube – watch the latter for a very cool cameo from Jin. And then came a Christmas present, as the Big Hit supremo, using his nickname Hitman Bang, introduced 'A Typical Trainee's Christmas'.

This half a song, with a self-edited video, was a teaser for his next Big Hit auditions. Once again, Rap Mon takes the mic, but this time Jin and Suga also take a turn.

On watching the video, it's apparent that these boys aren't playing the usual game. Here's a group who aren't afraid to answer back to their record company; a group who will reveal exactly how life is for the idol in training. While Jin sweetly covers the opening of the 1984 Wham! hit 'Last Christmas', the rap line complains of a lonely Christmas of endless practice and even asks how the group are supposed to write love songs when they are forbidden girlfriends.

On the same day the YouTube account had been created, BTS had entered the Twittersphere with the promise that the lead-up to their debut would be full of fun exploits. Who would have thought that in just a few years they would dominate Twitter! It was almost 2013 and BTS were out there – if you were a K-pop fan and were paying attention.

In January 2013 a new song found its way on to YouTube. A simply but artfully shot film employing a black background and extreme close-ups showed RM, Suga and Jin rapping. 'School of Tears' used the beats and flow of Kendrick Lamar's 'Swimming Pools', but the trio sang their own very personal lyrics. They talked of the dark side of school life: the bullying, and the fears of those who don't defend the bullied in case the same thing happens to them. Rap Mon is sporting the new dreadlocks he had put in for New Year (he took them out at the end of January) and he was reminded of this video in September 2016 when the others surprised him by playing it as part of his birthday celebrations.

Through the early months of the year, BTS members regularly sat down in the studio to record their diary entries. In these vlogs they were usually alone on screen, although we later learned that, of course, other group members were sometimes out of shot, pulling faces and teasing them. Frank and open, funny and sensitive, BTS showed they were ready to talk to their fans about anything – and that included their insecurities and their anxieties.

In one of his videos, RM tells us that he's upset to have been told that Big Hit doesn't believe he'll make it as a full-on solo rapper.

On 8 January, he complains that he's unable to come up with rap lines – he's exhausted, cold, wants to go home and isn't feeling inspired – but he knows the company expects him to come up with something. Jin, in his vlog, tells of being away from home and having to look after himself, and we can see the first signs of his interest in cooking. Then an adorably shy Jimin appears to do his first vlog and, having teased the others while they recorded theirs, can't think of anything to say.

In early February, Jung Kook made his first log entry. It's his middle-school graduation day and he says he knows he should be happy but, as the *maknae* (the youngest in the group, still only fifteen years old), he expresses just how homesick he feels – it's a heartbreaking entry. J-Hope is more upbeat as he states his pre-debut goals of making his rapping cooler and his dancing more professional, but throughout the early entries, often recorded late at night or in the early hours of the morning after a long day's work, the boys are very tired, quite shy and rather overwhelmed by the position they find themselves in.

The release of the joyous 'Graduation Song' video was therefore very welcome. Jung Kook, Jimin and J-Hope stepped forward to take their turn in the limelight. And boy did they shine – in and out of their school uniforms! Their snappy light-rap song covered Snoop Dogg, Wiz Khalifa and Bruno Mars' 'Young, Wild & Free'. The witty and upbeat replacement lyrics, written by J-Hope and producer Supreme Boi, celebrated the end of school and the freedoms of adult life. Even then, though, debut was on their mind – in one line, J-Hope even asks the boss if debuting is really meant to be this tough. This song, along with the vlogs, helped generate interest – it was vital that they had built a following before their first public appearance.

Lunar New Year is a big deal in Korea. In 2013 it fell on 10 February. Like Thanksgiving in the US, it's traditional to spend time with your family, and it couldn't have come at a better time for seven boys who had worked themselves into the ground. Having gone home, seen their families, slept and eaten well for a couple of days, they returned refreshed. Their debut was finally in sight and this came across in their vlogs: they were excited and all rededicated themselves to the BTS cause. Hard work was the mantra: we will work even harder to build a better Bangtan!

Throughout April and May, the exhausted Bangtan Boys appeared, discussing final choreography practices for their debut, recording tracks for their single album and filming their music video. It was getting closer! In his 14 May vlog, RM marked the shooting of his first ever music video as the end of their long trainee life. Then, a few days later, they all appeared together for the first time in a group vlog, talking about their video filming and reading out support messages from fans, adding that, although it was still nearly a month away, this would be the last vlog before their debut.

Okay. They all appeared together, but attentive ARMY will know there was one key member missing. Taehyung, known as V, was notable for his absence throughout the vlogs and videos. V had been part of BTS for over two years, training, singing and dancing with the others, but he was never announced as a member; he wasn't able to post a vlog and the others couldn't mention him. Poor V! He was the secret weapon and, in a clever play by Big Hit, knowledge of his existence was held back for maximum effect.

Debut is make or break time for K-pop groups and the pressure was building. For some this is the satisfying culmination of years of unrelenting hard work; for others it is simply incredibly nerve-racking, but as the big day approached it was the group's spirit and togetherness that saw them through.

On 21 May 2013, a countdown-to-debut clock was revealed on the website and the debut trailer released. It was a forty-five-second, black-and-white montage of the members' names and a series of hard-hitting slogans that formed into a firing revolver. Then, on 2 June, preview photos on the BTS page of the Big Hit website and on Facebook gave us the first pictures of Taehyung, looking suitably moody with shaggy, cropped blond hair. Big Hit's plan seemed to have worked and, by debut day, less than two weeks later, V already had five fan clubs of his own!

At the bottom of the home page, next to the countdown clock, was a simple tease asking: who's next? The answer came the very next day in the shape of Jin, Jimin and Jung Kook – which really got K-popsters chattering. Finally, a day after that, came the rap line. Fans were already familiar with RM, J-Hope and Suga through the tracks, videos and vlogs, but this was showtime – and they looked good!

All the pictures showed the members in their hip-hop and bad-boy gear: all leathers and logos, skate wear and sports clothes. J-Hope was in a studded mask; RM had shades, a medallion and dollar-sign cane; Suga wielded a skateboard; Jung Kook wore a hockey mask and gold hand-bone jewellery; Jimin was cute in his basketball kit; Jin looked every bit the b-boy in his backwards baseball cap and baggy shorts; and V posed in his black leather like the coolest kid in school. It was a look we would see again.

The training had finished for now. The teasers had been shown. The countdown was over. It was time. BTS, meet the world ... world, meet BTS. Their debut showcase took place on 12 June at the Ilchi Art Hall in Cheongdam-dong, in the Gangnam area of the city. But it was the following day that counted, when the band appeared live on stage for the first time on the TV shows *M Countdown* and *Music Bank*.

You can still watch the BTS debut-day video on YouTube and see seven unbelievably young Bangtan Boys about to face the public in a live premiere showcase. They are understandably nervous, hiding their anxieties by practising their routines one last time, teasing each other or just sitting quietly, each one a demonstration of just how dedicated these boys were. As V says, 'We only have one chance!'

Of course, once they were up on stage, throwing themselves into 'No More Dream', they were sharp and they were slick. Afterwards, ever the perfectionist, Jin was in tears after the microphone pack had made his trousers slip down, but his bandmates consoled him. He had no time to dwell on it as they were soon due back on stage for their other promoted song, 'We Are Bulletproof Pt. 2'.

On the YouTube clip, you can see by their faces when they had finished the day's performances that they'd given their all, and they knew they'd nailed it. Their energy, rap style and dance moves, especially Jung Kook's hat flick and Jimin's abs flash, had attracted attention. Like most debuting groups, BTS had set up a forum known as a 'fan café' – this had already swollen to 55,000 members.

For three years they had dreamed of the moment when they would take to the stage, so it was no wonder they had felt so nervous. They all said that when they finished and heard the cheers they were close to tears – V even confessed he actually cried. They were proud but admitted to having made mistakes and RM noted how heavy his legs felt on stage compared to the practice sessions, but they also knew that they had already learned so much over this brief debut period.

In the meantime, their first music video, 'No More Dream', had been released the day before debut. The hip-hop idol theme and attitude matched their teaser pictures and debut performances, and the scenario was one of upheaval and rebellion, where the group, sporting plenty of black and white, drive – and crash – the school bus, BMX riders roam the streets and a refashioned classroom has a skate ramp and walls covered in BTS graffiti.

BANGTAN BOMB

VJ
THE FIRST BANGTAN BOMB

On 19 June 2013, BANGTANTV posted a thirty-second video on YouTube. It showed Jung Kook filming Jimin, and in the corner was a small logo: a cartoon BTS bomb. This was the first of many bombs – bite-sized videos of behind-the-scenes footage, challenges or just the boys acting cute or messing around. They last for anything from twenty seconds to over ten minutes and give fans a fascinating insight into BTS away from the stage.

The choreography is very hip-hop, with a lot of low crouches, hip thrusts and lightning-fast pointing, and, helped by sharp editing, it keeps all the energy of the live performance. Those who saw the debut shows would have recognized Jung Kook carrying Jimin as he runs horizontally across the backs of the others and, of course, the Jimin abs-flashes that sent the live audience into meltdown.

This track would feature on *2 Cool 4 Skool*, the first BTS single album, which was released on the eve of their debut, 12 June 2013, and came in a stylish black-and-gold package. An attached photobook featured some glossy images similar to those revealed in the teasers, lyrics, a postcard and a flyer advertising the next Big Hit auditions. This 'single album' with seven tracks would be the first of a trilogy of releases that explored themes of not being ground down by the school system, having pride in yourself and facing the trials of being young.

In this album, RM declares the group's intention to talk to teens and twenty-somethings. This was what would set them apart from most other K-pop groups. BTS would be relevant and show they shared the aspirations and anxieties of their generation.

The album proper starts as 'We Are Bulletproof Pt. 2' sets out the band's stall as a group who could rap better than other idol bands and were as authentic as any Korean underground rapper. Next comes 'Skit: Circle Room Talk' (a skit is essentially members chatting – a feature of US hip-hop albums from De La Soul to Eminem), which gave the boys a chance to discuss their ideas and the themes of the album before diving straight into 'No More Dream', their debut single and the key track on the record. If the BTS mission statement was to speak to and for young people, then this went straight to the heart of the matter – it is assertive, heavy on the attitude and catchy as hell.

RM's opening lyrics announced the group to the world and from the resonant twang of the double bass, through Suga's sarcastic lines about the big house, big cars and big rings he wants, to the la-la-la singalong (the first of many), the sound was big, the beat kept pumping and the melodic hooks kept coming. Meanwhile, the rap line took the spotlight, working around the chant, which asks the listener about their dream. The lyrics spoke passionately of a frustration and anger that young people don't dream and are unable to break out from the mundane lives plotted for them by their parents and society.

After the brief 'Interlude' (a tune RM liked so much he used it in 'Monterlude' on his first mixtape), we are into 'Like' – and, what do you know, it's a pop song! Okay, there was still some rapping, but Jung Kook and Jin had put down some sweet melodies in a song about seeing photos of an ex-girlfriend on social media. The album rounded off with the light-hearted outro 'Circle Room Cypher' (a cypher being a hip-hop term for a freestyle rap session). However, those who bought the physical CD were treated to two extra tracks: 'On the Start Line', delivered by RM, and 'Path' (also known as 'Road'), featuring the whole crew. Both of these recalled the hardships of their trainee years, what they would be doing if they were not Bangtan and the strength they had gained from being together.

The debut period continued through the rest of June and July as the boys promoted their album via radio and TV broadcasts and through fan meets. There was one further notable milestone, though. On 9 July, on the BTS fan café, they announced a name for their fan club. From this time on, their fans would be called ARMY, an acronym for 'Adorable Representative MC for Youth'. They explained that an army needs its bulletproof armour, so the boys and their fans would always be bound together. BTS fans took to the name immediately – they had a cause to believe in and were now on the march.

After nearly fifty frenetic days, BTS's debut was finally over. They had not been an immediate sensation – lots of people had dismissed them as just another hip-hop group, having taken against their rebellious image and anti-conservative lyrics, or had slated their chances of success because they weren't a Big Three group. But they had established a group ethic, an image, a self-belief and, most importantly, a fan base that already stretched from Korea and elsewhere in Asia as far as the Americas, Europe and the Middle East. And there was more to come.

After their goodbye stage, which marks the end of a debut, heartfelt handwritten notes from all seven members of BTS appeared on their fan café. The band revealed how they felt when they set off on a journey without knowing the route or the destination. They described their debut as a whirlwind experience and said that although their training prepared them well for that experience, they knew they had so much more to offer. They were all overcome with gratitude for the support of the fans they had met in person and the fans whose messages they had read. Above everything, they said, this was what gave them the strength to enter the next stage of their career with confidence and optimism.

THREE

ROOKIE KINGS

They had debuted. The moment they had been dreaming of for so long had come and gone, but for the Bangtan Boys there was no let-up. There were fan meets, radio shows and dance practices to attend – and new tracks to record. It was a rollercoaster ride and they were hurtling along at full speed. Everybody needed to hold tight.

Within a few weeks of their goodbye stage, with *2 Cool 4 Skool* having reached number five in the South Korean Gaon album chart, BTS were recording new tracks. The Big Hit Entertainment countdown clock made its return on their website, along with a new trailer, released on 27 August 2013. In the trailer, BTS-branded trainers, a ring, mic and beatbox fall in slow motion as RM takes up the story where 'No More Dream' left off. Over a solemn backing track, he spells it out in English: it's time to live your own life, make your own decisions, now, before it's too late. As the beat kicks in, RM raps in his native tongue until the falling BTS items crash through glass.

A week later, there was more. A concept trailer saw the group, dressed in an all-black uniform of short-sleeved shirts, shorts and long BTS socks, surrounded and assassinated, one by one, by armed police. The idols lie fallen, until RM, who has sneakily escaped, returns to rouse them. Galvanized, they rip off their black shirts to reveal white, sleeveless tees. The dancing is fast and intense. They had clearly taken things up a level since the debut, with unbelievable popping and flawless synchronicity. It's a dance that's still ranked among their best ever.

Through their vlogs and tweets, the boys revealed not only the return of pre-debut nerves that had been lost in the adrenaline rush of their first performance, but also an expectation that they would all up their game. Could they? The answer is 'N.O', a track released on 10 September 2013. The video for 'N.O' finds them in a chilling, dystopian school, where uniformed, drugged and soulless students take lessons under armed guard. As Jung Kook leads a schoolroom rebellion, the video cuts to a bright, white studio and an outdoor scene with giant stone hands, where the dance action takes over. The choreography dials down the relentless energy and focuses on the emotional story, although there are still some stunning moves, not least when Jimin, so often teased for being the shortest, plays the hero. Jumping down from the back of the set, he executes an acrobatic mid-air spin and kick that lays low all of the oppressive police goons with one blow.

Most of all, though, the video celebrated the look of the group – collectively and individually. The new concept found them ditching the black for an angelic white, although, with V's distinctive faith chain, Suga's bandana and RM still in his shades, there was still plenty of bling and hip-hop style. The boys' hair had also changed: most noticeable was Jimin's new, smooth-as-silk coconut bowl, Suga had gone chocolate brown and curly, and V's hair was lighter with a purple tint.

Throughout September they were back promoting the new singles 'N.O' and 'Attack on Bangtan' (also known as 'The Rise of Bangtan'). The K-pop world is ridiculously competitive and BTS needed to work hard to build a following. They did this through hosting fan meetings in Korea, posting on social media, through the Bangtan Bombs on YouTube, and most importantly by appearing on the weekly television music shows where record sales, streams and viewers' votes all contributed to a show winner.

Though they were not yet in a position to compete with the massively popular heavyweights such as G-Dragon, BTS were getting noticed. On the *Music Bank* TV show, one performance gave fans an unexpected treat.

As the boys tear their uniforms off to reveal their white tees, RM and Jimin, giving their all, accidentally rip half their T-shirts off as well. You can still relive the excitement – search YouTube for 'Rap Mon and Jimin ripping their shirts'.

The new ten-track album – the second of what would become their school trilogy – titled *O!RUL8,2?* (meaning, of course, 'Oh! Are you late, too?') was released on 11 September 2013. The CD package included a poster and a booklet featuring photoshoots from the new concept as well as two random photocards and a cartoon biography of the BTS members. RM's first trailer turned out to be the album intro and led logically into 'N.O', the promoted single. The lyrics, as the video suggested, once again zeroed in on school. 'N.O' (which also stands for 'No Offence') is a refusal to conform to parents' educational expectations. It expands on the themes of 'No More Dream' by addressing the intense pressures and relentless routines imposed upon students, especially in South Korea. Can you be happy just being a 'studying machine'? The message was that there are other options open to you: don't leave the pursuit of your dreams until it is too late.

The music behind the message begins with a stirring orchestral sound, before letting the beat take over and the rapping and singing come to the fore. The lines are shared out pretty evenly among the group, with Jung Kook, growing into his 'Golden Maknae' nickname, even taking a rap turn.

Next up is 'We On'. This is a real gem with some very cool (and fast) understated rhymes in the rap line, contrasting with the sweetest of melodies from Jung Kook and Jimin. The song is a proud answer to the haters who dissed BTS but sought their attention now they'd debuted. The skit 'R U Happy Now?' that follows is a short chat where the band talk of how tired they are, but also how content they are with where they are.

'If I Ruled the World' takes the rap line into their wildest dreams of fame, success and confidence (dreams that have arguably now come true!) with a catchy chorus, enhanced by one of the first examples of V's delicious, velvet-voiced melodies. This track is followed by the contrasting 'Coffee', a teenage break-up song, in which the sweet taste of the caramel macchiato they shared contrasts with the bitterness of the Americano now drunk alone. Clever, eh?

'Cypher Pt. 1' is their first serious rap-off (after the previous album's jokey attempt). It's fun, assertive and certainly proves they can bust some rhymes, skills which they continue to put to good use in 'Attack on Bangtan', (a name referencing the popular Japanese manga series *Attack on Titan*). A live favourite, so upbeat and full of energy, it's another BTS 'la-la-la' song.

'Paldogangsan', one of the first songs recorded by an early BTS back in August 2011, is also known as 'Satoori Rap'. *Satoori* are Korean dialects and this is a rap battle between the different dialects of Suga, from Daegu, and J-Hope, from Gwangju, with RM intervening in a standard Seoul dialect. On stage, the group had fun pitching a team from the East (Gyeongsan) against one from the West (Jeolla and Seoul).

After all that rap, it's only fair that the vocal line has the final say. 'Outro: Luv in Skool' might only last a minute and a half, but it is beautifully sung and its high number of views on YouTube has surely been boosted by those repeatedly listening to the song's (and album's) final words: Jung Kook is asking you for a date!

What BTS really needed at this point was to show potential fans what they were about. The easiest way would be through a variety show. The Korean public love their television variety shows. Watching celebrities play games, attempt dances or try to complete absurd challenges is a national pastime. Of course, being a rookie group, it wasn't easy for BTS to get invited on such a show – so why not make a variety show themselves? South Korean broadcaster SBS's MTV channel had already had hits with the group Block B on *Match Up* and VIXX on *Plan V Diary*, but BTS were about to take the format and run with it.

Rookie King: Channel Bangtan, which appeared on South Korean music channel SBS MTV, was a parody of all the most successful Korean shows and it was very, very funny. Over eight fifty-minute episodes, BTS won the hearts of thousands more fans with their humour, easy-going nature and group friendship. The episodes are well worth watching online: from the first sketch, in which the boys dress in blue *hanbok* (traditional tunics) through to their version of *X-Man* (another popular South Korean game show), where one member is secretly selected to lose games (go on, guess who!), there's endless comedy and some great insight into the chemistry of BTS.

In between, there were some moments that reached mythic status. Episode one featured a hidden camera prank which saw each of the boys secretly filmed as a pretty young girl (an actress) entered their elevator in tears and pressed the button to every floor. Their reactions, from J-Hope's embarrassment at being caught dancing to Jin's touching concern, are all fascinating. And then there's the 'Open Your Heart' segment, which showed the boys screaming their most bitter complaints and confessions from a rooftop platform – including Suga revealing he stole Jung Kook's underwear!

O!RUL8,2? went to number four in the Korean charts and 'N.O' was a modest success, reaching number ninety-two, which is an improvement on 'No More Dream', but these were still challenging times for the group. Yes they had debuted well and had had some television exposure, but the K-pop world is incredibly competitive and many were critical of their rap style, their rebellious lyrics and a hip-hop sound that some thought dated. Furthermore, to stay at the top required major financial backing, which Big Hit were struggling to find. The pressure to keep on going was huge.

Many other talented K-pop groups hadn't been able to live with this kind of pressure and it's no surprise that around this time there were rumours that BTS were considering disbanding. Imagine all of the amazing stuff we would have missed out on! It was ARMY that prevented them quitting. Their messages of love and support, and the enthusiastic attendance at fan meets, kept the boys going through the hard times.

The November 2013 Melon Music Awards came as a fabulous boost, then, as BTS won Best New Artist. If the boys had had one dream when they debuted in June, it was to win this prestigious rookie award, which is based on digital sales, judges' scores and online votes. This was the recognition they were hoping for, but they couldn't quite believe it – as you can tell from the backstage YouTube video.

On the way back to the dressing room they bounced along the corridor. RM explained that he practised his speech that afternoon, praying that they might win. He had worked it all out and had been planning to mention their families, their dance teachers and Big Hit staff. However, on reaching the microphone, he was so overcome that he just bleated out 'Bang Si-hyuk PD-nim', the formal name of the Big Hit boss. Luckily, Suga whispered to him that they should also thank their parents.

N.O (TROT VER.) BY JUNGKOOK AND (OPERA VER.) BY BTS

This is *O!RUL8,2?*-era gold. Jung Kook is backstage, passing the time by singing a trot (a traditional Korean-style ballad) version of the 'N.O' refrain. Urged on by Suga, the others try different styles, topped by the most stunning operatic high note from J-Hope. You'll laugh –and be impressed!

If this was a good end to 2013, picking up the Rising Star prize at the Golden Disc Awards on 1 January was the perfect start to 2014. Winning the debut award at the oldest of the Korean music awards ceremonies put BTS in good company – successful groups such as Super Junior, SHINee and EXO had all been previous winners.

At the end of January, they picked up another rookie gong. Following in EXO's footsteps again, they won Best New Artist at the Seoul Music Awards. It was perfect timing, because the countdown to the final part of the trilogy – *Skool Luv Affair* – had begun. The concept teaser photos continued with the schoolboy theme, with the guys posing in school uniform and heavy eye make-up. The comeback trailer featured RM delivering a heavy rap over a fantastic animated sequence of old-school hip-hop iconography, including guys with beatboxes for heads. On 11 February came the live TV showcase for the mini-album, with the boys performing the track 'Jump' – with exuberant choreography to match, including a mid-air hand chair for Suga to sit and rap in – and, highlighted by a flying J-Hope, the lead track, 'Boy in Luv'.

The new concept positioned the group as the school bad boys, tough and wild but with tender hearts, as the EP took on the themes of young love and romance. The look was school uniform – black jackets (rebel Jimin ditching his for a leather one), white shirts and black trousers – worn with attitude. Jimin's coconut hair had gone and was now gelled up and messy, V went for an interesting bright orange, while RM sported a slicked-back silver quiff.

The video for 'Boy in Luv' followed the concept. They're a school gang. Jung Kook is the only one doing any schoolwork. The others are hiding away or messing about until the sight of a pretty girl walking down the corridor brings them together. To get her in front of Jung Kook, they rap in her face, grab her wrist and pull her along – it doesn't look great, but their attitudes to women will soon change for the better. In 2019, when they released 'Boy With Luv', RM would explain that the 2013 song was about teen love, and that now they had grown up they could write about real love.

On YouTube, they demonstrated 'Boy in Luv' for a 'Let's Dance' video. This series allows artists and groups to teach fans their dance moves. Taking us through their macho-romantic number, V and Jung Kook demonstrated the 'King Kong', all swinging arms and beating chests; Jin and Jimin showed us the 'Shaving Dance', a preening, posing routine ending on a 'hey!'; and finally the rap line showed us their as-yet-unnamed, tough-guy, grab-your-pants sequence. Just copy that rough but vulnerable look and you too can dance like BTS!

The CD package came in a smooth, green case with metallic pink lettering. As with the previous CD boxes, it was accompanied by an extensive photobook and collectible extras: a sticker pack of animated hip-hop monster Bangtans, a random group photocard and a random band member card backed with some 'scribbled' personal details, including their date of birth, blood group, favourite things and a signature.

Without abandoning their hip-hop style, in *Skool Luv Affair* the tracks have a stronger vocal element than previous releases. RM, Suga and J-Hope all contributed to the lyrics and Suga was involved in writing and arranging nearly all the songs.

Remember the 'Outro: Luv in Skool' backing track? Here it is again as 'Intro: Skool Luv Affair', which takes hold as the boys give us their personal take on romance. 'Boy in Luv' begins with classic BTS hip-hop, but after a minute or so something new happens and the mood completely changes. The usual electronic dance sound is suddenly replaced with electric guitars and drums – have BTS become a rock band? Well, no, but just nine months after debut they are showing they are willing and able to play around with their sound.

Previous BTS love songs fixated on past romances and the bittersweet memories of recently finished relationships, but this track is different. Here the guys are tough but humbled by a girl who seems tantalizingly unattainable. They are insecure, frustrated, confrontational, sensitive and vulnerable – all in one song! It's another great teen anthem in which RM gets angry for being made to look stupid in front of the girl, J-Hope tries to stay tough, while in a classic line Jung Kook asks his dad for advice. How did he ask his mum out? Did he write a letter? So sweet! 'Skit: Soulmate', a classic skit showing a discussion about what they are going to do for a skit – with rare appearances from special guests Supreme Boi and Bang PD – is up next, followed by 'Where You From?' with its super-bouncy and fun synth sound. The song is another *satoori* dialect-themed song as the boys compete with their chat-up lines.

'Just One Day' (which they promote in April as the second single from the album) is a smooth, lush track with a mid-tempo R&B-infused sound. Its dreamy lyrics describe a perfect twenty-four hours with their girl, although Suga, ever the realist, reminds us that with their busy schedule it is just a dream. When the video emerged – on a minimalist set with the boys in white cardigans, sitting on chairs and showing a new sweet and sensitive side – it undoubtedly recruited another legion of fans to ARMY.

But if you thought BTS had forsaken rap for good, think again. The next three tracks see them return to their hip-hop roots. 'Tomorrow' continues the 'follow your dream' theme as RM spits out some machine-gun fast rap, while 'Cypher Pt. 2: Triptych' lets the rap line loose, with Suga, intense and sincere, perhaps at his best. Then there's 'Spine Breaker', which has become a firm fan favourite. It is a classic, socially aware BTS song, which, over V's superb, deep melody, points to the cost – both financially and to society – of kids slavishly following expensive fashions.

BANGTAN BOMB

BOYS' CONFESSION THEIR OWN WAY

Watch this companion piece to 'Where You From?' in which each of them try out their 'love confession' chat-up lines to camera. Who's your winner? Would your heart be captured by Jin's intensity, Jimin's, er, cheesy acting, V's toughness, Jung Kook's smile or J-Hope's pure madness? (Let's be honest – Suga just isn't trying hard enough!)

The album draws to a conclusion with the excellent 'Jump', an up-tempo celebration of years of hard work that really comes into its own on stage. Finally, the vocal line is given a pure, two-minute ballad to sing out the album and for some, this is when Jin, effortlessly hitting those high notes, really shines for the first time. If there were any doubts about the course BTS were taking, *Skool Luv Affair* and 'Boy in Luv' had firmly dispelled them. The future was suddenly looking pretty rosy as the album went to number one in the Korean chart and number three in the Billboard World Albums Chart. 'Boy in Luv' also hit number five on the Billboard World Chart, which ranks the best-performing international digital singles in the US. As summer approached, with prime-time TV appearances and a trip to Japan coming up, there was little doubt – BTS really were the rookie kings.

MEMBER PROFILE

Name: Kim Namjoon

AKA: RM, Rap Monster, President Namjoon, God of Destruction, Dance Prodigy, Joonie

Date of birth: 12 September 1994

Birthplace: Seoul, South Korea

Height: 1.81 metres (5'11")

Education: Apgujeong High School, Global Cyber University

Chinese zodiac: Dog

Star sign: Virgo

Instagram: @rkive

FOUR

KIM NAMJOON/RM: THE MONSTER NO MORE

He's no monster, he's Kim Namjoon: the quietly spoken leader of BTS. The rapper is the tallest and one of the most stylish of the group, and has proved to be both sensitive and deep-thinking. So when, in September 2017, he announced he was changing his name to RM, it seemed a natural transition – the teenage rapper who had taken the macho name Rap Monster as a Big Hit trainee has since shown himself to be a super-intelligent and accomplished musician – more poet than monster.

Kim Namjoon was born in Seoul and grew up in Ilsan, an affluent satellite city of Seoul, with his mum, dad and younger sister. A happy boy, his smiling childhood photos reveal those same dimples that ARMY swoon over twenty years later. School was never a problem for a young Namjoon. Despite admitting to acting up as the class clown, he studied hard and consistently earned good grades. As far as his parents were concerned, a top university and a good job beckoned. Looking at Namjoon's middle-school graduation photo, with his shapeless pudding haircut and unfashionable glasses, you'd be forgiven for having him down as a future government official.

At home, his mother encouraged Namjoon to learn English. Together they would watch CNN and BBC News programmes, and when he was twelve he went to New Zealand to study for four months. As he revealed on the US *Ellen DeGeneres Show* in 2017, 'My English teacher was the sitcom *Friends*. Back in the day, when I was like fifteen, fourteen, it was quite like a syndrome for all the Korean parents to make their kids watch *Friends*.' He explained that his mother bought him all ten seasons on DVD: 'So firstly, I watched them with the Korean subtitles, and then next time I watched with the English subtitles, and then I just removed it.'

Around this time he discovered another English-language tutor: rap music, especially US artists like Nas and Eminem. He began to write his own rap lyrics on scraps of paper, hiding them between the pages of his schoolbooks so his parents didn't learn about his passion. He was occasionally found out, but no one really minded as long as he continued to receive stellar grades in his schoolwork. By now he was being encouraged to look way beyond his elementary school ambition of being a concierge (although he did eventually get to wear the uniform in the 'Dope' music video!).

Namjoon was developing fast as a rapper, too. He took the stage name Runch Randa, from an avatar in the video game *MapleStory*, and would hang out in Hongdae, the trendy neighbourhood of Seoul, where the hip-hop scene (known as the underground) was flourishing. Along with some others, including Kidoh (who later debuted with Topp Dogg), rapper Iron and future BTS producer Supreme Boi, he put together a rap crew named DaeNamHyup (or DNH), and later hooked up with other rising stars, including Zico, now leader of Block B.

Soon he was turning heads. In 2010, the hip-hop artist and TV celebrity Sleepy attended an underground crew audition and spotted this young kid with a gift for rapping. He got the phone number of Runch Randa, called Big Hit Entertainment and told them they might like to take a look at this talented high-school freshman.

But his teachers and parents still had other plans for him. In his Korean language, maths, foreign language and social studies exams, Namjoon really excelled. A test put his IQ at 148, and he came close to being in the top 1 per cent of students in the whole country. Crunch time was getting nearer for Namjoon, but how could he convince his parents that a career in music was the right path?

He told the Koreaboo website that he put forward a carefully crafted argument. 'My grades were about five-thousandth place in the country,' he recalled telling his mother. 'If I were to keep going on the path I was, I would've been a successful man with a plain job. But, no matter how smart people told me I was, I was five-thousandth in the country. However, I was positive I'd be number one in the country when it came to rap.' He asked his mum whether she wanted her son to be first or five-thousandth. What mother could refuse her child such an opportunity?

Namjoon passed his audition at Big Hit in 2010 and worked with the company as a solo rapper and then as they tried various combinations of rappers to create a hip-hop group called Bangtan Sonyeondan. Some left, frustrated with the process, while others quit when Big Hit decided to change the focus and develop an idol group.

And so began Namjoon's three long years as a trainee. These were tough, boring and repetitive days of hard work, which included dance, a new discipline for Namjoon. He hadn't signed on as a dancer, but that came as part of being an idol group, so he worked at it, picking up a new nickname, Dance Prodigy – an ironic reference to his struggles as a dancer – in the process.

It was as a trainee that he picked up the Rap Monster moniker. At the very end of one of his songs, he would yell out 'Rap Monster!', and company staff started calling him by that name for fun. It stuck and he took it as his stage name. It was one of many changes he would make as BTS approached debut. He was often criticized for selling out and abandoning the true underground rap path, and consequently had to defend himself for signing up as an idol and enjoying the opportunities it provided; he also sometimes found idol life difficult and wasn't always comfortable wearing smoky make-up, pulling cutsie *aegyo* poses and performing those highly choreographed dances.

Of course, there was one other major change that Namjoon had to deal with: he was named leader of BTS. This was a great honour, but it was also a position that came with a great deal of responsibility. In public appearances such as promotions, tours and comeback press conferences, awards acceptance speeches and TV interviews, he would have to take charge. He would have to be articulate and authoritative, but also make sure he included the rest of the group, giving them the opportunity to contribute and comment. Considering their astonishing future success in the rest of the world, it was a far-sighted move by Big Hit to give leadership of the group to its best English speaker.

The leader also has to represent the group to the company and the company to the group. In a fascinating episode of the Korean TV series *Problematic Men*, RM and Suho from boy group EXO discuss group leadership. RM explains how he was made leader because he was the first member of BTS and his ideas contributed to the musical direction of the group, despite not being the eldest. Jin, Suga and J-Hope are all his seniors (an important distinction in Korean society), which, when he has to take charge, can sometimes create a little friction. The way he deals with his responsibilities doesn't go unnoticed by the others, though. In the *Wings* concept book, a grateful V points out how RM takes many of the problems on his own shoulders and works hard to create an atmosphere in which the members of BTS get along well.

Despite being leader, RM is close to all of the members of the group. His naturally reserved nature, and his work as a songwriter and producer, mean that in backstage videos he is often seen quietly sitting in the background, preparing for the performance, but in the reality series *Gayo* or *Run BTS!* we can see how he takes part in playing games, silly dancing and messing around with the others. Of all the band members, he has known Suga the longest, having befriended the boy from Daegu when he turned up in the dorm in 2010 (the anniversary, 13 November, is now celebrated as 'Namgi Day' by ARMY). These two are the most serious musicians of the group and have a deep understanding of each other – RM has admitted that Suga is the one he turns to when he is worried. Then there are his other former roommates: Jung Kook, who has a special 'big brother' relationship with RM (watch V Live's 'One-Minute English' to see this in action as RM teaches the young *maknae* to say 'Pardon?'), and V, the member who seemed to miss him most when he had to return home early on the first *Bon Voyage* trip (one of BTS's unsupervised trips abroad). Namjoon and

Jin's bond is over their position as worst dancer! Jin told the TV show *Please Take Care of My Refrigerator* that in their choreography practice, the other five members learn from the dance instructor while he and RM are excluded and end up learning the moves in the corner.

In terms of pure personality, fellow 94-liner J-Hope (he and RM were both born in 1994) can always get RM laughing, particularly with his cheeky impressions of the leader. Indeed, RM has said J-Hope would be his ideal desert-island companion – because his constant talking would mean RM wouldn't need a radio!

J-Hope also features in one of RM's most memorable acting roles: as the mother to RM's hilarious BTS-loving, tantrum-throwing schoolgirl in the 2017 'House of Army' video. This clip would feature in any RM highlights roll, alongside his brilliant flailing-sleeve comic dance on *Weekly Idol*, in which he keeps a poker-straight face as bemused fellow members look on (except Suga, who can't bear to watch!), his tragic attempt at cutting an onion on the same programme and, of course, his inspired aeroplane seat utterance of 'Jimin, you got no jams'. Over the formative years of BTS, as well as the rapper and BTS leader RM, fans have also got to know the real Kim Namjoon. His clumsiness is legendary, causing the others to nickname him the God of Destruction. The video clip of him breaking his brand-new sunglasses became an instant meme, but over the years we've also heard of doors falling off in the dorm and out-takes show him effortlessly smashing video props. Similarly, RM has an ability to lose things so often that none of them seemed at all surprised when he lost his passport and had to cut short his *Bon Voyage* trip to Scandinavia. He hasn't changed over the years, either – in December 2019 he confessed to having lost a total of thirty-three pairs of AirPods!

Group members have also been quick to separate RM's stage persona from the Namjoon who shares their dorm. Suga said in an *Ize* magazine interview that, on stage, Rap Mon wears sunglasses and gives out a powerful image, but really he likes cute things. Indeed, Namjoon has a dog called Rapmon, an adorable fluffy white American Eskimo Dog, which he got as a puppy back in 2013. Then there is his obsession with Ryan, the lovable lion character from the instant messaging app KakaoTalk. He admitted to having at least thirteen stuffed Ryans in his dorm room, as well as a set of Ryan pyjamas, a Ryan eye mask and Ryan phone cases – and in 2016 the others even gave him a Ryan birthday cake.

JIMIN: I GOT YES JAM

Two minutes of joyous wigging out as RM bonds with Jimin in an all-out dance frenzy. An ARMY favourite, this bomb features a lot of jumping around, plenty of air-guitar action and proof that Kim Namjoon is as capable as anyone of just flipping out. And remember, as the man himself once said, it's R-A-P Monster, not D-A-N-C-E Monster!

ARMY might miss #KimDaily where RM used to post his outfits on Twitter (and will never forget his Minion dungarees outfit from 2015), but they still get to see plenty of pics of his high-fashion style. He tends to stick to neutral colours – forest greens, browns, beige and muted blues – and although he mixes street and boho styles with ease, he loves Japanese streetwear labels like VISVIM, WTAPS, Neighborhood and Yohji Yamamoto.

It is, however, the reflective side of Namjoon that many ARMY most admire. You will often find the words 'sexy brain' in posts from fans whose favourite is RM. He is interested in new ideas, philosophy and politics, and is a committed reader. He likes the Japanese authors Haruki Murakami and Hitomi Kanehara, writers such as Kafka and Camus, and has particularly recommended British novelist Jojo Moyes's love story *Me Before You*.

For many fans, part of the appeal is that he agonizes over details and takes issues to heart. Hurt by criticism in BTS's early days, he has apologized publicly for issues of perceived racism, sexism and plagiarism. For later concepts he undertook his own research, such as reading Tony Porter's thought-provoking *Breaking Out of the Man Box: The Next Generation of Manhood* and consulting with feminist academics.

This image of RM as a deep thinker emerges in his *Wings* song 'Reflection', in which he describes how, if he has something on his mind, he takes time out by going to Ttukseom Island in Seoul to think it through. In an interview in January 2018, he revealed that in the past he always coped with anxiety by immersing himself in music, but he has now developed other 'escapes', such as shopping for clothes, collecting toy figures and connecting with the real world by taking a random bus journey to a new place.

In 2015, Rap Monster, as he then was, dropped a mixtape (a type of non-commercial album favoured by rappers) that played on this introspection. The track 'Do You' debates whether to swim with or fight against the current, while 'Awakening' discloses his journey to being a proud idol rapper. *RM* would win a place in *Spin* magazine's list of the fifty best hip-hop albums of the year, and the mixtape proved that he could be both an idol star and a 'real' rapper; a status confirmed by subsequent collaborations with Wale, Fall Out Boy, Honne and legendary South Korean hip-hop artist Tiger JK.

A second mixtape, *mono.* – which collaborators Honne said stood for 'monster no more' – dropped in 2018 and took RM to the top of Billboard's Emerging Artists chart. The wistful collection of songs focused on loneliness and insecurities with 'seoul', 'moonchild' and 'forever rain' (which was given a monochromatic animated video) being acclaimed as highlights of the mixtape.

RM's growing influence as a songwriter and a solo artist was also evident in his contributions to the *Love Yourself* and *Map of the Soul* albums. 'Trivia: Love' was a bright and joyous celebration of the nature of love, while 'Intro: Persona', soon to be a fan favourite, bravely chose to get to the heart of the loving-yourself concept through a hard rap. His versatility as a rapper and a singer led to a series of appearances on other artists' songs. 'Seoul Town Road' used his contribution (and passable southern US accent) in a remix of Lil Nas X's 'Old Town Road'; he co-wrote and rapped on Younha's chart-topping 'Winter Flower'; his husky vocals added to eAeon's hit 'Don't' (which he also co-wrote); and Suga enlisted his lyrical skills for the *D-2* track 'Strange'.

It would, however, be three years before his next solo foray. 'Bicycle', dropped for the 2021 *festa*, was inspired by his love of cycling. He composed the track with jazz singer-songwriter John Eun, but wrote the lyrics himself while out on his bike. A relaxed, softly sung song, it tells of his enjoyment of riding as a metaphor for freedom, enjoying life and going along for the ride.

BANGTAN BOMB

RM'S VISIT TO 2022 BTS EXHIBITION: PROOF IN SEOUL

The BTS Exhibition: Proof in Seoul was on display at the Hybe Insight building in late 2022. It enabled fans to immerse themselves in a visual history of BTS using images, videos and costumes. RM's visit was very personal and moving as he took in their nine-year journey and commented with the honesty and eloquence we have come to expect. 'Loosen up will you?' he tells an early portrait of himself. He admits 'Butter' was his favourite concept, as it showed the most complete version of himself, and even gives staff a warning of his clumsiness.

He also earned a new nickname from ARMY, who began refer to him as 'President Namjoon'. He had always shown great leadership skills, but when he spoke at the United Nations General Assembly in New York in September 2018, he took this to another level. His iconic speech on the importance of self-confidence, finding your voice and following your dreams was widely acknowledged as powerful and inspirational and was soon being used in schools and colleges around the world. He would live up to the President name again in the coming years as he spoke in support of the Black Lives Matter campaign, led the group back to the UN General Assembly to speak in 2020 and 2021 and also to the White House to meet President Biden.

RM's intelligence, maturity and interest in the world are clear to all. In particular his interest in art has grown from visiting exhibitions to participating in informed podcasts to buying his own art. His taste is wide-ranging, but his personal collection focuses on modern art. It includes sculptures by US artists Roni Horn and Joel Shapiro and an impressive collection of the pop-art KAWS figurines, but is dominated by acclaimed Korean artists such as Yun Hyong-keun, Joung Young-ju and Kwon Jin-kyu. In December 2020, the Arts Council of Korea named him as a Patron of the Arts in recognition of his considerable donations to art-based charities.

Fans who followed RM's interests and hobbies came up with the concept of 'Namjooning' to describe the art of living like BTS's leader. This includes his love of travel and his visits to art galleries and museums, but also his love of the outdoors and his appreciation of the natural world. Nowhere is this more evident than on his Instagram account, @rkive, where he focuses on the people, art and nature he encounters.

As leader, it was also RM who was called upon to articulate the members' break from group activities during the *festa* dinner in 2022. On this occasion, his usual calm and deliberate style was derailed by his attempts to be completely transparent and honest about the situation. It led to him passionately and tearfully saying he felt trapped and needed time alone to think. As leader, it was also down to him to set matters straight the following day.

As the members focused on individual activities, RM announced that he was working on a solo album, but more immediately that a new collaboration single was about to drop. 'Sexy Nukim' was a single by the 'alternative K-pop' music collective Balming Tiger. RM wrote and rapped on the cool hip-hop track, appeared in the edgy MV and joined the group on stage for a performance at a charity event in Seoul.

On 2 December 2022, RM released his debut album (with a physical release, setting it apart from the digital-only *RM* and *mono.*). Using guest artists on all but two of the tracks, RM moved effortlessly from hip-hop to R&B and funk to folk as the lyrical material weaved together art, nature, hope, despondency, fame, identity, inspirations and aspirations. Among *Indigo*'s highlights were 'Yun', a soulful opening to the album with Erykah Badu and sample audio from iconic painter Yun Hyong-keun about being a human before you are an artist; 'Still Life', an ebullient funky workout with Anderson .Paak; and 'All Day', a rap-discussion in English and Korean on originality and freedom as an artist with Tablo, the leader of the legendary group Epik High. It was the lead single 'Wild Flower' that really stood out, though. A slow-tempo power-rap featuring Youjeen, vocalist of South Korean rock group Cherry Filter, it delivered an anguished and poetic evocation of the feelings RM touched on at the *festa* dinner.

RM talked about the album as the first-ever guest on Suga's YouTube chat show *Suchwita*. He said that J-Hope was the only person to have listened to it all before release (as RM had done with *Jack In The Box*). He explained that he had been working on *Indigo* for three years and said it served as his diary and archive since that time. The album was a deeply personal affair, an attempt to convey the inner life of a late-twenty-something mega-star.

He helped promote it with a short set on Tiny Desk (Home) Concert and a longer RM Live in Seoul concert in front of 250 lucky fans at Rolling Hall, and recorded four songs in different art installation spaces at Dia Beacon, a contemporary art museum in New York. *Indigo* said so much about RM's integrity, emotional intelligence and lyrical ability and was still a great success around the world.

Indigo reached number three in the Billboard 200, making RM the highest-charting Korean soloist ever (at the time). It wouldn't be long before he was back at the top of many charts with a collaboration with So!YoON!. RM had been a fan of the singer's indie rock band SE SO NEON since their debut in 2017 and contributed vocals and a rap verse to 'Smoke Sprite', as well as appearing in the MV for the single. A powerful and mesmerizing track, the rock sound was new ground for RM, but one which he fitted into seamlessly.

Me, Myself, & RM: Entirety, his contribution to the group's photo-folio project, portrayed a multi-faceted character as RM and Namjoon, as thoughtful and calm, as an artist and a young man. He soon grasped the freedom of the group's decision to focus on solo activities to embrace this entirety. He began to fulfil some of his long-standing ambitions. As well as the solo album, he met his musical hero Pharrell Williams for a candid exchange in a *Rolling Stone* magazine 'Musicians on Musicians' interview; he became an official ambassador for fashion brand Bottega Veneta, representing them at Milan Fashion Week and appearing on the cover of *Vogue Korea*, and he co-hosted the intelligent variety show *The Dictionary of Useless Human Knowledge*.

In a 2023 interview with *El País*, he said: 'As I'm about to turn 30, I like myself more than I did when I was 20. Now I will spend a year and a half in military service, which is a big deal in every Korean man's life. And after that, I am sure I will be a different human being, hopefully a better and wiser one.' It seemed he was beginning to feel his way into a new chapter in life. Just as he had grown out of Rap Monster to become RM, he was now on the way to finding Kim Namjoon.

FIVE

AMERICAN HUSTLERS

Korean television variety shows are essential exposure for K-pop bands making their way in the world, and on 1 April 2014, BTS were excited to make their TV debut on the *Beatles Code* show. They performed their Bangtan greeting in slow motion, J-Hope showed off his street-dancing skills and Jung Kook performed press-ups while singer Park Ji-yoon sat on him. For first-timers, they came across very well.

Then, on 30 April 2014, to great anticipation, BTS featured on the big one, the show that's a must for everyone who is anyone in K-pop: the long-running and popular variety show *Weekly Idol* where stars are interviewed but also teased and set amusing tasks. Dressed down in ripped jeans, tees and long shirts, they looked more comfortable than ever. In a rapping test, Jin hilariously shows why he's in the vocal line, while V completely smashed it, and in the random dance section, where the boys had to remember their own dance moves, poor Jimin got it all wrong and the presenters described him as a 'lost sheep'. It was very funny! Finally, the Initial Profiles section, where guests showcase their special skills, became the Jung Kook show. He danced move for move to half- and double-speed versions of 'Boy in Luv' and then danced brilliantly to Girl's Day's 'Something'. It's still a must-see for any Kookie lover. For young and still-shy boys, they had made a fine start. Having established a following in South Korea, it was now time for Bangtan to spread their wings. In mid-April they spent a few days in China, where they were amazed to find so many ARMY at the airport. Word had spread far and fast, and *China Job*, a documentary about the trip, showed them attending the V Chart Awards, where they performed in black suits and red sneakers, and picked up another newcomer award.

In early summer, the focus turned to Japan. Under the name Bōdan Shōnendan (the Japanese form of Bangtan Sonyeondan), they were about to release a Japanese version of 'No More Dream', and on 31 May they flew out to Tokyo to meet and perform the song for 5,000 of their Japanese ARMY at the Dome City Hall (adding an afternoon performance due to high demand). It was the start of something big there, and they would soon be back.

BANGTAN BOMB

LET'S SPEAK ENGLISH!

This is probably one of the most famous Bangtan Bombs. The boys are on the plane flying into LA and J-Hope decides they need to practise their English. Of course, RM, as a fluent English speaker, chats away and J-Hope gives it a go with some adorable broken English, but the others aren't really playing. Expressing his disappointment, J-Hope tells RM that Jimin really isn't any fun, to which RM makes the iconic reply: 'Jimin, you got no jams!' In Korean, *jaemi* means fun, so RM is making up his own English slang. It is now an essential part of BTS history.

Russia also got a look at the boys in June when the band travelled to the Bridge to Korea festival in Moscow. This event was designed to bring tourists to both countries, and they judged a K-pop dance competition and performed in front of the Kremlin to a crowd of over 10,000. Dressed in their grey cardigan outfits, they did a twenty-minute medley of hits followed by a joyous, out-of-tune, almost punk version of the traditional Korean folk song and unofficial anthem 'Arirang'.

A year had now gone by since BTS's debut – in fact it had flown by. On 13 June 2014, to mark the anniversary, they held their first *festa* (a Korean term for festival), releasing collections of photographs, dance videos and a fun-filled, hour-long radio-style discussion show.

They also put out a new commemorative song, a rap-led track called 'So 4 More', which found them looking back at the ups and downs of the past year and wondering, in classic BTS fashion, whether the hardships were all worthwhile.

Back in the summer of 2012, Jung Kook had travelled to Los Angeles to study at the famous Movement Lifestyle dance academy, but none of the others had set foot in the US. All Jung Kook could tell them was that the air there was different, but now they were about to find out for themselves: they were on their way to LA.

When the boys landed there, it was time for a little sightseeing. They went to a baseball game, where they caught countryman Hyun-jin Ryu pitching for the Dodgers (Suga would return to Dodger Stadium and meet him in 2019), and they hit the beach and showed off their dance moves in Santa Monica. As it was getting dark, they pulled into a parking lot and waited in the van while their manager went off to run an errand until, all of a sudden, in burst three scary-looking men. BTS were being kidnapped!

Was this for real? Well, no, fortunately it was a prank, filmed for the opening of their reality series *American Hustle Life*. Were the boys in on the joke? Possibly, but Jung Kook and J-Hope appeared genuinely terrified as, driven to what looked like a seedy part of town, the band members were hustled into a warehouse apartment and told to sleep. At 6 a.m., jet-lagged and dozy, they were woken by none other than

US rap star Coolio (who sadly passed away in 2022) and his team of rap mentors. They were about to get a crash course in American hip-hop life.

Over the eight episodes of *American Hustle Life* the boys are set challenges, but this isn't light and frothy, it's hardcore, and Coolio and his crew take the hip-hop boot-camp idea seriously. Poor V discovers this pretty quickly as he tries to lighten the mood by jokingly saying, 'Let's go party. Turn up!' He is immediately punished with twenty-five push-ups. 'Quit playing with me,' barks Coolio. 'If it wasn't for hip-hop, I'd be dead or in jail.' Suga and Jin also fall out with their mentor Dante so badly that after episode two he isn't seen again.

As they take on tasks including presenting a cooking segment, calling at strangers' homes to perform for them and finding girls to invite to dance in their music video, the boys sometimes appear confused, awkward and vulnerable. However, they are wonderful in their determination to please their mentors, the way they help each other along, and, of course, their charm and talent shines through. In the dance battle, J-Hope shows that despite the complexity of BTS choreography, he still has moves to spare; when he's not charming *noonas* (older ladies) in the market, V's vocals completely bowl over singing teacher Iris; and Suga comes into his own writing brilliant new lyrics for Warren G's 'Regulate'.

Seeing each of the group in trying situations does give us a great picture of BTS at this stage of their career. They clearly learn some lessons, especially in dealing with people. They have to meet ordinary folk and work mundane jobs, sometimes for mean bosses (Jimin and RM cleaning the bathroom is comedy gold), and they even have to talk to girls. As mentor Tony told the MoonROK website, 'I know the Korean entertainment culture is very strict about relationships, so when we put them in front of girls, they were so shy. They didn't know what to do.'

The bond that the great Warren G, who turns up in a stretch limo to give them a tour of his Long Beach hometown, has with his fans clearly resonated with the boys, especially as it was now time for BTS to meet their American public. Early in the morning on 13 July 2014 they announced on Twitter that the following day they would be playing a 'show and prove' concert at the Troubadour rock club in West Hollywood in which they would show what they had learned in the US. Entry was free – but was limited to just 200 people. No wonder the queue went right round the block. True to their word, they performed their singles along with covers of 'Regulate' and, with proud singing coach Iris (the real-life inspiration for *Sister Act 2*) watching from the balcony, the gospel classic 'Oh Happy Day!'.

In North America there is a large Korean-American population and K-pop is firmly established there, while K-pop groups are regularly promoted in East and Southeast Asia. These music industries provide a new group like BTS with a platform to build on. Europe, with its very limited exposure to K-pop, however, would provide a different set of challenges. Summer 2014 saw BTS making an attempt to crack Europe as they took their first trip there, with showcases and fan meets in Berlin and Stockholm. These shows were mobbed by small but very enthusiastic crowds as the boys performed their *Skool* trilogy hits. Their online presence and successes in other parts of the world were clearly getting BTS recognition in all corners of the globe.

In August, they made their first visit to Brazil, a country where they would find some of their most committed followers. In a short space of time they learned a lot about the country, including not to get off the plane in shorts and T-shirts when it's winter! In the Via Marquês club, BTS introduced themselves in Portuguese and talked about their impressions of Brazil, Jin saying he could already feel it was 'the country of passions' and Suga remarking that he had heard Brazil has many hot girls and, looking at the audience, he could now confirm that fact for himself! Wherever they went, they were making friends and gaining fans for life.

LA wasn't quite finished with BTS for the summer. In another big break for the now-no-longer rookie group, they were booked to play at KCON 2014. Over the course of a weekend, KCON, which began in 2012, celebrates K-drama, K-pop, Korean fashion and Korean food. This was their chance to show America what they were really about – and they didn't disappoint. Their red-carpet appearance delighted everyone; the BTS hi-touch and sign session was the hottest ticket around; and fans waited hours in the intense heat to catch their special appearance on *Danny From L.A.*, a US K-pop TV show.

However, the evening concerts were the highlight and, as anyone attending KCON 2014 soon realized from the fans' T-shirts and banners, BTS might not have been the headliners (they were G-Dragon and Girls' Generation), but they were a major attraction. The crowd, many of whom already seemed to know the chants and the members' names, were loud and wildly enthusiastic. The show went down a storm with those unfamiliar with BTS, too, and an *LA Times* correspondent commented, 'The group made the strongest impression of all the US debuting acts. This won't be the last time they play to thrilled crowds in the States.'

It had been a busy summer of filming and touring, but that was just the half of it. Wherever they went – Seoul, America, Europe, Brazil – they were writing and recording new material, and dancing to the point of exhaustion. And, when in LA, as well as the stress of *American Hustle Life*, they were laying down tracks in a studio set up in the garage of Bang Si-hyuk's apartment. The result was their first full-length album.

The comeback trailer for *Dark & Wild* was released on 5 August 2014. It featured RM's 'Intro: What Am I to You', a feverish track about a frustrated and insecure romance. A few days later, as a pre-release, they started streaming 'Let Me Know', another stirring, desperate song, on their website. Suga, who co-wrote the track, had promised fans they would love the song for its trance-like melody, and he wasn't wrong. ARMY held their breath for the full release.

The *Dark & Wild* concept photos revealed a more mature look that matched the more grown-up tone of the new songs. The bad-boy image was still there and they were back in black, but with stylish leather jackets and trousers with white T-shirts. The gold chains and rings had returned, but again in a more subdued way, and the boys looked serious and thoughtful as they stared into or away from the camera, despite the fact that Suga and J-Hope's hair was bright red and Jin's a subtle purple (which proved pretty popular with his fans).

The music video for 'Danger', the album's lead track, was released on 19 August 2014. The boys wore denim jackets and ripped jeans, but the overall feel was still dark. There is no real storyline this time, just brooding imagery. The settings are depressing – a disused subway and a derelict warehouse, partially flooded and littered with burning shopping carts – and the members play characters hurt by love. They try to distract themselves – RM writes, Suga plays basketball, J-Hope dances – but it's no use. As their frustrations spill over, Jimin lays into a punchbag, Jin plays with fire and Jung Kook smashes up a piano, while RM takes a tattoo needle to his arm and V sets about cutting his own hair.

눈,코,입 (EYES, NOSE, LIPS) OF BTS

Taeyang's 'Eyes, Nose, Lips', an emotional R&B-style track about remembering an ex, was the song of summer 2014 in Korea and beyond. In this priceless clip, the Bangtan Boys give us their own unique take on the song. Eavesdrop as they lip-sync, overact, fool around and even sing along. They all have a go, even RM, who initially turns his back to escape the camera, and Jung Kook, who overcomes his shyness in the end.

In the YouTube clip on the making of the music video you can see that they actually had a lot of fun portraying the darker side of youth. However, Jimin admits he's embarrassed about the boxing, RM notes that their trainers haven't dried from dancing in the water and V announces that, despite wearing a wig, he somehow managed to cut his real hair! Jung Kook also reveals later that he ripped open his index finger destroying the piano, so couldn't use the fingerprint recognition system to get into the dorm and for several weeks had to wait for someone else to let him in.

The most impressive aspect of the video has to be the choreography. It has the usual hip-hop character, but it's smoothed out and the b-boy moves have been incorporated to create a distinct BTS style. As ever, they stay perfectly in sync, but watch as they introduce the 'high blood pressure' part of the dance with an attention-grabbing neck-rub and shrug of the shoulder, then transform the macho arm fold or crouch into something more emotional and expressive. This may be where BTS dance came of age.

BANGTAN BOMB

RUNWAY IN THE NIGHT

What to do when you're all dressed up with nowhere to go? How about turning a corridor into your own model runway? That's the BTS answer as they wait around in their 'Danger' finery. From then on it's just a matter of who can goof around most. J-Hope's always a good bet, Jin certainly has the moves and V is, well, V.

The CD was presented in a glossy black card case with random scratch marks and an official-looking warning in English about the effects of love. The package contained a random individual photocard and group photocard, and a photobook with lyrics (in a bewitching handwritten style with doodles and underlinings).

In the album showcase, Suga stated that the previous single-album and mini-albums had been preparation for this, their first full album, and it should be listened to from beginning to end with the interlude bridging the change in tone from frustration to release. This was BTS growing up, no longer talking about school but focusing on the emotional stresses of youth.

So after RM's opening rap, 'Intro: What Am I to You', 'Danger', the lead track on *Dark & Wild*, zeroes straight in on the emotional damage caused by unrequited love. The group has developed lyrically and progressed from 'please go out with me' songs to songs about love that can really hurt when it goes wrong, and the music has matured, too. The vocal line has more room to explore their harmonies, the backing brings in a guitar sound that persists above the percussion, and the rap seems relaxed and less stylized.

Despite being poppy and infectious, in 'War of Hormone' BTS court controversy again with their honesty about the effects of hormones on young men. They admit they are girl crazy and, although they did receive some bad press for their attitude to women and tarnishing the squeaky-clean image of K-pop, this is clearly a hymn to girls and their tongues are firmly in their cheeks (J-Hope even has a line about popping a pimple!).

In 'Hip Hop Phile' we discover what BTS had learned from their summer school as, with a much more American feel than before, they name-drop their rap heroes and take us through their hip-hop education. Suga's pre-released 'Let Me Know' comes next, followed by 'Rain', an often underrated, melancholic, jazz-infused number with a fabulous cameo from J-Hope. The dark half of the album then closes with 'Cypher Pt. 3: Killer' featuring Supreme Boi, another circle-room rap session and, again, this seems more polished and less derivative than previous cyphers.

After a brief 1970s disco-inspired interlude that never quite takes off, we enter the wild side. They are a group building their fan base through social media, yet they are bold enough to ask, 'Could You Turn Off Your Cell Phone'? Do they look like your parents? No, but you can't deny the message: we're missing out on a personal connection if we live our lives through our phones.

'Embarrassed', aka 'Blanket Kick', is a song of frustrated embarrassment: a sweet confession of kicking at the bed sheets as you remember how weirdly you acted in order to impress or how you missed a once-in-a-lifetime opportunity. Now relax. It's '24/7=Heaven' and they are back in love again. To the poppiest of upbeat grooves, a fine line distribution enables every one of them to feel the romance.

Putting out a full album meant BTS could push their boundaries a little and the next track, 'Look Here', sounds exactly like a group who had spent their summer in the US, hanging out in LA listening to Pharrell's 'Come Get It Bae'. After the penultimate track, '2nd Grade', a fun freak-out with a magnificent 'bang it, bang it' refrain, the record closes with 'Outro: Does That Make Sense?' Here the album comes full circle to take up the theme of love grown cold once again. As on previous albums, the vocal line is called upon to finish, and right from Jung Kook's delicious 'listen', they are smooth as silk and totally in the groove.

On the TV music-show promotions, the group's performances got more air time and ARMY stepped up a gear with fan chants clearly audible to viewers. Nevertheless, the show victory that BTS craved still eluded them. In a typical response, they vowed to work even harder.

MEMBER PROFILE

Name:	Kim Seokjin
AKA:	Jin, Visual King, Third One From The Left, Worldwide Handsome, Car Door Guy, Flying Kiss Guy
Date of birth:	4 December 1992
Birthplace:	Angyang, Gyeonggi Province, South Korea
Height:	1.79 metres (5'10")
Education:	Bosung High School, Konkuk University, Global Cyber University
Chinese zodiac:	Monkey
Star sign:	Sagittarius
Instagram:	@jin

SIX

KIM SEOKJIN/JIN: WORLDWIDE HANDSOME

After the group's magenta carpet appearance at the Billboard Music Awards (BBMAs) in 2017, the hashtag #ThirdOneFromTheLeft suddenly went viral. It wasn't even the first time Jin had sent social media spinning. After his appearance at the 2015 Melon Awards, it was #CarDoorGuy that set Twitter ablaze. So what was he doing to attract such attention? Absolutely nothing. Unless you count being devastatingly good-looking. 'I think I'm worldwide handsome,' Jin explained. It wasn't exactly a modest statement, but nobody was arguing.

It was his looks – broad shoulders and a face with what plastic surgeons call a 'golden ratio' of symmetrical features – that originally brought him to BTS. SM, one of the Big Three entertainment companies, had selected him in a streetcast, but he ignored their invite to audition (some say he actually ran away from the scouts), believing it was a prank. When Big Hit invited him along, he turned up, auditioned as an actor and found himself as the first non-rapper to join the group.

Kim Seokjin grew up in Gwacheon City, just south of Seoul. His family was tight-knit and he describes his childhood as idyllic. They would take trips to places such as Japan, Australia and Europe, and his father would teach him golf and take him to ski resorts, where Jin found he had an aptitude for snowboarding. He had a warm if competitive relationship with his brother, who was just two years older, and in fact he remains close to all his family, especially his mother. For Parents' Day in 2015 he recorded a touching cover of Ra.D's track 'Mom', adding a sweet dedication to her.

At the Beautiful Moments concert in Seoul, his mother was in the audience and, as he welled up, he explained that his mum used to listen to her friends bragging about their sons without saying a word, so he really wanted to make his mum proud, and now, thanks to ARMY, he could. He is just as close to her today, with other members of the group remarking that he can stay on the phone to her for over an hour!

Jin's middle and high schools were both all-boy establishments and he admits to struggling to look girls in the eye, finally having to force himself to in order not to appear awkward in front of ARMY, but he did make plenty of friends, some of whom he is still in regular contact with despite his busy schedule. He enjoyed school, worked hard, played every possible sport and wanted to become a newspaper reporter.

That changed in 2009 when he watched the historical drama *The Great Queen Seondeok*, the most popular TV series in Korea. Like much of the nation, the young Seokjin was captivated, especially by the moving performance of actor Kim Nam-gil. It inspired the high-school student so much that he entered Konkuk University to major in acting at the Department of Film and Visual Arts. He had been studying for just three months when he got the call from Big Hit in April 2011.

For a young guy who had set his heart on acting, trainee life must have been a massive shock. Luckily Seokjin's easy-going nature helped. When Bang Si-hyuk asked him to choose a one-syllable name, as it is more intense, he simply shortened his own to Jin. He transformed himself from an aspiring actor into a trainee singer and dancer without fuss, saying he could always become an actor later. And he quickly got used to being the oldest in a group who could already dance, sing or rap. That was Jin, Mr No Worries.

But it wasn't easy. In the months before debut he found the dieting hard, and he struggled with performance skills, although he was always grateful to the other members of the group and the Big Hit staff who spent time helping him with his singing and his dance moves. Meanwhile, though, he had found his role in the dorm. It was soon evident that Jin was the one who would clean and tidy, put the groceries away and throw out rotten food. It was also clear that he loved cooking and creating meals to brighten up their somewhat tedious diet. No wonder he soon picked up the nickname 'Granny' from his younger bandmates!

Perhaps at first Jin's shyness made him seem stand-offish to some of the members of BTS, but when he and Jung Kook shared vocal lessons they quickly formed a bond. Jimin became his gym buddy and a love of animation brought him close to V. Suga never had any doubts: he shared a room with Jin and was adamant he never wanted to swap. Within the group, Jin was in an unfamiliar position: he was the eldest in this new 'family', having spent his life being the *maknae*, but again it didn't seem to bother him. He was quiet and serious with RM, J-Hope and Suga, and excitable and playful with the younger members, earning himself the label 'fake *maknae*'!

When they lived together in the dorm, Jin took on the 'parental' role. He often rose long before his bandmates to make sure they were awake and ready to start work on time (not always an easy task), cleaned up after them and, of course, liked to cook for them all. He continues to add to his collection of Super Mario figures (many given to him by fans) and relaxes by playing video games – *MapleStory* is a favourite. He also looked after Odeng, Eomuk and Gukmul, his adorable sugar gliders (a type of small possum), after coming across the animals while searching for 'Suga' on the internet. They have sadly now all passed away, but he was devoted to them.

Like all the members of BTS, Jin has lots of friends in other idol groups. He is close to Ken from VIXX and they are both part of a 92-liner chat group along with B.A.P's Youngjae, BTOB's Eunkwang, B1A4's Sanduel and Baro, EXID's Hani, and Moonbyul from Mamamoo, who has said it's Jin and Sandeul who always make the chat interesting!

By March 2013, Jin's singing had progressed enough for him to join RM and Suga in recording 'Adult Child', one of the first pre-debut BTS tracks, on which he provides a simple but sweetly sung interlude. All was going pretty well for the seemingly unflappable Jin, but debut was to provide a shock for the senior member. He has told interviewers that the *M Countdown* show was the first time he had worn a microphone pack, and he had climbed on stage with it attached to his trousers. However, he had not accounted for the weight of the pack. During 'We Are Bulletproof Pt. 2', in the section where they jump down, his trousers slipped all the way down to his thighs. He quickly pulled them back up, but they fell off a second time. He laughs about it now, but at the time the poor boy was inconsolable.

Jin had few worries about his dancing before the BTS debut, but the criticism he received afterwards – some called him the 'black hole of dance' – hit home. He's worked hard at his dancing and has shown real improvement, but remains very modest about his talents on the dancefloor. In 2017 he told a TV show, 'I think I am really bad at dancing,' but added, 'However, Rap Monster really cannot dance!'

An array of Seokjin talents have emerged since that debut day. No conversation with the Gwacheon boy seems to pass without an – often terrible – *ahjae* joke (literally an 'uncle joke', although in the West it's better known as a 'dad joke'). These are often Korean puns or a joke made by mixing English with Korean, such as: 'What does the dog say when it sees a wall?' The answer is 'wol-wol', which is Korean for the sound a dog makes. No wonder the other members of BTS often look bemused or cringe with embarrassment! Perhaps of more use is Jin's dexterity with his toes. On various reality shows he has demonstrated his ability to open bags of sweets or take off his socks without using his hands. And how can we forget his signature 'Traffic police dance'? A hilarious marching, hand-waving move that he has even taught to the rest of the group.

Actually, reality shows have proved Jin to be both resourceful and fun. In January 2017, he appeared on the tough survival show *Law of the Jungle*, which sends celebrities to survive in remote locations around the world. Along with other K-pop stars and K-drama actors, he was packed off to rural Indonesia. Despite having to leave early to go on tour with BTS, Jin acquitted himself brilliantly. He proved popular with the other stars, made wooden paddles with a hand saw, caught fish using an ARMY bomb (light stick) as a fishing reel and cooked them for his jungle family, as well as winning water for his team with an acrobatic triple spin dive.

Jin's humour and energy would prove just as popular in other shows such as *Hello Counselor* and *Please Take Care of My Refrigerator*, where he admitted the dorm fridge was mostly filled with cosmetics and skincare and that members would take food out to make room for them, and *Let's Eat Dinner Together*, where he entertained the crew with his *ahjae* humour and successfully found a Gangnam family willing to share their evening meal with him.

Ah, food! Jin loves his food. He loves cooking, eating and talking about food. His interest first surfaced on early Bangtan blogs when he would post 'Jin's Recipes' just to show how dull their debut diet food could be. This progressed to 'Jin's Cooking Diary', where he would detail more interesting meals, and eventually his occasional V Live series, *Eat Jin*. His version of *mukbang*, the popular videos where a host commentates as they eat, are a lot of fun, especially the episode where he attempts to consume an entire *jjajangmyeon* (noodles in black bean sauce, a dish favoured by Korean children) in one minute. In August 2018, Jin took his culinary interest even further when, with his brother, he opened Ossu Seiromushi, a restaurant specializing in Japanese steamed foods.

Jin's love for ARMY is also something else. He never fails to thank them for their support and has developed his own unique bond with them. It was Japanese ARMY who first called him 'Flying Kiss Guy' as they noticed his habit of blowing kisses off his hands to fans. He really has developed this into an art form, sending the most elegant and stylish kisses direct to every watching ARMY's heart.

For Jin really is the King of Hearts. It started with him putting out finger hearts to fans and drawing a heart on his hand next to the word 'ARMY', but it soon became his special contribution to live shows. In Hong Kong he reached into his shirt and produced a heart-shaped clothes hanger, in Anaheim he revealed a white heart taped over his heart, in

Sydney he flicked back his sleeves to show his heart-shaped felt bracelets. He would produce giant fold-out hearts, a long paper concertina of hearts or suddenly turn around to display his heart-adorned glasses. The other members enjoy these surprises as much as the fans, especially Jung Kook, who on tour in Osaka, Japan, searched Jin in vain for a heart, only to collapse in shocked laughter when the eldest member produced one from the microphone.

BTS WITH SPECIAL MC JIN @2017 KBS

In December 2017, Jin was selected as one of the MCs for the KBS Gayo Festival, a televised seasonal pop extravaganza featuring top Idol acts. Feast your eyes on Mr Worldwide Handsome as he prepares – very seriously – for his role and see the rest of the group support him as they watch him on their dressing-room TV.

Though some ARMY worry on Jin's behalf that he doesn't get enough singing lines or screen time, Jin himself seems to have a zen-like contentedness about his place in BTS. The *Wings* album included the first song where he had contributed to the writing and he was understandably proud of 'Awake', which he wrote with Pdogg. He says he worked hard on the writing and was very insistent his chorus was used. He was even reduced to tears when ARMY sang along to the song with him during a live performance.

That Jin was entrusted to sing 'Epiphany' spoke volumes to how his singing had progressed. The song previewed the *Love Yourself: Answer* album and Jin rose to the occasion with a measured and beautiful rendition. He continued to work tirelessly on his singing and the improvement was noted by all of the vocal line – Jimin noted how Jin would sometimes become stressed during recording sessions, but when they recorded *Map of the Soul: 7* it seemed he could use his voice in any genre. In 2021, he released his first solo OST with 'Yours', the theme song to the mystery thriller series *Jirisan*. It topped the iTunes charts in over eighty regions.

Jin had also worked hard on songwriting, which he used to convey deeply personal thoughts. Released for the 2019 *festa*, 'Tonight' focuses on loss, inspired by the death of his sugar gliders, then 'Moon' on *Map of the Soul: 7* was an upbeat hymn to ARMY. He contributed to the writing of 'Stay' along with RM and Jung Kook. He came up with the theme of missing ARMY during the pandemic and wrote the intro lyrics. His feelings in those trying times also resulted in his solo single, 'Abyss'. Released on SoundCloud just hours before his twenty-eighth birthday, it was a sensitive and brutally honest ballad that dealt with his insecurities during the pandemic, including imposter syndrome, where he doubted his talents and felt his success was undeserved.

The trio's performance of 'Stay' – surrounded on stage by the other members – became a highlight of the Permission to Dance concerts. However, Jin's participation in the Las Vegas shows was hampered by surgery after injuring the tendons on his index finger. Wearing a cast on his arm, he was forced to perform seated. Typically, he told the audience that felt he was a burden to the group, which compelled V to get up, give him a kick and tell him that he certainly wasn't.

When it came to their subsequent appearance at the Grammys, he carefully kept his arm hidden when on the red carpet (and still attracted attention as the 'Light Brown Suit Guy') and was cleverly integrated into the spy-themed 'Butter' performance. He looked a real special agent as he took a seat at the control board and, being a complete professional, he joined the group choreography in the finale without any fuss.

Jin has always remained dedicated to BTS. He seeks to improve his own contribution and often acts as the group's mood-maker, raising spirits and drawing members together. Away from group activities, he has no plan but simply does what he wants to do. It can take him to interesting places. He and Jung Kook apparently begged Suga to let them appear in the 'Daechwita' MV, where they stole a scene with their fighting (Jin said it made him realize he should never grow a beard). He also appeared on a great *Running Man* episode where he competed against the similarly named host, Jee Seok-jin, in foot volleyball, balloon popping on a slippery surface and other fun games.

One lighthearted diversion ended up giving him another – unexpected – hit. He came up with the excuse of wanting to write a modern fishing song in order to go fishing with friend and Seventeen-producer BUMZU, only to end up actually writing 'Super Tuna'. The short trot-style upbeat ditty was uploaded to SoundCloud as a gift to fans for his twenty-ninth birthday, but it was the video that helped it go viral. Everyone seemed to be copying Jin's fun moves and as a dance challenge it was a massive hit on TikTok.

Just weeks later, along with the other members, Jin launched his personal Instagram account under the name @jin. As a regular if not prolific poster, his photos portrayed his playful side, his love of golf, tennis and, of course, food and plenty of Worldwide Handsome shots and selfies. The account had only been running for a few months when, as an April Fool's joke, he switched the profile pic to his near namesake, Jhin, a villainous character from the videogame *League of Legends*. For the bio he even adapted a famous Jhin quote so it read: 'On stage [rather than the original 'In Carnage'] I bloom, like a flower in the dawn'.

Jin's love of gaming is no secret and fans know that *MapleStory* is his favourite game. However, no one suspected he would actually turn up in the game. In August 2022, a two-episode mini web series, *Office Warrior Kim Seok Jin*, published to the MapleStory_KR YouTube channel, featured Jin as a professional game planner. The character Jin was as charming, funny and full of creativity as real-life Jin as he presented ideas for game development and design to the Nexon company executives. And to prove that dreams can come true, he found himself in the game itself as an NPC dressed in his 'Super Tuna' dungarees.

After BTS announced they were to focus on solo activities in June 2022,

Jin reacted by engaging with projects that he said made him happy. One such endeavour was getting together with his good friend and drinking buddy TV chef Baek Jongwon to host The Drunken Truth, a four-episode food- and-drink-based reality series on YouTube's BANGTANTV. Drink was also taken when Jin appeared in a chaotic and memorable episode of Lee Young-ji's popular YouTube show *Nothing Much Prepared*. After drinks, hilarious questions, answers and games, the host retreated to the bathroom feeling a little ill. When she did not return, Jin took it upon himself to wrap up the show and left her a note that helpfully said: 'stop being drunk'.

Another longstanding love of his is instant ramen, and the conveniently named Jin Ramen brand in particular. 'I'll model for them someday,' he had declared back in 2016. Now that day had arrived. In 2022 he was declared the new face of Jin Ramen and was soon starring in their latest commercial, tucking into a steaming bowl of noodles.

The *Me, Myself, & Jin: Sea of JIN Island* photos for the group's photo-folio project enabled Jin to present different facets of his character. The ocean-based photographs portrayed him as a pirate in darkness, as a proud sea captain and as a working fisherman. Sensitive, seeking his own path and hard-working were all traits we had seen emerge in BTS's eldest member through the years. Now he would be the first member to undertake military service and needed to show his strength of character.

Jin soon displayed fortitude and a new self-confidence. 'Now, instead of, "How can I handle this?"' he said on Weverse, 'it's "I can handle this!" when I'm making songs for other people to listen to.' Just ten days later came his first official solo release, 'The Astronaut'. Jin had struck up a friendship with Chris Martin during BTS's collaboration with Coldplay for 'My Universe', and he co-wrote his new song with Chris and the rest of the group.

The romantic and sparkling rock ballad, which he described as being inspired by 'having to leave for a while and missing the band and fans', perfectly showcased Jin's charm and vocal ability. The music video was a beautifully sentimental portrait of an alien astronaut happily stranded on Earth (with a brief cameo from Chris Martin himself), and Jin even joined Coldplay on stage at their stadium concert in Argentina to perform the song live.

The single served as a bittersweet farewell, but Jin was not going away before leaving ARMY with a special treat. As part of 'The Astronaut' promotions, Jin had introduced a simple but cute astronaut character (having explained that 'RJ is so successful that he's busy') that he had named Wootteo (short for '*wooju tteodori*', meaning 'space wanderer'). Wootteo had his own Instagram account (@wootteo) where he told his story of playing on his planet before following a signal from earth to BTS's Busan concert, where he heard Jin talking about the single. He was an immediate hit with ARMY, and Jin hoped Wootteo would represent him well while he was away.

BANGTAN BOMB

JIN'S ENTRANCE CEREMONY WITH BTS

Everyone knew this moment was coming, but somehow we were still not prepared for it. On Tuesday 13 December 2022, Jin officially began his eighteen-month military service. The six other members turned up to wish him luck, all of them insisting on patting his newly shaved head for good luck. It was an emotional farewell, as Jin told them, 'I'll go and come back well', before being the last to fall in line and salute in the entrance ceremony. Who could look that good with a buzz cut and face mask? Private First Class Worldwide Handsome of course.

On his return from Argentina, Jin began his preparations for military service with 'The Astronaut' still charting all around the world. For him,

2022 had been such a momentous year. He had become the first BTS member to become an uncle (the baby given the nickname 'Kim Butter' by his brother) and had surgery to his hand; he had joined the group in their first full-audience concerts since the pandemic began; gone through the stress of the break announcement; had a hit single and found himself with buzz-cut hair and soldier's uniform before the year was out (soon earning extra vacation days for him and his team after they won a military talent show – with choreography he taught them!). Just like his whole career with BTS, Jin took it all in his stride. Nothing seems to faze him, but perhaps it's easy to keep things in perspective when you are Worldwide Handsome.

SEVEN

RED BULLETS

The city is in meltdown. An alien race of giant monsters is attacking Earth and we are defenceless. Our only hope is a tight-knit team of superheroes. With their special powers, they might just be able to fight off the mutant invaders. Fearless, self-sacrificing and incredibly handsome, they also look strangely familiar. Could this be BTS to the rescue?

We On: Be the Shield was an official Big Hit-promoted webtoon. It's a manga-style online comic telling the story of a team of superheroes determined to save the world. Think Marvel's *Avengers*, except this team has genius scientist RM; deadly accurate archer Jin; Suga, a warrior whose limbs become swords; J-Hope, the winged observer; Jimin, who can utilize the power of the natural world; Jung Kook, whose body becomes armour to protect the team; and V, the summoner of darkness, shadows and deadly black holes.

It has so much more detail than this and is a great read for those who like their sci-fi fantasy mixed in with their favourite K-pop group. Uploaded in September 2014, it was more evidence that BTS were making themselves known. *Dark & Wild* had recently reached number two in Korea and number three in the Billboard World Albums Chart, 'Danger' had climbed to number seven on the Billboard World Digital Songs Chart and in October they were to play in front of 5,000 fans in Seoul. They explained that BTS wanted to represent the energy of youth that will destroy obstacles and prejudice in the world, so the event was to be called 'The Red Bullet'. It was their first ever solo full-length concert.

The two AX Hall concerts sold out in five minutes, so an extra night was added. Headlining their own show was a big deal for BTS. 'Until now,' they told the press, 'we have stuck to the hip-hop genre and promoted concepts that differentiated us from other idol groups, so we are preparing a very unique concert.' And, sure enough, it was pretty special.

BANGTAN BOMB

'WAR OF HORMONE' IN HALLOWEEN

When you tire of watching the video for 'War of Hormone' (which, judging by some ARMY reactions, might take a while!) have a look at this special Bangtan Bomb. In a rehearsal room festooned with spiders' webs, a costumed-up BTS perform the choreography – in character. RM is a vampire, Suga is knife-wielding Chucky, Jimin has dressed as Charlie Chaplin, Jin as Captain Jack Sparrow, V plays the Joker, J-Hope is prisoner Papillon and a whip-slinging Jung Kook is anime character King of Terrors. Frightening? Not really. Fun? Totally!

On each night, from 17 October through to 19 October 2014, they played an introductory video set in a classroom, followed by 150 minutes of Bangtan magic. They sang, danced and joked their way through a set of twenty-four songs, including, of course, hits such as 'Boy in Luv', 'Danger' and 'Just One Day', but also other favourites like 'Let Me Know', 'If I Ruled the World' and 'Embarrassed', with its own bed and sofa on stage for extra *aegyo* and cuteness. The rappers, with a guest appearance from Supreme Boi, came together for 'Cypher Pt. 3: Killer', while the vocal line performed 'Outro: Propose' with a new second verse by Jin. As fans held up banners saying, in Korean, 'Let's walk on the same road together for life', they encored with a high-energy blast of 'Jump' and 'Attack on Bangtan', before finishing with the *satoori* dialect rap, 'Paldogangsan'.

The audiences were ecstatic and sang along with every word. Reflecting on the experience in their vlogs, the boys seemed shocked and slightly overwhelmed by the experience. They all admitted it was amazing, but felt it had passed like a dream. RM told the *Starcast* news channel, 'Our choreography is so extreme that it was a little bit scary, worrying whether we can really do it, but after the concert I felt much better, just like I had completed a bungee jump.' V picked 'War of Hormone' as the most memorable moment, saying, 'With other songs, it was full of tension, but when we sing this song, everyone was full of joy.'

Shortly after the concerts, on 23 October, BTS released 'War of Hormone' as a single, accompanied by a music video, which was the most fun they had had on screen to date. An impressive one-shot take in black and white, with some red splash added later for Jimin's trousers and the stripes on Jung Kook's jumper, it has energy, laughs and the cheekiest choreography.

The BTS Live Trilogy Episode II: The Red Bullet (to give it its full name) in Japan meant another first – a full concert in a different language. They had, however, cultivated a following in Japan, appearing on variety and music shows, and releasing Japanese-language singles of 'No More Dream', 'Boy in Luv' and 'Danger', all of which had made the Japanese top ten, so they were certainly among friends. Taking into consideration the traditionally reserved response of Japanese audiences, the shows in Kobe on 13 and 14 November and the 16 November performance in Tokyo were enthusiastically received – indeed, the fans knew all the words and sang along.

The boys returned to Seoul in time not only for Jin's birthday, which was coming up on 4 December, but also for the Mnet Asian Music Awards, which is arguably the most prestigious ceremony in the South Korean entertainment industry calendar. As the group were in their second year, it was thought to be unlikely that they would pick up a trophy, but BTS had been asked to perform. This alone was an achievement. J-Hope later told *Starcast*, 'To me, the stage at MAMA is the most memorable [event of the year]. When I performed at MAMA, I felt I had grown up … I was so happy and excited.'

BTS performed 'Boy in Luv' during the show and came back for a display which set Twitter and the forums on fire. This was a section billed as 'The Fight of the Century', which pitted BTS against Block B, a similarly successful seven-boy, hip-hop-style group. The face-off took the form of a dance battle, a rap duel, a group performance and a joint performance – and the Bangtan Boys did ARMY proud. RM, in a white suit and pink shirt, went face-to-face with Block B's Zico, BTS put their all into 'Danger' and the two groups combined brilliantly for the Black Eyed Peas' 'Let's Get It Started'.

But it was the dance-off that really got fans talking. First, J-Hope, who took to the stage like a man possessed, pulled some breathtaking moves, once again proving that few could match him on the dancefloor. Then Jimin spun on to the stage and ripped off his hoody and T-shirt. The move looked slightly inelegant, and he later lamented that it was ten times cooler at rehearsal, but as he continued dancing without his shirt there were few complaints from those watching! Who won the battle? In a poll conducted over the next two weeks, BTS took 90.1 per cent of the votes. It was a great victory for both BTS and ARMY – a combination that would be mobilized again and again …

Before the end of the year and the TV music show Christmas specials, the Bangtan Boys had time to fly out and perform three more concerts in what had been named the Red Bullet tour. In Manila (7 December), Singapore (13 December) and Bangkok (20 December), BTS, with RM now sporting flaming red hair, gave every bit as good a performance as they had at their first concert in Seoul, while, for the first time outside Seoul, ARMY responded with surprise banners, fan chants and synchronized light-stick waving.

It was their second Christmas since debuting. Despite many in Korea doubting BTS's ability to win over new fans, they continued to prove these people wrong as their profile continued to grow. This year they appeared for the first time on the prestigious K-pop Christmas specials, *M Countdown Christmas Special* and the *Show! Music Core End of the Year Special*. What's more, they were also invited to appear at *Seoul Countdown*, a New Year celebration outside the Lotte World Tower, Korea's tallest skyscraper. This was quite an honour, but if you look for Jung Kook in the video of their performance on YouTube you'll be disappointed – the Golden Maknae was still a minor and forbidden by law to work at such a late hour!

BANGTAN BOMB

SOMEONE LIKE YOU (SUNG & PRODUCED BY V)

As the very end of the year approaches, so does V's birthday. In 2014, he decided to give a present back to ARMY in the form of his first cover song. On Twitter he asked fans what he should pick and someone suggested Adele's 'Someone Like You'. This, he said, has the kind of emotional vocals that appeal to him so that's what he went for. And, what's more, he planned and directed the video himself, shooting it in the back alley by the dorm in just sixteen minutes.

For those who like seeing the Bangtan Boys scrubbed up and smart, take a look at the range of outfits on display during the January 2015 awards season. They collected their *bonsang* prize at the Seoul Music Awards in their school uniforms accessorized with waistcoats or cricket jumpers. To collect their World Rookie Award at the Gaon Chart K-Pop Awards they wore identical slimline, two-button grey jackets with black collars, black ties, black trousers and white shirts, while at the Golden Disc Awards they accepted their *bonsang* for *Dark & Wild* in more casual grey-brown jackets, green ties, white trousers and an assortment of shirts.

The fact that they were picking up *bonsangs* is a guide to where they ranked at this point in the K-pop standings. These are given for artists' achievements in the past year and it is not unusual for as many as ten *bonsangs* to be awarded in one category. BTS's ultimate ambition, however, was to win the *daesang* – the grand prize. To even dream of reaching that level they would first need to secure a win on a music show, which was now the immediate goal.

By the time 2015 really got underway, BTS had established themselves as one of the twenty best acts in Korea. That was pretty good for a group that lacked the backing of one of the Big Three, were helping write their own material and were still predominantly producing hip-hop-based music. But could they take their profile and performance up a notch? It was certainly possible. ARMY were getting stronger by the day and the fan café was close to celebrating 100,000 members. They were getting airtime both as a group and individually (January saw V co-presenting *Best of the Best* on MTV with Suejong from Lovelyz, and RM soon had a regular slot on the TV show *Problematic Men*), and were now looking to build their overseas following with tours to both Japan and the US. Yet there was perhaps a sense that it was now or never. If they didn't win a TV music show, produce a number-one album or win the coveted grand prize of a *daesang* this year, would they fall by the wayside like so many K-pop contenders before them?

One route to success lay in nearby Japan. Only the US music industry made more money than the Japanese; fans there were enthusiastic and the biggest buyers of physical CDs in the world, and they had a growing appetite for K-pop. BTS had laid down the foundations for success by recording Japanese versions of their hits and had taken the Red Bullet show to Kobe and Tokyo, but now they were preparing for a major assault on Japan.

The Japanese rapper KM-MARKIT, who has worked with some of the biggest names in Japanese hip-hop, had helped translate and rework BTS's

Korean lyrics, enabling them to release their debut Japanese-language album, *Wake Up*, at the end of 2014. It contained Japanese versions of all their most popular songs, as well as three new tracks: 'Pt. 2 – At That Place', an answer song to 'Like'; 'The Stars', featuring some vocals from Jin; and 'Wake Up', which blended a soft Japanese-style rap with the BTS sound.

BANGTAN BOMB

IT'S TRICKY IS TITLE! BTS, HERE WE GO! (BY RUN-D.M.C.)

They might be in their Donna Karan finest (RM clearly didn't get the memo!), but what is great about this bomb is they're still kids having fun. Run-DMC's classic is an old favourite of theirs and as it plays they put together some cheeky, cheesy and impressive moves. First Jimin realizes he's missing out, then RM decides he wants to join in too and, hey, what about Jin? Fun and funky, this could be one of the best Bangtan Bombs ever!

With the album reaching number two in the Japanese charts, BTS set off for Japan, where between 10 and 19 February they played to a total of 25,000 people in six sold-out concerts in Tokyo, Osaka, Nagoya and Fukuoka. Their set featured a sweet and funny video of them learning Japanese and, one by one, falling for the teacher, but each coming unstuck with their language mistakes, and they played the songs from *Wake Up* with some added surprises, such as pre-debut track 'Adult Child' and a cover of Mariah Carey's 'Beautiful'. As ever, they left the country with their profile enhanced and fans screaming for them to come back soon.

When they returned to Seoul, it was time for RM to take the limelight. And boy, was he busy! While recording a new mystery celebrity identity TV series called *Problematic Men* on which he was one of the hosts, he also released a collaborative single, 'P.D.D', with none other than Warren G, the pioneering rapper the group had met on *American Hustle Life*, and, finally, he dropped his long-awaited mixtape, *RM*.

Those paying close attention might have asked, 'If Red Bullet is Episode II, what happened to Episode I?' BTS answered this by announcing two concerts, on 28 and 29 March 2015, at the Olympic Hall in Seoul titled 'Live Trilogy Episode I: BTS Begins'. The show was a review of their career so far – from the birth of the group to the Red Bullet – and an opportunity to give a heartfelt thank you to ARMY and to their parents, some of whom were there, watching them perform live for the first time.

The boys, in piped blazers over white 'BTS Begins' hoodies, performed over twenty of their songs to an adoring audience. These included pre-debut songs like the Drake cover 'Too Much', as well as all their singles, and even a couple of sneak previews from their next short album. Two YouTube clips related to this concert are particular fan favourites. The first is a BANGTANTV video of J-Hope's astonishing dance practice for the event and the other is the clip of their last song of the evening: a fantastic performance of 'Born Singer', their pre-debut version of J. Cole's 'Born Sinner'. Watch them – they're brilliant!

MEMBER PROFILE

Name: Min Yoongi

AKA: Suga, Agust D, Genius, Motionless Min, Min PD, DJ Shup-D

Date of birth: 9 March 1993

Birthplace: Daegu, South Korea

Height: 1.74 metres (5'9")

Education: Daegu Taejeon Elementary School, Gwaneum Middle School, Kangbuk High School, Apgujeong High School, Global Cyber University

Chinese zodiac: Rooster

Star sign: Pisces

Instagram: @agustd

EIGHT

MIN YOONGI/SUGA: GENIUS AT WORK

ARMY know there's more than one Suga. There's the rapper from Daegu who doesn't give a hoot what anyone thinks; there's cute Yoongi with a smile that breaks hearts; and there's Motionless Min, the sleepaholic who says that in the next life he wants to be a rock and do absolutely nothing. And don't forget producer Suga, so obsessed with finding the perfect beat he'll work anywhere – in airport departure lounges, TV studio waiting rooms, even toilet cubicles. One man, so many roles – no wonder he's always tired! This is the guy who, when asked to describe himself, said, 'Min Suga, genius,' adding that no other words were needed. He's the rapper who, when the haters accused BTS of lip-syncing, deliberately stopped singing mid-song, and he's the mischievous member who breaks into English, just as RM finishes saying none of the others speak the language.

Min Yoongi, as he often likes to remind us, grew up in Daegu, in the North Gyeongsang Province. Men from the province are stereotyped as being temperamental and macho, and the dialect, in which he sometimes raps, can sound quite harsh to other Koreans. Like V, he spent some time being brought up by his grandmother and both seem to have had a tougher upbringing than the others. Suga has confessed that after debuting he went back to the dorm and sat staring blankly at the wall, amazed that a poor kid from Daegu could come so far.

The fact that he had was thanks to his determination and his musical talent. The song 'First Love' tells how he learned to play the piano at elementary school and, although he fared well at his studies, it was music that captured his interest. And in 2005, when he discovered South Korean groups Stony Skunk and Epik High, he caught a love of hip-hop – and caught it bad.

The teenage Min Yoongi set about finding out all he could about hip-hop. He taught himself how to operate music production software and by the age of seventeen he was working part-time at a recording studio, writing lyrics, and learning how to compose and arrange songs. He has recalled in interviews how he earned just enough for the bus to the studio and his food, sometimes having to walk home, which took two hours, if he'd spent too much on noodles.

Yoongi's hard work helped him make a name for himself in the Daegu music scene. He became a trusted source for 'beats' (backing tracks) for the city's rappers, produced their mixtapes and he even took a stage name, Gloss, and began rapping himself. In 2010, as part of the hip-hop crew D-Town, he produced and composed a song for a local festival. It commemorated the Gwangju Uprising, a 1980 pro-democracy demonstration in which hundreds of students were killed by the armed forces, and revealed the young songwriter's readiness to confront issues that others considered taboo.

Some months later, a flyer announcing that Bang Si-hyuk was holding a rap audition caught the eye of the high-school student. He passed the preliminary round, supposedly changing the beats he was given to rap over to his own arrangement, but only came second in the final rap battle. Fortunately, Big Hit had been impressed by his production skills and took him on anyway, and when the winner, i11evn, left the company, Yoongi found himself in the group, the second of the final BTS line-up to join.

In interviews, Suga has revealed that although his brother supported him from the start, his parents were initially against him following a career in music, but once they came round they became enthusiastic fans, even calling him by his stage name. His father jokingly told a fan meeting that he didn't understand why ARMY liked Suga so much! At the 2016 HYYH Epilogue concert, on spotting his parents in the crowd, Suga fell to his knees and bowed to them, and in 2017 he bought his mother a restaurant in Daegu called Big Hearted Grandma's Blood Sausage Soup … which probably sounds better in Korean!

When Yoongi became a trainee idol he needed an idol name and he's given two reasons why he chose the name Suga. One relates to his love of basketball. Even as a trainee, he played every week. His position was shooting guard and 'Su Ga' is an abbreviation of the term. However, he's also said he was given the name Suga because his skin is very white compared to that of many Koreans and he's so sweet – especially when he smiles. Of course, ARMY tend to favour the second explanation!

Suga found being a trainee pretty hard-going. He tells of how much he disliked Bang Si-hyuk at the time and how he once walked out of practice to confront the boss and tell him he was leaving the group. Luckily, after a blazing row, he rejoined his friends in the rehearsal room. He also did part-time work to earn extra money while a trainee, including making deliveries by bike. After an accident on the road, he injured his shoulder. He hid his injury from the company and thought of going home. But when they found out, they offered to help him financially and said they would wait until he had recovered and was able to resume his training.

That bond with the others helped him through those days. They affectionately called Suga 'Grandpa', as he's the one who changed the light bulbs, fixed doorknobs, mended the things RM broke – and because he's frequently to be found having a nap! Though sometimes the serious one of the group who doesn't always take part in the younger members' games (though he always puts up with them), Suga is respected and loved by the others. He has known and worked with RM since he joined Big Hit and, until moving into their final plush apartment, had roomed with Jin since the beginning, refusing to countenance any idea of swapping, believing Jin to be the perfect roommate.

Suga's bond with Jung Kook is the stuff of BTS legend. Suga himself has described him and the *maknae* as 'The Lamb Skewer Duo'. Ever since Suga introduced him to the meat-on-a-stick dish, it has been Jung Kook's favourite food. Their joke was that he has asked Suga to go out and buy him some so often that they were going to set up a lamb kebab restaurant. This business idea came up frequently until 2017, when Jung Kook told *ARMY* magazine that Suga's parents had told him it was an idea doomed to failure and Suga said he was looking at starting a furniture business instead!

BANGTAN BOMB

BTS'S VOCAL DUET 'SOPE-ME' STAGE BEHIND THE SCENE

Suga and J-Hope – SOPE – are a pairing fans love to see together. Their occasional V Live series 'Hwagae Market' is often laugh-out-loud funny, their photos in matching 'SOPE' orange tracksuits for the 2016 *festa* were inspired, while this bomb, in which the rappers try out as vocalists, shows just how well they get on.

ARMY have also taken the Suga/J-Hope friendship (called 'Sope') to heart. They loved the Hwagae Market vlogs they did together, the matching outfits and the on-stage tomfoolery during BTS's 2018 Love Yourself tour. Perhaps best of all was their April Fool's prank in 2019 when the duo took over the group's Twitter account, swapped the profile picture to a selfie of themselves, changed the name to SOPE and updated the profile to read: 'Contact via DM for event enquiries. We can go anywhere within the country. Get it!' The very next day they had a (fake) tearful live broadcast to announce they were 'disbanding' due to differences of opinion and musical styles.

Yoongi has a real passion for technology: his very first vlog for BTS was a review of the digital controller he used for making beats. Later we became used to seeing him with a camera, and a hashtag appeared on Twitter which fans translated as 'Suga's sight'. It featured photos of BTS members, curiosities or places he had travelled to with the group. He famously wrote on one upload that it was fine to re-upload or edit it 'because I'm cool :)'.

Suga's individual personality won him a special place in ARMY affections when he demonstrated his practice 'chat-up line' in *American Hustle Life*: 'You like this chain? Three dollars.' They love his use of the word 'infires', his version of 'inspires', and the nonsense rap line 'Min Suga genius jjang jjang man boong boong', a phrase immortalized when it accompanied Suga's photo on Jimin's phone. Other cherished Suga moments include when he dressed in uniform and a black bob wig as an incredibly pretty schoolgirl character, Min Yoonji, in *Run BTS!*, and finally, ARMY have never forgotten the clip from a BTS signing event where one overexcited fangirl hilariously screams at Suga that he is a dangerous man and threatens to sue him for hurting her by being so gorgeous.

'Yoongi marry me' has become a running joke between the group and ARMY. The phrase appears almost any time the members do a live broadcast. V in particular likes to read out the requests, which always leaves the members in hysterics, apart from Suga who remains cool and nonchalant (except for one famous occasion when he replied, 'Bring the documents'). It has become such an in-joke that fans bring proposal signs to concerts and events.

Because of his 'cool', reserved nature, Suga doesn't proclaim his love for ARMY as much as some of the others. He's Suga, he does it his own way. At a fan signing event back in 2014, he told ARMY that when he had made lots of money he would buy them meat. When, a year later, he was asked when he would keep his promise he named 9 March 2018, his twenty-fifth birthday, which was then still three years in the future, as the date. True to his word, on that day he donated Korean beef to thirty-nine orphanages, not in his own name, but in the name of ARMY.

In January 2014, Suga's appendix burst while the band were doing promotions in Japan. He flew back to Korea for treatment, but a day after being discharged he was back in Tokyo for a fan showcase. During the event, the members were supposed to read from letters they had written to the fans. Jin, however, chose to read a letter he had written to Suga. He said how much he admired Suga for his determination to perform for ARMY despite being frail, but he also reminded him that it was okay to feel weak and that the other members of BTS would always look after him.

These were words that fans would remember in December 2015 when BTS announced they were cancelling a concert, again in Japan, because V and Suga were suffering from nausea. Although V was indeed physically ill on the day of the concert, Suga would later admit that, for him, it was a crippling anxiety that meant he had simply not been able to face the audience that night. Suga's long series of tweets possibly suggested that he has suffered with depression-related issues since his teenage years. Nevertheless he felt he had let the fans down in Japan. He admitted being unable to sleep, to waking in a cold sweat and being tearful about not performing. His tweets over the next few weeks revealed an artist at a low point. When the group finally had a break in their schedule, he had gone to the venue alone to try to feel the emotions of the fans he felt he had disappointed. With real honesty, he described himself as a weak person who acts as though he's strong, and he thanked ARMY for staying with him.

In August 2016, Suga released a free-to-download or stream mixtape, both titled and recorded under the name Agust D (backwards it reads DT Suga, with DT standing for Daegu Town). Produced entirely by Yoongi, in tracks such as 'Agust D' and 'Give It To Me' we get full-barrelled brag rap that defends his idol status, the first of these boasting of his 'tongue technology', a term ARMY will relish forever, but what the mixtape really allows Suga to do is tell his story.

In tracks such as '724148' (named after the buses he took to school in

Daegu and Seoul), 'The Last' and 'Tony Montana' he really bares his soul about the hardships of trainee life and the anxieties that seem capable of eating him up.

The mixtape draws to a close with the slow, soulful and very popular 'So Far Away', in which Suga, accompanied by singer Suran, tells of the courage needed to follow and see through your dream. Suga went on to write and produce Suran's 2017 hit 'Wine', which won best Soul/R&B track of the year at the 2017 Melon Music Awards, and helped to launch his solo songwriting and production (for other artists) career.

BANGTAN BOMB

'뱁새' DANCE PRACTICE (흥 VERSION) – BTS (방탄소년단)

If you search for 'Bangtan Bomb festa dance practice 2016', you can watch Suga's hilarious reaction when he loses the rock, paper, scissors game during rehearsals for their 'Baepsae' dance for *festa* 2016. J-Hope usually performs the dance break when they perform the song, but now the 'honour' has fallen to the member who least likes the limelight. Suga, of course, brings his own, slightly different approach to the dance solo. Elegant? No. Emotional? Not in the slightest. Amusing? You betcha!

Around 2018, a different, more confident Suga had emerged. On his *Love Yourself: Answer* solo track 'Trivia: Seesaw', Suga delighted ARMY with his singing – a talent hitherto hidden from view. Then they were completely overjoyed when it emerged that he had a whole choreography for the live shows. Among the group's emotional acceptance speeches at that year's MAMAs, Suga's was incredibly positive. '2018 was a year that made me wonder if I could be this happy in my life,' he said.

He was now being taken very seriously by the industry as a producer. He had not only mastered the technical equipment involved in recording and making music, but was also increasingly adept at writing the instrumentals for songs and creating the arrangements for them. When Jung Kook once asked him if he sometimes might spent half a day in his studio, Suga replied: 'What do you mean half a day? I eat and sleep in this studio ...'

His skills were in demand. He produced 'Eternal Sunshine' for Epik High's 2019 EP *sleepless in* __________, was a composer, producer and lyricist for Heize's 'We Don't Talk Together' and, in December 2019, Halsey even namechecked him in the title when he rapped on her song 'SUGA's Interlude'. He was even more prolific in 2020, producing and featuring in IU's single 'Eight', which topped the World Digital Song Sales chart, while BTS took advantage of his talent too. Suga was involved in the production of many songs on *Map of the Soul: 7* and of course also wrote his own solo, 'Interlude: Shadow', and 'Respect', his rap duet with RM. The pair's performance of this at Bang Bang Con: The Live, dressed in fabulous retro baggy suits, was one of the highlights of the show.

Suga had been a busy man. No wonder his second mixtape had taken four years to complete. *D-2* was released in May 2020, again under the name of his alter ego Agust D. Speaking about the difference between Agust D and Suga, he told *Time* that with Agust D, 'There is a lot more that I can openly express and that I can show a more raw side to myself,' but added: 'What's similar is that both sing of dreams and hope.' Across the ten songs, he shared his experience and observations of the world around him, from fame, the music business, maturing as a person as well as dreams, choices and friendship.

On the album, Suga sang and rapped and recruited guest artists, including MAX, NiiHWA and Kim Jong-wan, and once again teamed up with his friend RM. Their collaboration, 'Strange', deals with moral and political issues in society, but there is a mature acceptance of different and sometimes conflicting perspectives on life. This is reflected in the rest of the album's songs with the exception of the completely solo lead track 'Daechwita', where an explosive instrumental and a skilful rap with a totally infectious chorus tell us just how confident he is, secure in his place in the rap pantheon.

'Daechwita' leaned heavily on the use of Korean instruments (the title refers to royal military marching music) and the MV followed in historical K-drama style. It features a clash between the king and a rebel gang leader (both played by Suga) and includes a highly appreciated and amusing cameo of a squabbling Jin and Jung Kook. The mixtape and the single saw Agust D become the first Korean solo artist to top the iTunes charts in over 100 countries.

SUGA'S 'DAECHWITA' SWORD-DANCE PRACTICE

For someone suffering shoulder pain, Suga wields the sword with gusto in his choreography lesson for the 'Daechwita' video shoot. With a real sword in hand – a gift from a Korean master craftsman – he gets to work, following his choreographer's every instruction and practising his moves. It's clearly hard work. Suga, with no make-up, wearing an old T-shirt with his undercut hair brushed away from his forehead, sweats as he puts in the hard yards. Ever the true professional, he shows dedication, a desire to learn and an amazing ability to memorize the moves – and clearly has a great time in the process.

Suga soon repaid US singer, model and actor MAX, who had featured on *D-2*'s 'Burn It', by adding a Korean verse to his song 'Blueberry Eyes', which helped it to number one on iTunes in over sixty countries (briefly knocking 'Dynamite' off the top!). However, in November 2020, much of his work came to a halt as he underwent surgery on his shoulder, which had caused him continuing discomfort since his injury.

The operation was a success but forced Suga to absent himself from a number of end-of-year award shows and performances. The group missed him but did their best to ensure he was there in spirit, carrying photos of him, mentioning him in speeches, leaving an empty space for him in group photos, and phoning him during their acceptance speech. At the 2020 MAMAs he even joined the 'Life Goes On' performance – as a hologram. Best of all was the 2020 *SBS Gayo Daejeon*, in his hometown of Daegu, where he was represented by a cute snowman who lip-synced Suga's verses!

In January Suga was back at last when BTS took to the stage at the Golden Disc Awards. Now fully recovered, he participated in the group's packed 2021 schedule but still found time for his production work. He reimagined 'Over the Horizon', Samsung's signature musical theme, produced 'You' for Japanese singer ØMI (the singer attributing the song's global success to Suga's involvement) and featured on 'Girl of My Dreams' by Juice WRLD. The US rapper had tragically died in December 2019, but Suga held him in high regard, recognizing their lyrics shared an honesty and rawness.

Two more notable Suga songwriting and production creations would emerge in 2022. First came Jung Kook's 'Stay Alive', an OS for the *7 Fates: Chakho* webtoon, which (along with 'Girl of My Dreams' lyrics) he wrote on the plane to the US for BTS's 2021 LA concert. Then Suga came up with the wonderfully fun and energetic 'That That' for K-pop legend Psy. He had originally planned only to write and produce it but Psy convinced him to feature too – and even to appear in the Western-style MV, acting out a fist fight with the veteran star while dressed in a white suit and leopard-print shirt. The track was a massive hit and took the Best Collaboration award at that year's MAMAs.

It is now clear how exhausted the whole group were when they made their decision to take a break from group activities. It was Suga who brought the subject up at the *festa* dinner and encouraged RM to explain how they would focus on solo activities in the months ahead. Suga was already known to be working on a follow-up to *D-2* and fans were relieved to hear they were not in for another four-year wait.

After the announcement, Suga seemed to begin to enjoy his newfound freedom. ARMY know all about his love of basketball and were pleased to see him attending the NBA match between the Los Angeles Lakers and Dallas Mavericks, where he met Lakers star Luka Dončić. As well as being subsequently appointed as an NBA ambassador to help promote the sport, he was named as the new face of the luxury Italian fashion house Valentino and attended his first-ever Paris Fashion Week show in February 2023.

He then hosted his own talk show on YouTube called *Suchwita*, which roughly translates as 'Time to get drunk with Suga'. He invited some of his favourite stars for sincere and sometimes revealing in-depth chats about their careers and their future plans (and some drinking). RM was his first guest, but further shows featured Taeyang from Big Bang, Hoshi from Seventeen and Suga's all-time hero, Tablo from Epik High. Eventually he got round to the show's biggest fan, Jimin, in a near perfect heart-warming and tearjerking thirty minutes.

Suga deleted his first Instagram post and complained that 'IG is hard', but by 2023, @agustd was getting the hang of it and even posting reels when on tour in the US. By then his photo folio *Me, Myself, & SUGA: Wholly or Whole Me* had been released. The photos – including some of his own polaroids – featured a red-haired Suga enjoying the great outdoors in California. With the beautiful backdrop of the Sierra Nevada mountains, it's a soft-edged Suga that we've rarely seen before as he sets off in his SUV to explore the wilderness: hiking, spending time with the adorable dog Shelby and relaxing with his guitar by the campfire.

In early April 2023, Agust D returned. In anticipation of a forthcoming new solo album, a new single, 'People Pt. 2', was released. In an interview with *Billboard*, Suga explained how the song – an extension of the fan-favourite 'People' from *D-2* – was an attempt to 'sync the person SUGA and Agust D' to change expectations of the new album. To help achieve this he enlisted the help of IU, who he had collaborated with before on her hit song 'Eight'. Her vocals added an enchanting vibe to the emotional song's reflections on love and relationships.

Weeks later, Suga released his first full-length album. *D-Day* is the final instalment of the Agust D trilogy (although Suga doesn't rule out his alter ego reappearing in the future). The release of the album was accompanied by a Disney+ full-length documentary, *SUGA: Road to D-Day*. More than just a behind-the-scenes look at the making of the album, it was a fascinating account of the artist's creative process and his search for inspiration.

D-Day revealed a mature artist whose musical instincts and songwriting skills enabled him to confront the deepest of issues. He had moved on from the anger of *Agust D* and *D-2*, attempting to find resolution and acceptance in an album that explores liberation in its many forms. It confirms Suga as a masterful songwriter. He has an amazing capacity to confront both emotional issues and social commentary with honesty, passion and expression that can be direct or deeply poetic.

D-Day opens with a statement of intent in the strident 'D-Day', but the album is as much contemplative as it is assertive. This is evident in 'People Pt. 2'; the deeply personal 'Amygdala', which references his mother's heart surgery, his father's cancer and having to keep his own delivery-driving accident secret; and the smooth and atmospheric 'SDL', which uses past love to question just what we choose to remember.

Suga becomes more polemic when he confronts people's hypocrisy and prejudice. Some of the anger returns when he teams up with J-Hope on the fiery 'HUH?!', a full-on attack on baseless insults and ignorant judgement, while the more anguished boom-bap hip-hop track 'Polar Night' (where it is dark even in the middle of the day) questions people's entrenched one-sided views.

The album concludes with two uplifting tracks. 'Snooze' finds Suga positioning himself as an older brother, talking of the bitter lessons he has learned and offering support to those following their dreams. Kim Woo-sung of The Rose provides vocals on the track, which also features the legendary composer Ryuichi Sakamoto. Suga revealed that he had been sampling Sakamoto's compositions since seventh grade and had always dreamed of meeting him. Their encounter is a highlight of the documentary film but, sadly, Sakamoto died aged seventy-one, a month before the album's release. The album concludes with a different version of BTS's 'Life Goes On', which is as calmly positive as the opening track is strident.

'Haegeum', the second song on the album, is a raucous title track offering defiant optimism in its refusal to be defined or hurt by the past. While a *haegeum* is a traditional Korean string instrument (which is used in the song), it is also a word meaning 'the lifting of a ban'. The song is about achieving freedom from self-imposed and societal restrictions, from prejudices and conformity to information technology.

The MV sees Suga re-employ the dual-character motif he used in 'Daechwita', this time playing a cop and a gangster, who are both versions of his Agust D persona. It's a thrilling action movie in miniature and helped 'Haegeum' to hit the top of the iTunes chart in eighty-six countries and reach number one on the Billboard Digital Songs Chart. Meanwhile, *D-Day* debuted at number two on the Billboard 200 Album Chart and recorded the highest-ever first-day sales for a solo artist on the Korean Hanteo chart, with over a million copies sold on day one.

At the end of April, Suga set off on a Suga/Agust D Tour that saw him playing twenty-five dates across the USA and Asia. It must have been a daunting experience as a solo artist: not only the huge arena shows without his bandmates, but TV appearances too, such as his interview and performance on *The Tonight Show Starring Jimmy Fallon* in May. Suga seemed relaxed and confident throughout. He had promised a tour beyond people's expectations and from day one he was not about to disappoint.

The show began with a dramatic opening which recalled his motorbike accident and left Suga lying prone on the stage. After leaping up as the 'Haegeum' beat started, the energy levels shot up. The staging was stunning, constantly changing as sections rose to the heavens to reveal a new setting or a special effect, like the pyrotechnics accompanying *D-2*'s 'Burn It'. Meanwhile Suga sang, played piano, performed an acoustic version of 'Trivia: Seesaw' on a guitar signed by all the BTS members, and of course rapped through a setlist featuring a selection of Agust D tracks along with BTS songs, including 'Cypher Pt. 3: Killer', 'UGH!',

'Moonlight' and 'Interlude: Shadow', and finishing with 'The Last'. It was a virtuoso performance and as *NME's* rave review declared, 'a show-stopping statement of artistic intent'.

When Valentino, who provided custom clothing for his tour, selected Suga to be an ambassador for their fashion house, they did not just choose him for his sense of style. They admired him as 'a multifaceted artist' whose 'diversity, inclusivity, creativity and passion' embodied all the values of their 'Different Values' campaign. Their statement captured much of what fans had grown to love about the boy from Daegu. Whether it's as BTS's rapper Suga, alter ego Agust D, super-producer Min PD, Lil Meow Meow, the sleep-loving Grandpa or just simply Yoongi, he's still their 'Min Suga, Genius'.

NINE

BEAUTIFUL MOMENTS

Comeback day dawned – and it looked like it could be the most crucial comeback of the boys' careers. They wanted that music-show win so much. It was mentioned in so many of the interviews they did in spring 2015 and was even brought up in the skit on their forthcoming album. It was easier said than done, though. There were so many popular K-pop artists on the scene. They needed to produce something very special.

The new mini-album, *The Most Beautiful Moment in Life, Pt. 1*, was announced with the now familiar teasers for the end of April 2015. The trailer was once again a rap, but this time from Suga not RM, and with it was a beautiful Japanese-style animation featuring a young man hiding from the realities of life as he played alone on the basketball court. It ended with lyrics which explained that, even in times of hardship, happiness can be found in 'beautiful moments'. RM thought long and hard about the theme that would cover this and the next release, before choosing the phrase *Hwa yang yeon hwa* (often abbreviated to HYYH) to sum up the philosophy behind the album. The phrase is related to a Chinese saying meaning 'flower years' and is usually interpreted as 'the age of blossoms', a metaphor for the passing of youth, beauty and love, but, in keeping with BTS's mission to talk directly about the anxieties and problems of the young, the group opted for a slightly different translation for their album title: 'The Most Beautiful Moment in Life'. Later, during live performances, RM elaborated on the theme, emphasizing how the young must cherish their moments of joy and beauty, even though they may be struggling in school, in a job, with their parents or in a relationship. The concert DVD's English subtitles translate his words as: 'If you know and feel this moment truthfully with the heart, and that you're ready to accept the moment, then from the time when you're born, the entire life can be beautiful.'

Shortly after the trailer came the new concept photos. A set was revealed for each of the two album designs – a pink version and a white version. The first version contrasted splashes of colour in the boys' clothes, the green grass and flowers, and the sakura trees of Gyeongju National Park with their sombre mood. The second set, this time shot in black and white, reflected a similar mood, but was taken at Yeongdeok on the East Sea with a wintery seaside backdrop. On 29 April 2015, before the album and video drop at midnight, BTS appeared on *Starcast* in their own hour-long live show, called 'I Need U BTS on Air', where they talked about the photoshoot and the album, and performed a stunning 'slow jam' live version of 'I Need U'. Seeing them laughing and joking together in such a carefree way made the sombre posing seem almost unbelievable but, as we were about to discover, as well as singing and dancing superbly, these boys were also pretty good actors.

There was no dancing in the 'I Need U' music video, just a dark, dark story. It's actually so dark that the original video was re-edited, because it contained scenes that could shock or upset younger viewers (the original version was later uploaded with a 19+ age rating by the title; the re-cut version is rated 15). It takes the idea of the fragility of youth to a grim conclusion: a descent into violence, overdosing on pills and even hints of suicide. The frustrations of 'Danger' are nothing compared to the extremes depicted here, as each of the group are given their individual stories, all with a theme of desperation and despair.

Shot through a blue filter, the melancholic scenes really give the boys the chance to play a role – Jimin burns letters as he sits in the bath, Jung Kook is set upon by thugs, V reacts violently to his abusive father – and they're very believable. The images are laden with symbolism about leaving childhood behind and plummeting self-esteem, so it's unsurprising that ARMY continue to come up with theories about the meaning of the video.

The atmosphere of loneliness contrasts perfectly with clips of the group as a whole. Here they are not alone, but laughing, hugging, play-fighting and enjoying each other's company. Dressed in English-style casual wear – a Fred Perry polo shirt for Jimin, punk band T-shirt for V, check shirt with braces for RM, and bomber jacket and white tee for Suga – they come across as ordinary lads out having fun.

The video did its job. Within hours #INeedU was trending across social media and the stage was set for the mini-album release. The pink and white versions of the CD were both packaged with an exquisite 120-page photobook full of even more pictures from both the flower and the seaside photoshoots, as well as the usual random member photo and a group picture.

Suga's forceful rap from the trailer serves as the album's intro. It's a passionate rant against the voices of self-doubt, which is driven by the beat of the bouncing basketball and heightened by the sound of sneakers squeaking on the court. This leads straight into the single, 'I Need U', which sets the electro-pop sound and emotional intensity levels for the rest of the album and returns to the familiar theme of longing for a love that has ended. This, however, is a more mature reflection on the topic. They are no longer boys in 'luv'; this is serious, and for the first time they are prepared to use the word 'love'.

Those who discovered BTS at this point may not have quite appreciated that this was when it all came together. The transitions between singers and rappers are so much smoother. They move further away from hip-hop and towards a softer pop style, but they keep the beat alive. It isn't an imitation of US rap and it isn't Korean hip-hop or pure K-pop. They were forging a sound which was truly their own and 'I Need U' was their most complete single yet.

However, anyone missing the dance element in the music video didn't have to wait long. Just a few days after release, Big Hit put out a dance practice video for the song. This was more subtle than many of their dances and the general effect is of waves of movement until the chorus, when that amazing sharp and angular dance action comes to the fore. The excitement heightened in anticipation of the music-show promotions to come.

Track three, 'Hold Me Tight', marked V's songwriting debut. Having watched the rap line at work for such a long time, he had waited patiently before emerging with this gentle piano and synth love song. The revealing 'Skit: Expectation!' follows, in which the band discuss their hopes for the album or, indeed, whether they dare hope at all.

This shows the group's insecurity; that they really want to believe they have a chance of success, but are held back by modesty or perhaps a lack of real self-belief. There was, however, a lovely interview with Jin on the TV show *Pops in Seoul* in which he claimed he knew 'I Need U' would be a hit, because whenever J-Hope says something will be a flop, it does well, and J-Hope had predicted disappointing results for the new single!

'Welcome. First time with BTS?' asks RM, greeting the ever-growing new recruits to ARMY, at the beginning of 'Dope'. The energy returns in this, track five of the album, and with it comes the most popular song BTS had recorded to date. *Billboard*'s Jeff Benjamin, one of the group's earliest mainstream champions in the US, praised the song's 'aggressive lyrics, party-ready production and exotic horn-laden breakdown'. America was starting to take notice of BTS. And how could it not? In a really upbeat track, BTS parade their ability to merge a string synth sound, a jazzy break and a pounding beat as they sing about defeating their critics and celebrating their success. It's as if, despite their modest expectations, they knew this was going to work all along.

What you want at this point is a feel-good foot-stomper and along comes 'Boyz with Fun', which is exactly that. Once they performed this good-time bop on music shows it became a firm live favourite with its relatively easy to imitate choreography and the crowd-pleasing tradition in which V invents a move the others have to copy.

'Boyz with Fun' and the next track, 'Converse High', had both been previewed in the concerts at Seoul's Olympic Hall in March. The subject of the latter, written by RM, was familiar to those who had heard him interviewed about his ideal type: he likes a girl who wears red Converse high-top trainers. In this smooth, R&B-infused song he manages to convince the rest of the band of the excellence of his preferred make of footwear – except (of course) for Suga, who won't be told, and has his own verse dissing them!

In spring 2015 the boys had finally moved dorms. They originally shared a small dorm with all seven of them sleeping in one room, but with their success they had moved to a bigger, three-bedroom dorm where Jin and Suga shared one space, RM and Jung Kook another, and J-Hope, Jimin and V a third. So in the next song, 'Moving On', a light hip-hop-with-guitars track, they talk about their change of dorms, their memories – happy and sad – of the last place, and use moving as a metaphor for going up the rankings as idols.

The ninth and final track, 'Outro: Love Is Not Over', continues the tradition of the vocal line closing the album. This piano-accompanied ballad was Jin and Jung Kook's opportunity to shine in the songwriting department and they did just that, with a beautiful, soul-wrenching denial of the end of a romance.

From the outset, BTS have attempted to create a unique relationship with their fans through social network sites and YouTube. From summer 2015, although the bombs, dance practices and other videos continued to be uploaded to YouTube, other BTS videos appeared on the newly launched V Live. This platform enabled K-pop groups to post live and recorded videos (with English translations) and even chat to their fans in real time. (At the end of 2022, V Live was phased out, with Weverse becoming the official communication channel for BTS and many other K-pop artists.)

The first BTS series that appeared on V Live consisted of five ten-minute episodes called *BTS Bokbulbok*. The title translates as *Lucky Draw* or *Lucky or Not* and the group pick a random game – it could be a boxing video game, mini table tennis or cup stacking – to play in their dance studio. Check out the first episode where they play charades, with Jung Kook, Jin and Jimin being kangaroos, or episode three in which a blindfolded V scoots around the dancefloor in a hilarious round of hide-and-seek.

In August 2015, V Live began broadcasting a fun music-based series called *BTS Gayo*. In the eight episodes (or 'tracks' as they're called here) the challenges see them perform girl-group dances or try to recognize members' impressions of other K-pop singers. ARMY especially love track two, where the boys re-enact romantic scenes from Korean movies, and track six, where a quest to find the worst dancer in BTS ends in a fabulous impromptu dance battle between Suga and J-Hope.

Another V Live series, *Run BTS!*, saw the boys freed from the studio, and given even more scope for games, challenges and activities. If you wonder whether J-Hope ever stops smiling, then watch him on the rollercoaster when they all visit a theme park in episode three. And, if you believe they're tough guys, just watch them sweat on the elevator to the bungee jump in episode nine!

V Live would become an important outlet for BTS. Individual members had their own live shows such as 'Eat Jin', Suga and J-Hope's 'Hwagae Market', J-Hope's 'Hope on the Street' and Jimin and V's 'What are the 95z Doing?'. The group also regularly broadcast live on the app, whether backstage at awards ceremonies, in the dressing room before TV variety shows, on every member's birthday, and before and even after concerts all around the world.

Meanwhile, BTS hadn't forgotten the importance of television. With the video for 'I Need U' reaching 1 million views in sixteen hours and number five in the Gaon charts, and the mini-album going in at number two, they prepared their stages for the Korean TV music shows. Could they finally take that elusive show victory?

MEMBER PROFILE

Name:	Jung Hoseok
AKA:	J-Hope, Hobi, Smile Hoya
Date of birth:	18 February 1994
Birthplace:	Gwangju, South Korea
Height:	1.77 metres (5'10")
Education:	Ilgok Middle School, Kukje High School, Global Cyber University
Chinese zodiac:	Dog
Star sign:	Aquarius
Instagram:	@uarmyhope

TEN

JUNG HOSEOK/J-HOPE: MORE THAN SUNSHINE

Even if you're new to BTS, J-Hope is easy to spot in any group interview. He'll be the one with the beaming smile. What if a few of them are smiling? No worries. Wait a minute or so and one of them will start whooping, waving or, if you're lucky, dancing. That'll be J-Hope.

Right from debut, J-Hope's energy and exuberance has driven BTS. In interviews, vlogs, Bangtan Bombs and performances, his good nature is a given. In a *festa* conversation Suga once suggested that this wasn't the case when they were trainees and that it was the 'Hope' name that took Hoseok into optimism overdrive. Whether that's true or not, J-Hope is proud to be BTS's ray of sunshine, often introducing himself with 'I'm your hope, you're my hope, I'm J-Hope!'

Of course, J-Hope is so much more than a happy mascot for BTS. He takes his place on the rap line, has contributed to the writing and production of over a hundred songs (including his solo work) and is the main dancer. It is J-Hope who takes the lead in dance rehearsals, helping the others master the steps in the long practice sessions.

Unlike some others in the group, J-Hope arrived at Big Hit as an accomplished dancer. He had been dancing since he was at elementary school, and he recalled his thrill at the reaction he received when he performed on stage in a talent competition there. The love of music and expressing himself through dance would never leave him. Young Hoseok and his older sister, Ji-woo (who has a clothing line called Mejiwoo), grew up in a loving family in Gwangju, a city in the south-west corner of South Korea. When an early enthusiasm for tennis faded, inspired by dance videos he saw a perfect outlet for his passion for music and performance. In middle school, he kept up his studies, but was already building a reputation among his friends for his dancing ability, and even won a national dance competition.

At high school, he claims to have been well behaved, but he probably had little choice – his father was a literature teacher there. He didn't achieve particularly high grades, but he did excel at hip-hop-style popping. By fifteen he was learning dance at an academy, performing regularly with a local street dance team called Neuron, and even auditioned for JYP Entertainment. V later recalled that when BTS debuted, his friends asked if J-Hope was that dancer from the academy in Gwangju (at that time his stage name had been 'Smile Hoya'). 'That's how famous he was,' V concluded.

According to J-Hope, it was his love of dance and his willingness to work hard that brought him to Big Hit's attention. Legend has it that after a Big Hit dance video audition in his home town, when staff returned several hours later to pack up they found him still hard at work practising, so word went back to Seoul that here was one dedicated talent.

In December 2010, J-Hope became the third of the final BTS line-up to sign with Big Hit. He arrived in the dorm on Christmas Eve and was soon hit by the reality of trainee life: long hours of intense practice and sleeping in the dorm. It was Suga who looked after him in those tough early days, even turning up with fried chicken when J-Hope faced a New Year's Eve alone in the dorm.

Our man took the 'J' from his name Jung and added 'Hope' because he wanted to be the optimistic member of the group, which he's certainly succeeded at being. He was not only recruited as a dancer, but as one of the rap line, too. This was a new skill for him, but he worked diligently to develop his own distinct style and was especially grateful for the time Suga spent helping him.

Like all the members, J-Hope found the trainee period arduous and became frustrated waiting for debut day. In the *Burn the Stage* YouTube documentary, the group discuss the time when he decided to leave the group. We hear how Jung Kook sobbed and RM talked to Big Hit to persuade him to stay. He says he only returned because he trusted that the group would eventually find success.

ARMY are so grateful that he did. Hobi, as they often call him, has astonished with his performances on so many occasions. His amazing dance skills stole the stage in the MAMA battles in 2014 and 2015, and his solo display in 'Boy Meets Evil' just takes your breath away. As the main dancer, he's often credited for his part in creating and interpreting the complex choreography BTS are given, and in a V Live special for 'DNA', V said J-Hope could do the trickiest choreography they'd ever attempted in just ten minutes.

Not that he is just a dancer. His smooth and sometimes incredibly fast rap style provides a contrast to the rougher tones of RM and Suga. Listen to 'Whalien 52', 'Ma City', 'Cypher Pt. 3: Killer', 'Let Me Know' or 'Boy Meets Evil' and it's hard to believe he's a rap convert. And in tracks such as 'Rain', 'Tomorrow' and especially his ode to his mother, 'Mama', when he does sing he shows exactly how well he would fit in on the vocal line. Indeed, many ARMY have specifically complimented his backing vocals on 'Spring Day'.

J-Hope's love of dance inspired his V Live videos 'Hope on the Street' (now viewable on YouTube). These feature J-Hope dancing and giving dance tips to viewers, but mainly just having a good time. He's joined by Jung Kook in one episode and in another Jimin arrives on a hoverboard and, eventually, V turns up on a bike and they have some freestyle fun.

Born in 1994, Hobi forms a natural bridge between the older members and the 95 line. Open and good-humoured, he seems to get along effortlessly with the rest of the group. It's been noted that when everyone else has failed, he's the one who can always get Suga laughing, and their SOPE friendship is clear in the Hwagae Market vlogs, the SOPE-ME duet and the fab orange tracksuits.

The other obvious connection is with Jimin, as the 95-liner was the first to bond with him, helped by the time they spent at dance practice together. J-Hope and Jimin also roomed together, initially along with V, but even when they moved into their luxury apartment and everyone else got their own room, Jimin and J-Hope chose to share the largest of the rooms. J-Hope has said, 'I'm the older one and Jimin really does listen to me. We don't usually say this to each other face-to-face, but I'm always grateful to him.' Jimin, by turn, is thankful that J-Hope falls asleep instantly as soon as he gets into bed and he trusts his *hyung* so much that he offered him sole responsibility for cleaning the room. J-Hope declined the offer!

Jimin has also said that J-Hope can make friends with anyone. Among his K-pop friends are Ravi from VIXX, Hyungwon of Monsta X, Astro's Eunwoo, rapper Jessi and Jo Kwon (a pre-debut J-Hope rapped and danced on the video for his track 'Animal'). More recently, Becky G cited him as a BFF and his launch party for *Jack In The Box* in 2023 was attended by many South Korean stars of TV, movie and music.

His charisma, caring nature and exuberance (not to mention his ability to pull the most amazing facial expressions) have naturally endeared him to BTS fans, too. In the early variety shows when the other members were often a little reserved, J-Hope was always willing to put himself out there. Few can forget the 2015 episode of *Yaman TV* when he performed a jaw-dropping dance medley of girl-group choreographies, most impressively of Red Velvet's 'Ice Cream Cake'. Go find it now – and while you are looking you might just come across the word 'snake'.

BTS's 2015 Summer Package included a trip to the zoo, where J-Hope was introduced to a particularly large snake. As it's draped around his shoulders, he's obviously terrified, but his reaction is very funny – and indeed became a favourite fan meme. It soon became clear that this was just one of his fears. In various *Run BTS!* episodes he has a similar reaction to riding a rollercoaster and bungee-jumping, scrunching his face and frowning in what ARMY would enjoy calling the 'Nope Face'.

When interviewed about the snake incident on SBS Asia, J-Hope came out with the classic phrase, 'I hate snakeu!' Now, he's no fool, and can speak a number of languages (particularly Japanese), but his own brand of English has produced some moments that ARMY cherish. Of course, he was the instigator of the whole 'Jimin's got no jams' conversation, with his instruction to 'All English speakeu', and that also produced gems such as, 'Oh my hearteu is, my hearteu is …' and, 'Oh Jimin is very no fun!'

BANGTAN BOMB

J-HOPE VS 95Z

Don't be fooled by the title. It's not a dance-off and it isn't a singing challenge. This is just what happens when you wake a sleeping ray of sunshine. J-Hope is the one senior member who the 95 line know they can rely on for a bit of fun – but just how far can they push him? Quite far, as it turns out in this charming caper.

For a long time, J-Hope was known for his promise to produce a mixtape. Over the years the idea progressed from 'dream' to 'on my 2017 to-do list' to 'working on it' and some believed it would never happen, but it just turned out to be the longest teaser in history, because on 1 March 2018 *Hope World* was dropped – and boy, was it worth waiting for!

The cartoon-like, vibrantly coloured cover sets the tone immediately and the 'hixtape', as *Hope World* was nicknamed by ARMY, features seven tracks that span pop, tropical, EDM, trap and hard rap (or as hard as J-Hope goes, with BTS producer Supreme Boi adding some grit to one number), all adorned with a sweetly sung J-Hope take on the world. There's no intro here, just the title track 'Hope World', a dance number that uses his favourite book from childhood, Jules Verne's *Twenty Thousand Leagues Under the Sea*, to introduce him and his perspective on life.

'Daydream' is the first of the lead tracks. The vivid, heightened-colour video is a perfect match for the funky, bounce-along track and a real gift for J-Hope fans, featuring him in all his guises from sleepy Hobi to rapper to sharp-suited singer. The other lead track, 'Airplane', accompanied by a music video featuring a more thoughtful J-Hope, has a much more mellow vibe as he reflects on how his life has panned out. He told *Time* magazine, 'I was sitting in an airplane when I was writing these verses, a first-class seat no less, and it dawned on me that I was living the glorious life I'd only dreamed about when I was young and had somehow gotten used to now. But then and now, I'm still the same person, the same J-Hope.'

The mixtape is 100 per cent Hobi, and you can feel his warmth and personality in every track. Throughout, we can feel the idea of a guy who finds enjoyment in the moment, but also someone who is sensitive to the struggles and trouble of others. He is also never far from BTS, admitting his success is part of a group achievement; they are even present in the backing chants of 'Airplane'.

The positive vibe, catchy melodies and lyrical depth of *Hope World* seemed to surprise even J-Hope's biggest fans. It went to number one in the iTunes charts in over seventy countries and broke the top forty in the Billboard 200. Meanwhile, the 'Daydream' video amassed 20 million views on YouTube in just a few days.

Despite this success, a year later J-Hope was still denying he was ready for a collaboration, saying he lacked a depth of understanding about music. 'Chicken Noodle Soup', a single released in September 2019, proved this wrong, as it was a banging Latin-meets-K-pop cover, a collaboration with Mexican-American singer Becky G (both singers confessed the 2006 original was the first song they had danced to). The track made Hobi the youngest Korean artist ever to reach the Billboard Hot 100, the fastest to top the iTunes chart and the first to pass 2 million spins on Spotify.

J-Hope had earned 2018's most liked tweet in the world (1.7 million likes) when he responded to Drake's 'In My Feelings Challenge'. Now it was his turn as he and Becky issued a 'Chicken Noodle Soup' dance challenge using their adapted choreography. Jung Kook, Jimin and V all tried on V Live, while the craze went viral on TikTok.

By this point, J-Hope had picked up a new nickname: 'Jung Team

Leader'. He was a perfectionist on the dancefloor, put in the hard hours in the dance studio and expected the others to do the same. In an episode of *Run BTS!*, they all commented on how strict he was and that he noted every mistake – Jin adding that he did the same after a performance – and they showed the scared face they made when he caught their eye.

Meanwhile, J-Hope was still impressing with his own dance performances. His 'Dynamite' dance break at the 2020 MMAs was a particular favourite. In the Michael Jackson-inspired dance, his smooth, clean moves, dynamism, facial expressions and gestures were simply sensational. He looked so good in his open-necked purple velvet jumpsuit and hat that the clip went viral. 'To be honest,' the usually modest J-Hope said in an interview with *The Atlantic*, 'I think that performance was close to perfection.'

J-Hope had been involved in the writing of some BTS tracks since their early days, but he was eager to show how his skills and persona had developed. He wrote the searching lyrics for his solo 'Outro: Ego' on *Map of the Soul: 7*, which explored his twin identities as performer and person. He then released a new full-length version of 'Blueside', the short outro from *Hope World*. He explained that he now felt he had the ability to express how he could connect with his younger self and enjoy the comfort it gave.

It was a new facet of the member known for his joyfulness. 'I realized I'm not just some always-cheery person – I experience hardship, too.' He said in a Weverse interview. 'So I thought I could grow closer with listeners by sharing little parts of me that I had been hiding away.' This was also the origin of J-Hope's lyrics for 'Dis-ease', the old-school funk track from *BE*, where he went to the diary of emotions he kept during the pandemic for inspiration.

J-Hope tested positive for Covid-19 just a few days before BTS's historic 2022 Grammy performance. With Jin already side-lined with an injured hand, he was desperate to perform – and recovered with one day to spare. Ever the perfectionist, he confessed to feeling disappointed in his part in what was a generally acclaimed performance. He also revealed that the whole group were on the verge of mental exhaustion, which would soon contribute for their decision to take a break from group activities.

In July 2022, J-Hope became the first member to release an official solo album with *Jack In The Box*. He was the songwriter for all the full-length tracks on the album, which took the myth of Pandora's Box – which when opened unleashed all the evils of the world – as a metaphor for the pressures and hardships of fame that J-Hope had endured. It also explains the origin of his stage name, as hope was the only thing left when the lid of the box was finally put back.

BANGTAN BOMB

J-HOPE 'JACK IN THE BOX' LISTENING PARTY EVENT SKETCH

It's J-Hope's big day as he launches his solo album at a party attended by stars and friends. In this behind-the-scenes film we see just how meticulously he prepares. He is totally invested in getting every little detail right, making sure the set is perfect and rehearsing his speech thoroughly. Hobi looks a million dollars and acts the perfect host when his guests arrive, including all the Bangtans (except Suga, who was ill and gutted to miss it) who turn up to give him their support.

This is J-Hope setting the 'sunshine' persona aside, and some of the lyrics can be dark and discomforting. 'Pandora's Box' tells of the struggle to keep up the persona; the rock-infused 'More', a pre-release single, finds J-Hope growling and shouting of his driving ambition to grow as a musician and the danger that passion can rage out of control; and 'Safety Zone', his own favourite of the tracks, searches for somewhere he can feel secure. But there is also optimism in tracks such as 'Stop', which counters the litany of humanity's ills by holding on to the idea that people are inherently good and change is possible, '= (Equal Sign)', a plea for kindness with a lush soul backing vocal, which he described as Part 2 of *Hope World*'s 'P.O.P (Piece of Peace), Pt. 1', and 'Future', with its call to go forward with bravery, self-belief and, of course, hope.

The album ends with the lead single 'Arson'. In-your-face and explosive, J-Hope uses his own voice to brilliant effect to move from a haunting reassurance to a menacing rasp as he describes the raging fire he is starting in his solo career and how he won't be able to stop it. It's a thrilling finale and was accompanied by an equally powerful MV with J-Hope emerging energized from a fire-ravaged scene in a shocking ending.

Jack In The Box never hides its hip-hop credentials, but infusions of rock, R&B and other genres, even a children's choir, keep each track fresh. And J-Hope changing his style of delivery from song to song is just one of the components that make it such a deep and multi-faceted album. Both singles charted in the US Billboard 100 and topped iTunes charts in over fifty countries, while the album found similar chart success and considerable critical acclaim, including *NME*, who, having described how J-Hope had set fire to his previous persona, observed that from the ashes 'comes a star more thrilling and formidable than ever and seemingly unstoppable.'

J-Hope's solo schedule was high-profile. His release party was attended by South Korea's top rappers, singers and producers as well as fellow group members, and he guested on the YouTube series *IU's Palette* in which the host, Korean musical royalty IU, sang with him on '= (Equal Sign)'. Most exciting, however, was his historic appearance at Chicago's Lollapalooza music festival, where he became the first South Korean solo artist to headline a main stage at a US festival.

Lollapalooza was a triumph. J-Hope had the crowd in the palm of his hand from the moment he leapt out of a giant box to start the show, hailed as one of the performances of the year. In an eighteen-song set, he not only played his latest songs, but favourites from *Hope World*, BTS's rarely-performed 'Cypher Pt. 1' ('for the OG ARMY'), the tropical remix of 'Dynamite' with brand-new choreography, and welcomed a surprise guest in Becky G for their first live duet of 'Chicken Noodle Soup'. The

100,000 on site (including the supportive Jimin) and nearly 15 million watching the livestream were just enthralled.

He was also the main attraction at the 2022 MAMAs. He owned the red carpet in a stylish all-black look, with open shirt, swept-back hair and the coolest shades and gave show-stopping performances of his two solo singles. He took home the award for most popular male artist and was nominated for best collaboration for his part in the funky hip-hop single 'Rush Hour' by Korean rapper Crush (including a video where he brings in some classic BTS choreography), but narrowly missed out to Suga and Psy's 'That That'.

J-Hope was still hitting headlines as 2023 dawned. He was in New York performing '= (Equal Sign)', 'Chicken Noodle Soup' and 'Butter' on *Dick Clark's New Year's Rockin' Eve with Ryan Seacrest*; saw the documentary film *J-Hope in the Box* released on Disney+; and was a star attraction at Louis Vuitton, Hermès and Dior events in Paris, with *Vogue* calling him 'the MVP of Fashion Week'.

The posts on Hobi's Instagram account @uarmyhope exude a colourful, street vibe, but his photo folio, *Me, Myself, & j-hope: All New Hope* gave fans something very different. He was seen with amazing long, purple-tinted hair in flowing white robes in a beautiful field of flowers (prompting many a 'Legolas' comparison) and then cut a contrasting figure dressed all in black with short dark hair amid a fire-ravaged rocky wasteland. It portrayed, he explained, a rebirth into a strong character with new hope from a previous precarious existence.

Though ARMY knew the time would soon arrive, it was still a shock when J-Hope announced that he had initiated his military enlistment process at the end of February. Typically, he went on Weverse to reassure fans and promise his support to the other members. 'I decided that the sooner I go in,' he wrote, 'the sooner I can return and show you something good.'

Days later, he left them something good as a parting gift in the shape of a new single, 'On the Street', a collaboration with J. Cole, who had been a longtime hero of J-Hope. He references him on 'Hip Hop Phile', and *Hope World* is named as a nod to the legendary US rapper's *Cole World*. Both rap about their journey as artists, but J-Hope in particular emphasizes his bond with his fans. The single – accompanied by a video shot on the streets of New York where J-Hope dances to J. Cole's verse just as he did when he was a teenager and a trainee – was especially successful in the UK, as J-Hope became the first Korean soloist to debut in the Top 40.

'On the Street' was a return to Sunshine Hope, but fans now knew that he was more than just an idol who always had a smile on his face. It was true that he had constantly been a caring friend to and cheerleader for the other members and was the first to provide an optimistic outlook, but as his work as a songwriter and soloist developed, another picture had emerged. Alongside J-Hope, the supreme dancer, fabulous rapper and integral group member, there was an intelligent solo artist, who could convey the hardships and darkness of life as well as the joy and the light. And ARMY loves them both.

ELEVEN

ALL AROUND THE WORLD

Different Korean music shows have slightly different ways of calculating their weekly winners, but all follow a generally similar format. They take into consideration digital downloads, music video views, experts' reviews and album sales to select the nominees, and then allow live votes to contribute to the result. In the case of *The Show Choice*, 15 per cent of the points come from live voting. Up against the previous week's winners EXID and Block B subunit BASTARZ, BTS faced a huge challenge; they needed their fans to respond. And ARMY did – magnificently.

'The 27th The Show Choice was won by BTS!! Congratulations on winning your first music show #1! We hope you continue to be the best!! Congratulations to ARMY, too!' That tweet was sent out by SBS MTV's *The Show Choice* on the evening of 5 May 2015, confirming what many had already found out: BTS had done it. 'I Need U' had won them their first show number one.

Two days later, they won again. This time on *M Countdown* and again, the following day, at *Music Bank*, to their sheer disbelief. After eight days they had won a total of five shows, including returning to win *The Show Choice* for a second time.

With the album reaching number one in the weekly Gaon chart, and the group performing in May at Dream 2015, the Seoul World Cup Stadium K-pop festival, which only invites the very best acts, naturally they were all on top of the world. Fittingly, it was the perfect time to celebrate, with their second *festa* (their debut anniversary celebrations – keep up!) coming in June. This time, with ARMY three times bigger than last year, they embarked on a two-week bonding session with the fans who had delivered them the big prize.

AFTER M!COUNTDOWN 1ST PLACE T—T

Just in case it wasn't clear what achieving that winning position meant to them, here's the boys' reaction after their second win. With red-smudged lips, after they have fulfilled a promise to perform their encore in lipstick if they win, they jump around, gush, hug, stare in disbelief and, in the case of Jimin, find a quiet corner in which to have a little cry. Beautiful.

The *festa* began with a fabulous new track on YouTube, 'Hug Me', a sensitive ballad cover song performed by V with an added rap from J-Hope. Once again, they all got together to chat for an hour-long radio broadcast that included a hilarious version of 'I Need U' in which the rap line and the vocal line swapped parts, and a segment where they chose their ambition for the coming year. While Jimin wanted them to play an even bigger stadium, V dreamed of them making a cycling trip together, RM suggested a group vacation, and Jung Kook had plans for them all to learn Wing Chun, a Chinese martial art.

Other *festa* festivities saw them post a series of 'real family pictures' on Facebook. Some showed them all deliberately looking stiff and awkward with forced smiles as they posed in matching suits, while others featured J-Hope, Jimin, Jin and Jung Kook standing behind one another in a typical dorky 'brothers' pose. And the treats didn't finish there. Two special new dance practices were uploaded on YouTube. The first was 'War of Hormone' (see Bangtan Bomb overleaf) and the second a version of 'Embarrassed' with the boys having fun going full-on *aegyo* – acting shy and cute.

While ARMY were still reeling from *festa*, along came the release of 'Dope' as a single and an accompanying music video. In August 2017, this would become the first BTS video to pass 200 million views, but in June 2015 it did the job of keeping up the BTS profile. The video is vintage Bangtan, beautifully filmed in what is made to look like a one-camera continuous shoot. The boys look great in their fantasy costumes – RM as a concierge, J-Hope a racing-car driver, Jung Kook a police officer, Suga (now sporting a blond look) a naval officer, V a manga comic Detective Conan, Jin a doctor and Jimin (whose hair colour J-Hope calls strawberry ice cream) a businessman. And the choreography is phenomenal. It is the first time they have worked with the legendary Keone Madrid and it is their most intense, powerful and synchronized routine yet.

As they promoted the single, the costumes became wonderfully random: J-Hope appeared as a tennis player, Jin as an aircraft pilot, Jung Kook as an engineer, Suga as a secret agent, or they could all appear together in military uniform. It was as if they were saying, 'We can be anything we want to be.' And as the video picked up views, something else was happening, too: the song reached number three in the Billboard World Digital Song Sales chart. It was the best-performing BTS single in this category so far.

The USA wasn't the only English-speaking country where ARMY was growing rapidly. In mid-July BTS took their Red Bullet tour to Australia, where concerts in Sydney and Melbourne had sold out in minutes. In Australia, BTS seemed chilled. On the Australian music show *SBS Pop Asia* they named their favourite Australian animals, impersonated each other (as well as RM doing a great Marge Simpson impression) and even tried some of the nation's favourite spread, Vegemite. Jin seemed to like it, but for once J-Hope wasn't smiling!

As was becoming the norm, long queues formed early on the day before each concert Down Under. It was worth the wait. The opening video – here a classroom registration of the members, all of whom were absent – produced feverish excitement, and a crescendo of screams, yells, fan chants and waving light sticks greeted the boys' appearance on stage. In a breathless opening medley they played 'N.O', 'We Are Bulletproof Pt. 2', 'We On' and 'Hip Hop Phile', before slowing the pace with 'Let Me Know' and 'Rain'.

BANGTAN BOMB

'호르몬전쟁' DANCE PERFORMANCE (REAL WAR VER.)

Fifty million views don't lie. This second *festa* gift is a massive ARMY favourite. It's the 'War of Hormone' choreography, but not as we know it. This is the 'boys go crazy' version, which they refer to as 'real war', and they're out to have as much fun as possible. It doesn't matter who your bias is, they all have their moments here – but it's hard to ignore V, who is enjoying himself way beyond the legal limit!

Although almost drowned out by the audience, the songs were spot on and the dances were slick. They were punctuated by various members trying out their English. As the concerts progressed through a twenty-four-song, two-hour set, various surprises ensued. The boys introduced a karaoke section for fans to sing along to 'Miss Right' and 'Like', and they played rock, paper, scissors to determine who had to perform the cute dance to K-pop classic 'The Gwiyomi Song'. The shows came to a close with 'I Need U' and 'Boy in Luv', but there was no way these Aussie – or any other – fans were letting them go just yet.

The encore began with another video, this time of the pre-debut Bangtan Boys hard at work, and then they performed 'Dope' live for the first time, before ending on the high-energy 'Boyz with Fun' and 'Attack on Bangtan'. In Sydney, the boys left the stage one by one – Jimin staying until last, until V returned to drag him off. The audience and the band were euphoric, but completely drained.

And so the Red Bullet sped on. BTS were returning to the US. That meant In-N-Out, Shake Shack, hot dogs, doughnuts and Korean food just as good as at home – oh, and the small matter of ARMY impatient to see their heroes. To prove it, they snaffled up the 12,500 tickets in minutes.

As ARMY brought Times Square to a standstill with a flash-mob dance, the group flew in to New York for the first ever time to perform on 16 July 2015 at the Best Buy Theater. They got the customary rapturous reception and fans raised a banner reading, in Korean, 'Just One Day with BTS', which made the boys all smile. However, the night was not without controversy. After coming back for an encore, the group played just one more number and then left suddenly. Even worse, they cancelled the after-show hi-touch event as well. It appeared there were safety concerns after threats had been made to the group on social media, and, although these proved to be groundless, the BTS management felt they couldn't take any chances.

Nevertheless, the show left an impression for the right reasons on those who had seen it. *Billboard*'s review admired how the group hadn't rigidly stuck to the synchronized dances, but had freestyled from as early as the third song. Jeff Benjamin, the publication's K-pop specialist, remarked how natural, casual and fun this had made the show feel.

The tour continued to Dallas on 18 July and Chicago on 24 July, before landing the boys back in LA on 26 July at the 2,300-seat venue Club Nokia. There, Suga told the crowd that LA was his 'second home' and they brought the house down once again. Watching and waiting for them afterwards was Tony, their mentor from *American Hustle Life*. He celebrated by posting a photo of his reunion with the band on Instagram and Twitter with the legend, 'Great show, lil' bros killed it tonight at Club Nokia.'

Like all crowds on the Red Bullet tour, those in LA were excited and exuberant, but something about the fans had changed. A year ago, when they had played in the City of Angels at their 'secret' *American Hustle Life* concert or at KCON, the boys had performed to a largely Korean-American audience. In 2015, although Korean-Americans were still out in force, there was a diverse ethnic mix and even some guys and older fans! No longer niche, BTS were heading mainstream.

Down in Central and South America, the locals were ahead of the game and the continent had already taken K-pop to its heart. Exactly what caused *hallyu*, or the 'Korean wave', to take such a hold there has been the subject of much debate. Of course, as in other regions of the world, fans in South America could watch an enormous volume of high-quality material – songs, shows, videos – online, but they were now very grateful that BTS, live and in person, were coming their way. From the end of July to early August there were concerts in Mexico, Chile and Brazil, at the biggest venues they had played outside Japan, and people flocked to the shows, not just from those countries, but from adjacent nations such as Argentina, Peru and Colombia. The enthusiasm of the fans certainly made an impression on the boys. Jung Kook picked the concert in São Paolo as one of the highlights of the tour, while RM spoke of Brazilian and Chilean ARMY as the most passionate BTS fans in the world.

Eventually, though, it was time to head home. The Red Bullet tour was nearly over, with just two concerts in Thailand and Hong Kong remaining. In eleven months, BTS had played to packed, sold-out venues in fourteen different countries over five continents. There was no stopping them now.

MEMBER PROFILE

Name:	Park Jimin
AKA:	Jimin, Jiminie, Little Prince, Chim Chim, Dooly, Mochi, Manggae, Ddochi
Date of birth:	13 October 1995
Birthplace:	Busan, South Korea
Height:	1.73 metres (5'8")
Education:	Heodang Elementary School, Yoonsan Middle School, Busan High School of Arts, Korean Arts High School, Global Cyber University
Chinese zodiac:	Pig
Star sign:	Libra
Instagram:	@j.m

TWELVE

PARK JIMIN: MAN OR MOCHI?

Park Jimin was the last piece of the BTS jigsaw. Brought in just months before the BTS line-up was confirmed, he had thrilling dance skills, a singing voice with such potential and the looks of an angel. And yet there were some at Big Hit who didn't think this piece of the jigsaw fitted. At the *Love Yourself: Her* showcase, he revealed that in his short time as a trainee he was kicked off the team eight times (V reckons it was more like fifteen!), and Suga seems to think he was almost left out on the day before their debut – but just try to imagine a BTS without Jimin. Not only are his vocals now seen as an essential ingredient of BTS songs and his dancing as a highlight of video and stage performances, he is also one of the most fun and playful members of the group. He was known in the early years for frequently posting to BTS social media accounts, updating ARMY with messages, photos and videos, although ARMY would certainly like him to be more active on Instagram. While RM may have famously implied that Jimin was no fun when he pronounced that Jimin's 'got no jams', every ARMY knows that in fact Jimin has jams to spare.

Jimin describes his childhood in the South Korean port city of Busan as happy. Home life was spent having fun with his brother, who is only a couple of years younger, as they played games and watched movies together. He sounds such a boy as he remembers wanting to be a chef, a pirate or the driver of the space train *Galaxy Express 999*. He was the same happy-go-lucky character at school, enjoying his studies and getting on with all his classmates.

He says he fell in love with dancing in his early teens, while in the second year of middle school. Inspired by Korean pop superstar Rain, he set his sights on becoming an idol. He spent more and more time at the dance academy after school and by the time he was to choose a high school, his mind was made up. He would go to Busan High School of Arts and major in modern dance. Then, in the spring of 2012, on the advice of his middle-school dance teacher, he tried out for Big Hit.

In a 2013 interview with *Cuvism* magazine, Jimin recalled, 'It was my first ever audition so my hands were shaking a lot when I opened the door. I also remember that my voice shook a lot while singing, but because I started dancing at a young age, I danced very confidently. I sang "I Have a Lover".' RM has teased him about this, because at the time it was the most popular karaoke song among middle-schoolers, but Jimin says at that point he hadn't learned how to sing and just didn't have a clue what to pick.

By May of that year he was on his way to Seoul to become a trainee. Jimin remembers J-Hope being the first person he met, and recalls that he was welcomed into the dorm with the words, 'Let's work hard together!' And he would soon find out just what hard work was. Having joined Big Hit, Jimin transferred to a school in Seoul and found himself at the same high school as V, the two of them leaving for it together in the morning in their uniforms (Jimin wore V's actual uniform in the 'Graduation Song' video). Although they were in different classes, V helped out his shy new friend by getting his classmates to talk to him.

Suga would recall that his first impression of Jimin was that he must be an excellent singer or dancer because this round-faced boy in thick glasses certainly wasn't a visual. But he would soon see another facet of the then-sixteen-year-old: determination. Jimin would do a full day at school, practise until three or four in the morning and have a few hours' sleep before getting up to do an hour's singing and then setting off for school again.

As tough as it was, Jimin valued his trainee time. Those around him soon noted his perfectionism and how eager he was to improve. He also appreciated spending time and eating with the other trainees. He says he still carries an amusement park admission ticket in his wallet, a souvenir of one of their first trips out together.

When doubts arose about him before debut, it was the rest of the members who seem to have argued to keep Jimin in the group, and he says that in the darker days it was their confidence in him that drove him to work harder and believe in himself. He even had the confidence, with the backing of the other members, to turn down the stage names Big Hit suggested for him, which included Baby J and Young Kid. He said he was hoping for something better, so instead plumped to use his own name.

By the time debut day arrived, Jimin had the star dance role: running across the others' backs. It was a real thrill, but nerve-racking for him as he didn't want to kick his friends too hard. And then came the transformed 'chocolate abs', the toned stomach muscles that look like the divided parts of a chocolate bar (a 'six pack'). At first, the naturally shy Jimin was embarrassed at showing off his ripped torso on the dance floor, but he's also someone who likes to please his audience and, as early as the first *festa*, J-Hope revealed that when Jimin saw the reaction he was getting from flashing his abs, his shyness disappeared pretty quickly! When they decided he would tear his shirt off at the 2014 MAMAs performance, his determination kicked in again and he began exercising even more, visiting the gym before going to sleep even when they were on tour in Asia.

Jimin's looks changed more than those of any other member in BTS's rise to superstardom. This was the chubby-cheeked boy who was nicknamed Ddochi by his middle-school friends after a cartoon ostrich who puffs his cheeks out, and *manggae* (soft rice cakes) by ARMY, who loved his squishy face, but when the 'Blood Sweat & Tears' video was released, a different

Jimin emerged. Through intense dieting, he had lost the puppy features. He's a guy who cares about his looks – and he's not the only one.

Whether it is his soft, thick lips that produce the perfect pout and smile, his large eyes that take so well to the smoky eyeliner look, or his fluffy hair that induced gasps when he dyed it candy-floss pink, Jimin has what it takes to excite an audience. He also knows how to work a crowd from the stage. Tony Jones, his mentor in *American Hustle Life* and the first to name him Chim Chim, nailed it in an interview with the MoonROK website when he said, 'When he's performing and winking, he's got all that fan service down. His attitude is so positive. I'd say charming … and he just knows how to give the crowd what they want.' Just watch videos of him on stage as he shrugs his shirt off his shoulders and you'll understand how Jimin always has the audience in the palm of his hand.

BANGTAN BOMB

'WINGS' SHORT FILM SPECIAL – LIE (JIMIN SOLO DANCE)

This is Jimin's dance video for 'Lie', the track he co-wrote on the *Wings* album. It's simply shot and showcases his dancing skills perfectly as he delivers a controlled performance of elegance, passion and superb technical footwork. It's also an emotional piece which Jimin throws himself into with such energy that he needs a lie-down when he finishes, and judging from the comments, he wasn't the only one!

It helps that Jimin is an amazing dancer. Having studied modern dance at high school, when he joined Big Hit he switched to street dance, but perhaps it's that contemporary dance background that adds an elegant quality to BTS's style. Just watch his blindfolded dance with J-Hope in 'Boy Meets Evil' at MAMA 2016, his incredible solo to 'Butterfly' or his smooth moves to 'Let Go' at 2019's Magic Shop concert in Osaka. For such a shy boy, Jimin really comes alive when he performs. It has now reached the point where the others joke that in the live shows he always seems to hog centre-stage!

Jimin definitely has his self-doubts, though. During the promotion of *Wings*, he explained that the high notes in 'Lie' made it difficult for him to sing and he warned fans that he would never be able to perform it live, but of course he did – beautifully. Similarly, on their *Bon Voyage* trip to Hawaii, when the boys look at the stars and make a wish, Jimin's wish was that he could sing. Jung Kook's immediate reply was that he sings pretty well and Jin told him his singing is perfect. This, after all, is the guy who sang 'Serendipity', who performed a wonderful cover duet with Jung Kook of 'We Don't Talk Anymore' and whose smooth tones embellish so many BTS tracks.

Jimin's early *selca* (selfie) obsession developed into an interest in instant Polaroid pictures. He once listed looking at his Polaroid collection (he mounts and labels them in a book) of him and other band members as the number-one recreation on his happiness list. ARMY have their own list of cherished Jimin moments, many of them gifs of him looking super-cute, smiling, looking shy, fiddling with his hair or revealing that mischievous grin. Such posts amass thousands of likes on social media and it's not surprising that among many ARMY, Jimin is known as the group's recruiting fairy, because he attracts so many new fans.

Jimin's self-assumed role as the social media king of BTS has led to a great relationship with ARMY. In 2017, when he talked openly about his extreme dieting and how it caused him to collapse in dance practice, ARMY ensured that #JiminYouArePerfect was all over Twitter. Then in January 2018 they got #ThankYouJimin trending worldwide on Twitter. It took Jimin completely by surprise, causing him to reply, 'What is this? hehe logged in because I wanted to leave something and saw this.'

Among the treasured videos for Jimin fans are the April 2017 'Eat Jin' episode where he sings along to 'Butterfly' as Jin plays guitar; the *Run BTS!* karting episode where his punishment for coming last includes dancing to 'Blood Sweat & Tears' while getting doused in water and then having to clean the floor; when he plays with Brandley the cat in the 2017 summer package; when he sneakily cheated on Jimmy Fallon's Subway Olympics in 2021 or when he says 'I love you' to a cringing Suga in 2021's *Let's BTS*.

Who wouldn't love such a cute and playful young man? Certainly not the other BTS members, although they do endlessly tease him. Jimin even declared that 'being teased' was his speciality in the group. He's forever being reminded that he is the smallest of them all (although he claims he's now taller than Suga), that he has tiny hands (they are quite petite) and that he constantly runs his hands through his hair (guilty as charged). But who do they all go to when they're feeling stressed? Jimin's ability to listen to others' troubles seems to be one of the key elements that makes BTS so strong. Jung Kook is often the teaser-in-chief. It's a strange role for the *maknae*, but perhaps he can get away with it because Jimin loves Jung Kook like a little brother. Not that Jimin doesn't strike back. He often accuses Jung Kook of copying him: being born in the same city, wearing the same earrings and having the same colour contact lenses. They are often seen messing about with each other and in November 2017 they took a trip together to Japan. You can see their holiday film on YouTube, shot and edited by Jung Kook (so it's pretty much all Jimin!) and called *G.C.F in Tokyo*.

If Jung Kook is his younger brother, then V is Jimin's twin. Together they make up the 95 line. They attended high school together, graduated together (check out the song '95 Graduation' they recorded as they couldn't make the ceremony) and continued to be best buddies as BTS went stratospheric. They are seen all over the Bangtan Bombs, dancing, teasing other members and play-fighting. They send each other touching tweets, look out for each other when they've fallen on stage, and V even bought a thousand-dollar Gucci jumper for Jimin on his birthday in 2016. Their V Live 'Mandaggo' shows, in theory about amusing regional differences between Jimin's Busan and V's Daegu dialects, show just how comfortable they are in each other's company.

Just after midnight in Seoul on 31 December 2018, Jimin surprised

ARMY with his first solo release on SoundCloud. 'Promise' was a song he had co-composed with Slow Rabbit and co-written with RM – even V had chipped in with the photography for the cover art. He nervously tweeted that it was his first song and was still maybe a little early; Jimin later explained that he had begun writing a dark song that reflected his mood and that of the group at the time. As the vibe in the group changed, he put it aside, but RM encouraged him to return to it and it became a tender, comforting message.

ARMY loved it, amassing 8.5 million streams in twenty-four hours – a new SoundCloud record. This was no surprise: Jimin is a real favourite. He regularly inspires trending hashtags such as when he performed the *buchaechum* fan dance at the 2018 MMAs; when a seven-second video of him on stage in LA with an ethereal gaze and beguiling smile went viral; when the whole group laughed as his jacket got caught over his head on the New Year's Eve performance in Times Square in 2019 and when his body wave and air-slap to 'Airplane Pt. 2' at Permission to Dance on Stage: Seoul turned into a dance trend on TikTok!

ARMY never tire of hearing about Jimin and he constantly picks up new nicknames, including Little Prince, Stage King, Dooly (the cartoon dinosaur), Global It Boy and even Bagel Man (from a Korean term meaning 'man with a baby face but a glamorous body') and Angel. The latter was given to him not just because of his soft features, soothing vocals and graceful movements, but also for his caring nature and sensitive disposition.

Jimin is popular the world over, but the love he receives in the US led the Korean media to coin the nickname 'Jimmerica'. Stars such as Cardi B, Jennifer Aniston and John Oliver have all picked him out as a favourite; he has befriended chat-show hosts Jimmy Fallon and James Corden (who Jimin calls 'Papa Mochi') and his solo songs perform particularly well. 'Filter', his Latin-infused solo track on *Map of the Soul: 7*, sold over 500,000 units in the country, matching 'Lie' and 'Serendipity' and making him the only male K-pop soloist to reach that landmark with three songs.

That album also featured 'Friends', a track that Jimin co-wrote and co-produced. A duet between Jimin and V, the song is a celebration of their friendship. It even references the 'dumpling incident' – a massive two-week falling out over when to eat their dumplings. To be fair, Jimin has since referred to that incident, saying: 'Taehyung and I don't fight anymore. You only fight when you're young.'

BANGTAN BOMB

YOU HAVE A MEOW-SITOR!

Jimin's fondness for animals has led to some ARMY calling him *Gangyangi*, a combination of the Korean words for puppy and cat. It is the feline side that comes to the fore here in a totally indulgent look at Jimin's interaction with a cat that has found its way into the studio during the 2021 *festa* photoshoot. Those who recall his encounters with Curry the calico cat in the 'Serendipity' MV or the stray cat in Malta in *Bon Voyage* will know just how gentle and playful he is with them and this is no exception – they just can't get enough belly rubs!

'Vmin', as ARMY call them, continue to give fans heart-warming friendship goals, such as running into each other's arms and rolling in the snow in *Bon Voyage 4*; wearing school uniforms and backpacks and entwining pinkies when they sang 'Friends' at Bang Bang Con: The Live and, most emotionally, when V reads his letter to Jimin at the end of *Bon Voyage 2* and says, 'When I am in the bathroom crying, you cry with me. You also come to see me at dawn to laugh with me. You care about me and have me in your thoughts. You work hard for me and you understand me.'

Jimin had good need of his close friends in the difficult period after the pandemic began. He opened up to ARMY in a September 2021 Weverse interview, saying that he had recently gone through a difficult time. He returned to this theme when he guested on Suga's chat show *Suchwita* in 2023. He recalled how he had drifted away from friends during this time and when Suga, referring to lyrics claiming he was living like a fool, asked if he really was, Jimin replied, 'You should know.' Suga's 'I do' response suggested Jimin's troubles were more than evident to his friends.

Helped by his parents and friends, he seemed to be returning to good spirits as 2022 began, but after enduring severe abdominal pains he was admitted to hospital for an acute appendicitis surgery. To make matters worse, he contracted Covid-19 while in the hospital. Amazingly the Stage King recovered swiftly and was back performing just a few weeks later in the Permission to Dance on Stage: Seoul concert.

Soon Jimin was back in the charts around the world with a duet with Ha Sung-woon, formerly of the boy groups Hotshot and Wanna One. 'With You', sung in English and Korean, was an OST for the TV series *Our Blues*. Both vocalists wring the emotion from a deeply romantic ballad, sung to a simple acoustic instrumental, with Jimin's honey-coated tones bringing out the best in his vocal partner. The song went on to garner nominations for best OST and Song of the Year at the 2022 MAMAs.

When BTS's *Proof* came out in June, fans were delighted to find it included a studio version of Agust D (aka Suga)'s 'Tony Montana' featuring Jimin. The live version of the two performing the song at the third muster in 2016 had always been an ARMY favourite. The album also featured both 'Filter' and 'Friends', tracks Jimin had chosen himself to show his different sides. 'I still have many different colours to share,' he added. Such a claim appeared as a statement of intent in the light of their imminent decision to focus on solo activities. 'I think now we're starting to think about what kind of artists we each want to be remembered as by our fans,' Jimin said on Weverse. 'We're trying to find our identity and that's an exhausting and long process.'

Jimin was one of the first to get his '7' friendship tattoo. His was done on his index finger, but wasn't noticed at the concert in Busan as, he joked, his hands were too small to display it when he held the microphone. His tattoos often seemed to involve an element of teasing. Back in December 2014, ARMY spotted a 'Nevermind' tattoo on his torso; it was only temporary, but later he had the same thing done for real, sparking months of speculation over whether he had actually got inked this time. In 2020 he revealed a '13' (his birthday and BTS's debut day) on his wrist, 'Young' and 'Forever' above his elbows and 'Youth' behind his ear, while a crescent moon on his neck was done in time for the 2022 Permission to Dance on Stage: Seoul concert. In March 2023, he revealed that was a tease of a kind too – he had in fact extended it to a series of moons running down his spine after V had shown him some fanart that he liked so much he made it a reality.

Jimin is not a prolific poster on his Instagram account ('I can't go on it,' he once said, 'because I'm scared I might press something wrong'), but he took full advantage of his self-created photo folio, *Me, Myself, & Jimin: ID: Chaos* to embrace the many facets of his inner self. The photos, many inspired by Greek mythology, are breathtaking and included a vulnerable Jimin surrounded by broken mannequins; besuited and super cool with his 'Tailor of Chaos' neck tattoo, and most stunningly, dressed in black leather, masked and horned with his dark hair wet and sleek.

Jimin's first official solo project was a monumental one. In January 2023, he released a single with K-pop legend Taeyang. The Big Bang singer was trainee-Jimin's idol and his inspiration: 'It wouldn't be an exaggeration to say,' he admitted, 'that I've come this far with the goal of one day working on music with him.' Back in 2014, Jimin had half-jokingly covered Taeyang's 'Eyes, Nose, Lips' in a hilarious Bangtan Bomb, but now the superstar had invited him to work on a song together. 'Vibe' is a funky bop bursting with star quality. Taeyang brings his charisma and control, while Jimin compliments him wonderfully with his softer, higher register adding a whole new dimension to the song. Similarly, in the MV, Jimin in a stunning red leather jacket, a white polo-neck or a black collar suit was a perfect contrast to the more hard-edged Taeyang.

When BTS's group commitment to Louis Vuitton expired at the end of 2022, members were able to become solo fashion ambassadors. Jimin was the first to take up the opportunity and in January 2023 become the first Asian male brand ambassador for Dior. He was no stranger to the luxury brand, having stunned onlookers of various red carpets wearing their creations in the past, and by the end of the month he was turning heads at their Paris Fashion Week Show. Unsurprisingly, Jimin was in high demand – shortly after the Dior announcement, he was unveiled as a brand ambassador for high-end jewellery brand Tiffany & Co. too.

Those who follow Jimin closely know that behind his playful persona lies a sometimes introverted, thoughtful and vulnerable young man. He told *Rolling Stone* magazine how he had spoken of his self-doubts and insecurities to the rest of the group while in Las Vegas for their Permission to Dance shows. They had responded by encouraging him to express his feelings through music. The result was his first solo album, *Face*, released in March 2023. The first single, 'Set Me Free Pt.2' (linked thematically to *D-2*'s 'Set Me Free') came out a week before the album. In a full-on hip-hop anthem, Jimin was backed by a choir, a hard-hitting beat and pumping horns as he sang of securing his own freedom and moving forward. In an accompanying MV, he was surrounded by a plethora of dancers as a complex choreography played out the transition against a background that subtly changed from dark to light.

Jimin used his vocal technique and range and employed auto-tune to great effect in the song as he conveyed feelings of deep anxiety, anger and a determination to move on. The other five tracks of *Face* follow this exploration of the conflicting feelings of the artist and the person. It is a grown-up album with complex thoughts and adult language – sung with the voice of an angel. There is an outpouring of raw emotion: from the angry trap-pop 'Face-off' where he uses a break-up song as a metaphor for his frustrations; to the ethereal 'Dive', which blends Jimin's on-stage words and ARMY cheers with sounds from his everyday life; to a ballad, 'Alone', reflecting on the loneliness and fear of losing himself that he felt during the pandemic.

The album's lead single, 'Like Crazy', references the 2011 movie of the same name, which tells of falling in love and losing control. In a soothing, dreamy, disco track, Jimin sees these themes mirroring his own ideas of escapism, self-identity and the struggle to find yourself. The MV was exquisite. Dreamy, surreal and enigmatic, one interpretation suggests Jimin is trying to flee the torment of his break-up by drinking and dancing in a crowded club but is constantly being pulled back to the reality of his loneliness and the inescapable muddy grip of his love.

Jimin performed the song on *The Tonight Show Starring Jimmy Fallon* the day after release, as well as on *M Countdown* and *Music Bank*, where he registered four wins and an acoustic performance on *LeeMujin Service*, a YouTube chat show. 'Like Crazy' topped the number-one position in ninety countries on the iTunes chart worldwide, gave Jimin a top-ten place in the UK and went straight to number one on the Billboard Hot 100. *Face* also had stunning success: number one in South Korea and Japan, number two in the US and a top-ten hit around the world.

Sitting pretty in the charts, Jimin took his turn to sit and chat with Suga on *Suchwita*. It became clear that Jimin had not found recording the album easy. It had required him to open his heart and soul and the process had taken him ten months to produce. The conversation was wide-ranging and revealing, from how Suga had convinced him to be part of BTS when he was inclined not to join the original team to their ambitions for the future. 'My only dream is to make this team last a long time, until I can barely move,' he told Suga. 'Personally, even when we're old, I think it'd be nice if the seven of us were sitting around, and our fans sitting too, just talking and singing.'

Seeing the themes of depression, escape, introspection, loneliness and emergence expressed by Jimin in and around the *Face* album helped fans appreciate who the grown-up Jimin really is. He is still that cute boy who they loved for his sense of fun and silliness, he is still a fabulous dancer and singer as well as a caring and lovable friend to the group and to fans. He is still a vital piece of the BTS jigsaw. But now they can also understand that he is his own man, able to find and choose his own direction in life. And they will continue to support him forever, because the ARMY adage remains true: 'Once you Jimin, you can't Jimout!'

THIRTEEN

RUNNING MEN

BTS could now call themselves not just idols but international stars who draw huge crowds to their concerts all around the world. Some fans at home might have been worried that success would change them. After all, this was a group who wrote songs from their own experiences as young people and who had built a unique relationship with ARMY through openness and communication. Would that suffer as they became more and more popular and their fan base expanded exponentially?

Not with these guys. One of the first things they did when they got back to Seoul was take a group of fans to the movies. Have you ever known a group to do that before? What's more, it was BTS keeping a promise they had made before they released 'I Need U'. Back then they had sworn that if they won a music show they would treat some fans to a night out with them at the movies (it was V's idea), and here they were, being true to their word.

The choice of movie was easy. After receiving good reviews for his solo mixtape and the 'P.D.D' collaboration with Warren G, RM was invited by Marvel to contribute to the soundtrack for the movie *Fantastic Four*. The result was 'Fantastic', which featured Mandy Ventrice, an American singer who had worked with Snoop Dogg, Jay-Z and Kanye West. So, along with

200 fans, who were probably more interested in the occupants of the front row than the superhero movie, on 12 August the boys attended a special screening at the CGV Cinema in Wangsimni, Seoul, to support (and poke a little fun at!) their leader.

BANGTAN BOMB

400-METER RELAY RACE @ ISAC

Having missed the Idol Star Athletics Championships in February 2015 because they were on tour in Japan, BTS eagerly return to the competition in August to defend their position as kings of the relay. With a team comprising Jimin, Jung Kook, V and J-Hope, they had high expectations as they lined up against Seventeen, B1A4 and Teen Top. Have a look at this Bangtan Bomb to see if they beat their K-pop rivals.

The fun and games couldn't last forever, though, and it wasn't long before the hard-working Bangtan were again on the plane to Japan. Back in June, BTS had achieved their first number-one single in Japan with a track written only in Japanese called 'For You'. The song has a soft, lyrical flow and a slow beat provided, somewhat unusually, by a plink-plonk piano and whistle. It's catchy and light, and the music video is a gem – worth catching if only to see Jung Kook in a giant teddy bear outfit!

In contrast to the darkness of 'I Need U', the vibe here is warm and feel-good. In the smooth choreography sections the boys are dressed in black and white, but without the swag look, and the hip-hop moves are almost completely gone, too. They find solace in each other's company once more, but this time it's as a relief from the drudgery of their jobs: Suga is delivering pizzas, Jin is cleaning cars, V works in a convenience store, J-Hope waits on tables, Jimin is a washer-up, RM is still at the gas station and teddy bear Jung Kook is handing out leaflets. Aww!

After wrapping up the Red Bullet tour to a rapturous reception in Hong Kong on 29 August, it was time for a very special occasion: Jung Kook was going to be a Bangtan man! His eighteenth birthday fell on 1 September 2015 and, on the stroke of midnight, the other members surprised him with a strawberry birthday cake and promises of presents ranging from Timberlands (J-Hope) to a kiss (Jimin), while ARMY responded as only they can, getting #HappyJungkookDay trending worldwide on Twitter.

Little more than a month after leaving, BTS returned to North America in September to play some short sets in a Highlight Tour as part of their association with New York streetwear brand Community54. They went to San Francisco, Houston, Atlanta and, in a first trip to Canada, Toronto. Although they played 'N.O', 'Boy in Luv', 'Dope' and 'I Need U' with their customary energy and charisma, they had little onstage time to communicate with their audiences and poor organization of the events meant that unfortunately many fans didn't have a very positive experience.

As they continued to play festivals in Korea throughout the autumn, some intriguing teaser releases focused all eyes on the next comeback. The images for this were called *Papillon* (French for 'butterfly) and the feel was much lighter. Gone were the frowns and there was even a playfulness in some of the pictures. In fact, these concept photos were arguably the best yet. In the ones taken in a rural setting the boys seem very much at ease with themselves, while other pictures, titled *Je Ne Regrette Rien* (French for 'I regret nothing', but also titled 'No Regrets') feature a more industrial scene and a punkier look – but even though pink-haired RM and mint-haired Suga pose and pout, the smiles escape nonetheless.

Want to see something even more spectacular? Search for 'BTS on Stage: Prologue'. You should find a twelve-minute film posted by Big Hit. Don't worry about the language barrier, you just have to listen and watch and you'll be captivated. Released out of the blue at the beginning of October, it was an immediate hit with ARMY, who, of course, came up with their own theories about what's going on in the film (and their own subtitled versions).

As the film begins with a blood-splattered V cleaning himself up, is it safe to assume this is the aftermath of the 'I Need U' video, in which V became violent – perhaps killing his abusive father? Moving to another scenario, we see the boys hanging out and messing around, on one last, crazy road trip. There is a sense of wild abandon as they arm-wrestle and sword-fight, but there is also a forlorn undercurrent related to the music and the view through the lens of Jin's camcorder, especially as V plunges from a pier into the sea at the end.

Most theories assume that this is a ghost story. Big Hit posted, but later replaced, a version where, at the end of the credits, Jin is alone at the beach looking at the picture RM put in the glove compartment. Suga has disappeared in the photo. Could it be that, V aside, some or all of them died at the end of the music video? Is Jin trying to capture a time or emotion that has actually already passed?

Whatever the theory, the film set up the new album perfectly. The boys looked great, dressed down but bringing energy and charisma to every scene, the cinematography was spot on, and the previews of four of the tracks from the new mini-album provided a superb soundtrack. On 29 November 2015, the nine-hundredth day since their debut, BTS played the last of a three-night stint at the Olympic Handball Gymnasium in Seoul. The 5,000-capacity venue was the largest they had played yet in Seoul but, of course, every night sold out instantly. They made use of the huge performing area, running around the T-shaped stage and even the aisles. They sang new arrangements of 'No More Dream' and 'N.O' and, less confined by strict choreography, they performed in a straight line, which enabled them to interact with their fans in a new way.

That this was a thank you to the home ARMY was made evident when they premiered their new songs not on a TV music show or an online video, but in front of those very fans. 'You guys are the first in the world to hear and see this performance,' was how Suga announced their new single, 'Run'. To a sea of chanting, light-stick wielding devotees, they then went on to sing, also for the first time, 'Intro: Never Mind', 'Butterfly' and 'Ma

City'. If the audience reaction was anything to go by, the new mini-album was going to be a runaway success.

The *Korea Herald* reported that at the press conference for the concerts, RM had talked about the new songs, saying, 'No matter how old you are, you can slip and make mistakes, but I think society has become too harsh to judge those mistakes.' He went on to explain, 'We wanted to say that it's okay to fall down, to get hurt. All you have to do is get back up and keep running.' The 'never give up' message had already been seen in the album trailer. It featured simple, stylized outlines and bold colours featuring a boy, a basketball and hoop, and a butterfly with Suga at his most passionate and heartfelt yet, reflecting on his youth and delivering, in a raw shout, the key line: if you think you're going to crash, go faster. The day after the final Handball Gymnasium concert saw the release of the music video for 'Run'. It amassed nearly 2 million YouTube views in the first twenty-four hours. A kind of sequel to 'I Need U', 'Run' was another collage of the boys having fun, partying, getting emotional and causing havoc. From V's backward fall into dark water at the start to Jimin being thrown fully clothed into a bath at the end, it was five minutes of high-octane action with bad boy BTS back vandalizing cars, spray-paint-tagging and fighting. It was not without wistful looks and meaningful stares, but the message about living your life, falling down and getting up again, came across strongly.

The Most Beautiful Moment in Life, Pt. 2 was released on 30 November 2015. Once again, it came in a choice of cover designs, this time peach or blue, and included a photobook featuring beautiful photos of the boys from both their nature and urban shoots. With this mini-album, BTS showed their mettle and proved the doubters wrong: not only had they continued to write their own top-quality songs, but the sophistication of both music and lyrics had improved, as had their attention to the smallest details in the production. More than one reviewer noted their bravery in pushing the boundaries of their musical style and continuing to produce amazing tracks.

Suga's opening rap, 'Intro: Never Mind', which, as was now customary, had been used as a trailer, lays out the mini-album's theme, and the next track 'Run' takes up the baton. Another step towards a full-on lush pop sound, 'Run' brings the rappers and the vocal line closer again. With a subtle instrumental dance backing, toned-down rap and punchy chorus, it seems BTS have established a new style that combines passion and energy with a sentimental feel. As the practice choreography video for 'Run', released in early December, also showed, their dancing was maturing as well, because without the hip-hop posturing they could utilize their acting skills and be more expressive.

The next track, the artfully arranged 'Butterfly', features a soft synth backing track that allows the vocals, especially Jung Kook and V's, to spread smoothly and sweetly across the song like honey. More than this, though, it again shows how Suga's gift for lyrics is blossoming and the way he compares love to a fragile and elusive butterfly marks him out as a poet who is growing in stature.

The following track on the mini-album uses a different animal to communicate a concept. 'Whalien 52' is about the 52-hertz whale, a real creature that sings at a unique frequency other whales cannot hear and has been described as the loneliest whale in the world. The tune is lilting and hypnotic and, although the metaphor is not as subtle as 'Butterfly', Bangtan turn it into an empathetic exploration of feeling alone, which is just as effective.

Next it's all aboard for the train to 'Ma City'. A live favourite, this is a non-stop express ride with a driving beat and a retro, almost disco, feel. As the group members eulogize about their home towns (with Suga admitting he brags about Daegu on every album), it's a reminder that BTS feel free to use their local dialects and are not ashamed of where they come from.

Don't ignore the track '뱁새' that follows just because there is no direct English translation. It's officially known as 'Silver Spoon' but often called 'Baepsae' – which is a small Korean bird also known as a crow-tit. According to a Korean saying, if a crow-tit walks like the long-legged stork, it will damage its legs, and BTS portray their generation as the crow-tits expected to walk like their stork parents, even though expectations have changed. Set to a South-East-Asian-sounding beat, it is one of BTS's angriest songs yet, as RM almost spits out how, thanks to those who came before them, his generation has suffered. It would become a firm fan favourite.

The skit features a light-hearted chat about how far they have come, before two final tracks, some say the best of the album. 'Autumn Leaves' (sometimes known as 'Dead Leaves' or 'Fallen Leaves') gives us another metaphor as the season changes and leaves hanging on to branches mirror a love growing cold and hanging on desperately. With an even line distribution, the song highlights the vocal talents of every single member.

The high production standards are maintained right through to the outro, a song titled 'House of Cards', which compares a fragile love affair to a structure precariously built from playing cards. To a dreamy string backing track, voices weave in and out in the smoothest of transitions as we pick out V's falsetto, Jin's pleas, Jimin's raspy tone and Jung Kook's alluring, almost cracked voice.

BANGTAN BOMB

'RUN' CHRISTMAS VERSION

Suga in a Santa cap ... Jimin in antlers ... Jin in pink ear muffs ... This isn't 'Run' as we know it. There's no enigmatic storyline, no heavy make-up, no sensational choreography, but instead there are a lot of laughs and we're treated to Jung Kook sleeping sweetly and Suga definitely not running. If you're in need of Christmas cheer, this is the bomb for you.

BTS had treated the Seoul ARMY to the first live performance of 'Run', but the comeback stage was pretty special, too. At the 2015 MAMAs in early December, although the *daesang* grand prize escaped them again

(Big Bang and EXO took the honours), BTS picked up a special award for best worldwide performer – one of the first signs that their global popularity could mean they would eclipse other groups.

For those who enjoyed the previous year's Block B collaboration, this time they took on GOT7 in a special stage. The performance of 'Virtual Boys' began with a rap battle between RM and GOT7's Jackson, then a dance-off with J-Hope and Yugyeom, before both groups, BTS in white and GOT7 in black, united in a superbly synchronized display. The video of the joint group owning the MAMA stage is still cherished by ARMY, perhaps because of all K-pop groups, GOT7 seemed closest to BTS. Then, as BTS followed with their own comeback stage, they again brought the audience to their feet. MAMA was becoming a pretty special event for the boys.

Once they had persuaded J-Hope to say the single would flop, there really was no doubt it was going to be a hit. The video secured wins on music awards programmes *Show Champion* and *The Show Choice* while the boys were busy in Japan, although they were back in time to perform on *Music Bank* and see their track win again, despite fierce competition from Psy. Three wins in a week! And to think that just a year ago they were desperate for even a solitary victory. They had come a long way.

BANGTAN BOMB

IT'S THE POSE WHEN BTS SLEEP NORMALLY

If you've watched any BTS interviews you'll know by now that BTS's favourite thing (after ARMY, obviously) is sleeping. So here's a Bangtan Bomb from their time in Chile about sleeping, or trying to sleep, or waking, or walking on your hands (J-Hope is one excellent hand walker!). Whatever. It's Jimin on camera and more super-charming goofing around from J-Hope, Jung Kook and Suga.

'Run' reached number eight in the Korean singles charts, while *The Most Beautiful Moment in Life, Pt. 2* matched *Pt. 1* by topping the album charts. However, it was the splash they made stateside that was most remarkable. Over there, the mini-album topped the Billboard Heatseekers and World Albums charts for four weeks, a record for a South Korean act. And they weren't finished there; when the Billboard 200 came out in the week before Christmas, BTS was at 171! Although ten K-pop acts had already matched that position, BTS were the first to achieve it without being a Big Three group.

In Japan, BTS had followed their June 2015 number-one hit 'For You' with a Japanese version of 'I Need U', which reached number two in December. That month, 25,000 fans had attended two sold-out concerts in Yokohama, Japan's second-largest city. Meanwhile, out in the USA, *The Most Beautiful Moment in Life, Pt. 2*, spent a total of sixteen weeks on Billboard's World Albums Chart. Even Europe was catching on to BTS as they took Best Korean Act at the 2015 MTV Europe Music Awards.

At home a victory on *Music Bank* at the end of the promotion on 8 January 2016 marked their fifth triumph of the comeback and their tenth to date. The awards season over, the Christmas period had also proved fruitful as they picked up *bonsangs* at the Golden Disc Awards and the Seoul Music Awards. That yearned-for *daesang* was tantalizingly close but still eluded them.

V

MEMBER PROFILE

Name:	Kim Taehyung
AKA:	V, Tae, Taetae, Human Gucci, Vante
Date of birth:	30 December 1995
Birthplace:	Daegu, South Korea
Height:	1.79 metres (5'10")
Education:	Changnam Elementary School, Geochang Middle School, Daegu First High School, Korean Arts High School, Global Cyber University
Chinese zodiac:	Pig
Star sign:	Capricorn
Instagram:	@thv

FOURTEEN

KIM TAEHYUNG/V: PRINCE OF DUALITY

They are both devilishly good-looking, stylish and love to sing. But there the similarity between Kim Taehyung and BTS's singer and dancer, V, ends. Yes, they might be one and the same 95-line boy from Daegu, but Taehyung's persona changes radically when he goes out on that stage. Watch any BTS performance and you'll see V being cool, sophisticated and professional; watch a Bangtan Bomb or an offstage video and you'll often discover the lovably dorkish Taetae, messing about, being plain silly or lost in a world of his own.

In November 2016, during the encore of a BTS concert in the Gocheok Sky Dome in Korea, it was V who came to the front of the stage to address the 17,000 fans. In a heartbreaking speech, he explained that recently, when the group was in the Philippines, he had received news that his grandmother had died. Fans and group members shed tears with him as he told of his love for her and how he had planned to send her a special message when the group were on television, but now would never get the chance.

Taehyung had been particularly close to his paternal grandmother. She had brought him up for fourteen years as his parents, traditional Korean farmers, were busy working. He was a boy who loved to play outside, but paid attention to his studies too. Then, as he went to middle school, still not quite a teenager, he began to dream. He wanted to be a singer.

Taking his father's advice to learn an instrument, Taehyung took up the saxophone. He worked at it and became a competent player, winning first prize in a regional competition. With his eye already on becoming an idol, he joined a dance club and soon gave up the sax to spend more time on the dance floor.

He had joined a dance academy, but a few months after starting high school in Daegu in 2011, his life changed – dramatically. When Big Hit held auditions in Daegu, Taehyung had no intention of trying out, but went along with a friend. There, the good-looking young lad was spotted by one of the Big Hit staff. She encouraged him to audition, but Taehyung declined as he didn't have his parents' consent. Sensing the boy might have something, she called his parents, got permission and he was quickly on stage, dancing, rapping and even telling jokes. He didn't believe he had a chance, but Big Hit contacted him and told him he had passed – the only one from that audition who had.

So Taehyung moved into the Big Hit dorm and, wearing the padded red jacket his mother had sent him so he stood out, enrolled in high school in Seoul (where he was joined by Jimin). Trainee days don't seem to have scarred Taehyung as much as the others. He liked school, loved the dance lessons and although he admits to missing his family, he was having fun with his new friends at school and in the company. He seems to have been happy living in the present, taking his place in BTS in his stride and not wondering when they would debut. Although it was hard work and intense, Taehyung was living his dream and was determined to enjoy it.

Finally debut did appear on the horizon and Taehyung chose a name. He rejected Six and Lex and went with V for victory, but he was in for a shock. Big Hit had decided his membership of BTS would be kept secret until just before debut. His identity would be hidden, no photos of him would be released and he couldn't record vlogs like the others. He went to RM and Jung Kook's graduations, his back had appeared in Jimin's selfie (everyone had assumed it was Jung Kook) and Jimin had even taken his school uniform (while V was sleeping!) to wear in the 'Graduation Song' video. Poor V would sometimes sit by himself and pretend to do a vlog and, as if that wasn't sad enough, as they were recording their final pre-debut group vlog, V was actually in the room, standing in the corner keeping out of shot!

However, once he was revealed, V was an immediate hit with fans. They liked the handsome figure who flicked off his glasses during the 'No More Dream' performance, although they noted that offstage he could be a little, well, strange. He'd sometimes speak a made-up language, have an incredibly blank expression, wave his hands or make off-the-wall comments like saying his chosen superpower would be to be able to talk to cars. It was charming and K-pop fans have a word for it: 4D.

There is a K-pop tradition of describing artists as '4D' and it's a flattering term, meaning they are quirky and different, and have added personality and charisma. Suga later said he originally thought Taehyung was acting, that people like that didn't exist, but came to realize his unique behaviour was authentic, and ARMY affectionately began calling him '4D', 'Alien' or 'Blank Tae'. However, even as early as summer 2015, Taehyung let it be known that he didn't really like those names and most fans respectfully stopped using them.

Nevertheless, he has remained the most unconventional member of the group and in a 2015 interview with Korean magazine *The Star*, Taehyung said, 'I am not scared of looking ugly and I'm thankful that [my fans] like me even when I pull weird faces. I don't plan on looking handsome in an unnatural way. That would be a burden.'

There is one look that everyone loves: V with a slightly tilted head, wide eyes and a tight-lipped half smile. The 'Tata Mic face' meme originated when V tried to persuade staff to give him a Baby Tata (V's BT21 character) bluetooth microphone during the 2021 *festa*. It has since become a favourite ARMY spot seen in various *Run BTS!* episodes, at Bang Bang Con: The Live during his 'Friends' duet with Jimin and even in a photo of V as a baby.

Taetae (a name he seems happy with) has a great relationship with ARMY. This is the guy who came up with the 'I purple you' phrase in 2016, explaining that as purple is the last colour in the rainbow it means 'I will love you forever'. He has delighted fans on V Live with his DJ TaeTae FM sessions where he lip-syncs and dances to songs and has been a regular contributor to the BTS Weverse forum. In January 2020, when he posted just-woke-up pictures with the comments, 'My face is pancake u know?' and, 'bbut! you still like it right?' ARMYs were already swooning, but when he replied to a fan enquiry, saying, 'I'm tying up my hair,' it was all too much and the site crashed!

Taehyung's out-there persona extends to his fashion sense. He doesn't follow the crowd, but always manages to look stylish, whatever he wears. Back in the early days he developed a quirky but chic look by combining various styles that might include any combination of round glasses, roll-neck jumpers, French-style, striped long-sleeved shirts and oversized coats. As BTS became successful V earned another nickname: 'Human Gucci'. He loved the brand; not only the clothes but the shades, rings, neck bows and watches. However, he would move on again. In a 2022 interview with *Vogue Korea*, he said he now preferred 'something more simple and casual' than the classic 'British style' he had been sporting.

Like all the members, Taehyung has given ARMY many moments to cherish. *American Hustle Life* provided memes of the classic 'Beach! Bitch?' misunderstanding with Jimin, as well as his misjudged attempt to impress Coolio with his enthusiastic 'Turn Up!' exclamation. A much-loved TV episode of *Star King* (the clip is on YouTube) saw him pull off some serious dance moves while wearing twelve-centimetre (four-and-a-half-inch) heels. Various videos show how soft Tae gets when kids and babies are in the vicinity and ARMY just love it when he kisses the camera.

Tae has a way of wearing glasses that no one can match. Every pair in his vast collection just looks so right. In Japan he went viral as 'The Guy with Glasses' after a 'Stay Gold' performance and he was an unbeatable Ending Fairy when he put on his sunglasses at the end of the 'Dynamite' MV (although the eyebrow raise at the end of the 2020 MAMAs performance is a worthy challenger).

His tweets also reveal V's love of art, from the Van Gogh *Starry Night* picture hanging on his wall in the dorm to his professed love of Jean-Michel

Basquiat and Egon Schiele. In November 2022, he revealed that he was a fan of 11-year-old US artist Andres Valencia and added her portrait of him to his collection. He is also a big fan of Australian photographer Ante Badzim, whose simple but beautiful photos inspired V to take his own pictures. He uploaded some of them with the hashtag #Vante (another nickname!) and came to the attention of the photographer himself, who dedicated a photo to V in return. In 2019 the cover art for V's solo track 'Scenery' even featured shots of Tae taking photographs.

The other group members all love V too, even if Jin complains he is a little noisy and Suga says he sometimes just doesn't get him. A love of gaming and a light-hearted approach to life has led him to bond with ace gamer and super-*maknae* Jung Kook, but Taehyung and Jimin possibly have the closest friendship in the whole group, and V's heartfelt letter to his friend on the *Bon Voyage 2* boat revealed just how grateful he is for his fellow 95-liner's care and affection. In 2020, on their 'Carpool Karaoke' trip, Suga named Jimin and V as the group's biggest arguers. When asked what they disagreed about, Jung Kook said, 'Dumplings!' – a source of conflict which was confirmed in their duet 'Friends'.

Taehyung is a real social butterfly. He has so many friends outside BTS and is regularly pictured with celebrities and idols. He seems to be able to make friends anywhere, having befriended BTOB's Sungjae, singer Jang Moon-bok and Block B's Park Kyung during rest breaks, while Park Hyung-sik and Park Seo-joon, friends he made on the set of *Hwarang*, would soon form part of his 'Wooga Squad' friendship group. He has also emerged as an inspiration to other K-pop artists. Younghoon of The Boyz, Ateez's Yeosang and Mingi, Treasure's Haruto, Golden Child's Jaehyun and Jangjun, Cravity's Serim and Jungmo, TXT's Beomgyu and so many others who look up to him have confirmed his status as the 'Idol of Idols'.

In December 2017, we were introduced to Tae's latest friend. Jin was conducting a live stream for his birthday when V appeared at the window holding the cutest puppy imaginable. We soon found out that this was his new dog, a Pomeranian that he named Yeontan (which translates as 'charcoal briquette'). Because of BTS's busy schedule, Yeontan left the dorm to stay with Taehyung's parents, but they still see each other regularly. In the 2018 *festa* interview, Taehyung revealed how the puppy now follows him around but runs away when he tries to catch him – and that 'Tan' had gained too much puppy fat!

As ARMY got to know Taehyung, so they became accustomed to V. It surprised many to hear those deep, soulful notes coming from someone so adept at *aygeo* cute faces, but V's rich tone adds contrast to the higher register of the other vocalists, although he can take it up the scale with ease, too. There are so many examples of his singing talent, but his solo tracks 'Stigma' and 'Singularity', his collaboration with RM, '4 O'Clock', or his cover of Adele's 'Someone Like You' are exquisite.

V's stage presence is also pretty awesome. He feels the emotion of every word he sings and he works the crowd with a perfectly placed, but not overused, wink, smile or subtle lick of the lips. His dancing is sharp and confident, and he created a moment audiences anticipate with great excitement in 'Boyz with Fun', where the other members (and sometimes backing dancers) have to copy his improvised choreography.

BANGTAN BOMB

V'S DREAM CAME TRUE – 'HIS CYPHER PT. 3 SOLO STAGE'

When J-Hope took the third place in BTS's rap line, V's status as vocalist in the group was confirmed, but he remained a frustrated rapper. He raps in the practice room and at fan meets, and sometimes seems to bristle with jealousy during the cyphers. He has admitted he wanted to switch bodies with Suga for 'Cypher Pt. 3', so imagine his glee when he was given the solo part in the 2016 *festa* performance. This bomb shows not only his memorable rap, but also how the other members help him prepare for his big moment.

In 2016, V temporarily got himself another name: Han Sung. He was cast in a historical drama television series called *Hwarang: The Poet Warrior Youth*, which focused on the lives and loves of a group of young men in Korea around 1,500 years ago. Taehyung's portrayal of a lovable and innocent character, the youngest of the group, was appreciated by audiences (and not just ARMY), especially in the scenes of high emotion, and his fellow actors commented on his natural talent and his work ethic.

Like his fellow members, V has been given solo opportunities as the group have progressed. In January 2019 he released 'Scenery' on SoundCloud, a soulful and sweet ballad he wrote and composed. In just over two weeks, it became the fastest song to hit 100 million streams on the platform. Later that year, 'Winter Bear', another beautiful self-composed solo, this time sung completely in English, was released along with a self-directed video that celebrated his love of nature and photography. It would remain a fan favourite, reaching 100 million views on YouTube in August 2022.

Fans eager for more solo releases from V had a long wait, but it was worth it. His self-penned 'Sweet Night', another English-language song, was released in March 2020 for the OST of the popular K-drama *Itaewon Class*. A warm and emotional track that displayed sighing, whistling and humming from the singer, it topped iTunes charts around the world and was awarded the 'Most Streamed Drama OST Category' for two consecutive years in 2020 and 2021 by Spotify Wrapped.

In the summer of 2020, V first mentioned that he was working on a mixtape. Excited ARMY named it *KTH1*, but even a year later V was telling *Rolling Stone* magazine that the release plan 'turned out to be [much] harder and more complex than I imagined that it would be'. For now, fans had to be content with festive solo tracks in the jazzy 'Snow Flower', a song recorded with his friend Peakboy, and December 2021's 'Christmas Tree'.

The last of these became a particular ARMY favourite. 'Christmas Tree' was an OST for the romantic comedy TV series *Our Beloved Summer*. It was written specifically for V by the show's music director, and he perfectly delivers the breathy, fragile English lyrics to a soft instrumental, creating a tender love song that touched the soul of fans. The track debuted at number seventy-nine on the Billboard Hot 100, making it V's first solo entry on the chart.

The idea of a mixtape hadn't disappeared. In episode five of the first series of *In the Soop*, a song by V played over footage of him sitting along in a canoe in the middle of the lake. The sensitive and beautiful track was revealed to be an English-language version of 'Blue & Grey' that he had written about feeling burned-out and down during lockdown, and was originally intended for his solo release. When the group heard the song, they liked it so much that they reworked as a track for *BE*. For many, it was the stand-out track on the album, but it was also one fewer song for the mythical mixtape.

BANGTAN BOMB

HELP V CHOOSE A PAIR OF SUNGLASSES

Taehyung loves his sunglasses, whether classy, classic or unique, and ARMY love to see him wearing them. So here's a treat. He has twenty-six pairs to choose from and, of course, has to try them all on. He first asks J-Hope for advice and when he gets bored he summons Jimin, who hilariously suggests, 'It'd be nice if you could hurry and pick one.' Jungkook and various staff members are enlisted to help but we seem no closer to a choice. While ARMY are thinking, 'We don't care, he looks great in them all,' Jimin comes to a decision. But is it one V will respect ... ?

Along with the other BTS members, V launched his own Instagram account (@thv) in December 2021. His first posts displayed the quirky and cute sides of the singer beloved by ARMY. His first was a small animal skeleton in mid-air (it was South Korean artist Hyungkoo Lee's artwork of cartoon character Wile E. Coyote) and the second was a selfie in his bathroom. Both made an incredible impact. He was the first member to use Instagram stories and his pictures of his dog Yeontan (or Tannie, as he is often known), his own artistic, enigmatic and beautiful photographs and, of course, his selfies have made his a go-to account. He is acknowledged as the 'King of Instagram', having become the fastest person in the world to pass 1 million (43 minutes) and 40 million (135 days) followers; and, in 2023, he was the first and only artist in the world with over 10 million likes on each post and had the highest Instagram-influencer value in the world.

Unsurprisingly, V's contribution to BTS's photo-folio series, '*Me, Myself, & V: Veautiful Days*', was greeted with rapturous attention. It features V in a series of impeccably styled outfits. Eschewing modern fashion, V cast himself in matching cream trousers and waistcoat while riding a bike with a basket of flowers; looking like a nineteenth-century dandy in a royal-blue tailcoat and top hat; and sitting thoughtfully on the stairs in a soft brown suit and chequered cravat. 'I think that a classic look always comes back,' he said. And he proved his point.

The announcement that the members would focus on solo activities for the near future from autumn 2022 brought a similar reaction from V as the rest of the group. 'For the past ten years, we kept on looking upwards, and I realized it was scary,' he wrote, and explained how he shared the feelings of exhaustion and constraint. There were many things he had wanted to try in the previous years, but group commitments and loyalty to his fellow members had made him hold back. Now he hoped to show fans new aspects of himself.

It wasn't long before they were seeing just that as V brought his friendship group to the screen. V's renowned ability to make good friends had led him to team up with other big names in Korean entertainment. The 'Wooga Squad', as they became known, was originally formed by actor Park Seo-joon. He met V and former boy-group ZE:A singer turned actor Park Hyung-sik on the set of *Hwarang* in 2016. Later, he introduced them to Korean-Canadian actor Choi Woo-shik (of Oscar-winning *Parasite* fame) and rapper Peakboy. V would explain that 'Wooga' was short for the Korean phrase, '*Woori-ga gajok-inga*?' which translates as 'Are we family?'

They weren't related, but they did act like a true band of brothers, spending holidays and Christmases together and supporting each other's work – even all taking cameo parts in Peakboy's 'Gyopo Hairstyle' MV. In July 2022, all five of them starred in *In the Soop: Friendcation*, a spin-off of the getaway reality series that BTS (and Seventeen) had appeared in. Like the BTS and Seventeen seasons, it follows the group relaxing, playing, cooking and eating, as well as some heartfelt discussions. Especially moving were the scenes with V crying in the night and the squad consoling him over the difficult year that had been troubling him.

A few of the squad soon returned to TV. In the series *Jinny's Kitchen*, available on Amazon Prime, Park Seo-joon, V and Choi Woo-shik took on a culinary challenge. The reality series finds TV celebrity Lee Seo-jin opening a Korean street-food restaurant in Bacalar, Mexico, and employing the trio as interns and kitchen assistants. V (as anyone who has seen any cooking-challenge episodes of *Run BTS!* will know) is not a natural in the kitchen. He admitted, 'In BTS I'm the worst cook, so I wondered why they asked me to cook on the show.' The show confirmed that his cooking isn't great, but that he can be a whole lot of fun – and that he really, really likes a corndog.

As other members revealed plans for solo albums, V's fans were finally able to forget a possible mixtape and wait for an official solo album instead. In the meantime, they did receive a Christmas surprise. In what was now becoming a tradition, V dropped a Christmas song for fans: a cover of the Christmas classic 'It's Beginning to Look a Lot Like Christmas'. V brought his jazz side to the fore with a beautiful warm tone to his voice, sending the track straight to number one on SoundCloud, and the simple video of V singing, wrapped up warm in his hoodie, racking up the views on YouTube.

Back in the summer of 2022, V had been all over social media when he attended the Celine showcase at Paris Fashion Week along with Lisa from Blackpink and actor Park Bo-gum. He clearly had an affinity with the menswear brand and for their April 2023 edition, *ELLE Korea* announced that he would represent the luxury brand as a global ambassador and produced three different covers of V looking completely stunning. The magazine also revealed that he had come up with the concepts himself and had helped direct the shoot.

Over and over, V has amazed with his chameleon-like ability to effortlessly manifest diverse concepts and take on differing personas. He can appear as an innocent and sweet boy and transform almost instantly into a gorgeous and sensuous young man; he can be goofy and fun and then deadly serious and studious. Sometimes, he does all this just by taking off his glasses and shaking out his hair! Thank heavens that Big Hit staff member was so determined to get his parents' approval for the original audition. Taehyung brings so much more to BTS than his vocals and dance skills; he provides a vibrant personality, a unique and stylish visual sense, and performance talents that give the group an extra dimension. V and Kim Taehyung: let's celebrate the duality!

FIFTEEN

BTS ON FIRE!

In late 2015, just before the release of *The Most Beautiful Moment in Life, Pt. 2*, the sports brand Puma announced an endorsement deal with BTS. Brand endorsement is a major part of K-pop and the fact that a multinational company as massive as Puma chose to sign up the Bangtan Boys tells us a lot about how far they had come since their debut. Even if their initial advert, which featured them wearing Puma and dancing in the street to a rewritten version of 'Run', was a little cheesy!

Cheesy was something BTS might have to get used to as major idols. Early in 2016 they were invited to appear with top girl group GFriend in a song for Family Love Day, a campaign encouraging families to spend at least one day a week together. On YouTube the song's title is translated as 'Family Song' and, well, it may not be BTS's finest three and a half minutes (you get the sense Suga doesn't really want to be there!), but they all look cute in their smart school uniforms and, if you're looking for a straightforward BTS dance to learn, this is a good place to start. The 'making of' video also has some particularly cute pics of the guys as young children.

In February, BTS returned to the Idol Star Athletics Championships in a team called Beat to the End with their friends GOT7 and girl groups Twice and Bestie. They retained their relay kings title, with J-Hope, Jimin,

Jung Kook and V taking gold in the 4 × 100 metres, and then took part in the eight-team *ssireum* tournament. This traditional Korean form of wrestling involves each competitor wearing a loose belt which is gripped by his opponent, who attempts to bring him down. A team of V, Jung Kook and Jin saw off BTOB and Teen Top to meet VIXX in the final. Jung Kook won the first bout, but V couldn't wrap the tournament up so it was all down to Jin, who met singer Ken in the final bout. Although there were a lot of smiles, it was tense as the two faced off. They moved around the ring holding each other like ballroom dancers before Ken, sensing his moment, forced the slightly off-balance Jin to the floor. Never mind, he still looked good!

BANGTAN BOMB

BTS'S RHYTHMICAL FARCE! LOL

This bomb is a big favourite of ARMY all around the world. In a backstage area, various combinations of Bangtan Boys pretend to meet each other. Their reactions are exaggerated and usually accompanied by a scream of 'Yahhhh'. What are they doing? Working out a new form of greeting? Some form of improvised drama? Or perhaps it's just inspired messing around? Whatever. It's ninety seconds of nonsense that you'll watch again and again.

No one actually died as a result of Big Hit posting comeback concept photos for their compilation album in April 2016. But given ARMY's online reaction to the new blond Jin, you'd be forgiven for thinking someone had. With a wavy, backcombed look, Jin wrecked biases in seconds as he posed in the photoshoot. Not that he was the only one to change his hair colour; Suga kept the grey but all the others had been at the dye. RM had gone for blue-grey, Jimin was back to black, V's hair had taken on a pinky-orange hue, Jung Kook's messy locks were dark brown and J-Hope sported a layered, light brown style.

For the day and night sets of concept photos for *The Most Beautiful Moment in Life: Young Forever*, they posed in a clearing on Jeju, an island off the Korean peninsula. They were on an adventure involving a campervan and a hot-air balloon, and the location choice allowed the boys' bright colours to contrast against a washed-out landscape and a big sky, with a Polaroid format adding an extra effect on the night photos.

The shoot presented a change of style for the Bangtan crew. Gone was the punked-up look we saw in *Pt. 2* and in its place was finery – and shorts! The clothes were dominated by Gucci, with frilly shirts, ribbons, neck clasps and berets, but there were also smart, tight-fitting, two-button suits, V carrying off a powder-blue version with particular aplomb. It was the sophistication of a bygone era combined with camp, humour and a carefree attitude. Most ARMY barely seemed to notice, though. They were still getting over Suga's freckles, the return of Jimin's dimples and – wow – Jin's hair!

Young Forever, BTS's April 2016 release, was a twenty-three-track compilation album featuring the songs from both *The Most Beautiful Moment in Life* albums, with six remixes and full versions of the previous two albums' outros, as well as three new tracks. However, the fact that it was a compilation didn't stop Big Hit giving it the full build-up with teasers and previews.

They also trailed and announced BTS's first solo concerts of 2016, BTS Live The Most Beautiful Moment in Life On Stage: Epilogue, to be held at the Olympic Gymnastics Arena in South Korea where, once again, ARMY would be the first to witness the new choreography live. Their first ever concerts at the 15,000-capacity venue played only by K-pop giants sold out instantly. The trailer for the shows featured the smartly suited band members facing the flashing lights of the paparazzi as they trod the red carpet. It was an experience they were going to have to get used to in real life.

Each of the three new tracks on *Young Forever* were released with their own music videos, beginning with 'Epilogue: Young Forever'. The video showed flashbacks to 'I Need U' and 'Run', along with images of individual members trapped in, and eventually breaking free from, a wire fence maze. The song builds from a softly spoken statement about living in the now, enjoying the moment but not being scared to move on, to the unashamed optimism of the anthemic chorus, an almost irresistible singalong that dominates the final section.

In the first week of May, BTS dropped the music video for 'Fire'. Basically a dance video set in a now almost familiar derelict warehouse, it was further enlivened by Suga remotely exploding a dark figure, uncontrollable flames, a falling car slamming to the ground and some great acting. Jung Kook's wide-eyed look, V's video game-playing and even Jimin's 'Ow!' were highlights that demonstrated a new level of confidence in front of the camera. The video hit 1 million views in just six hours and in just over two days had amassed 10 million views. It was the best reaction yet. 'Fire' is a rocking, beat-thumping number that charges out of the starting blocks and incorporates all those elements that make their high-tempo tracks so exciting. A rap intro – check (good job, J-Hope and Suga); a singalong chorus – check; an infectious la-la-la – check; a cheeky insert – check; a false stop and a renewed start – check. The lyrics pick up the themes from the whole trilogy. They ask their listeners to run with them, to not be afraid to live, to embrace the fire and burn everything up – with passion, desire, risk and ambition.

The accompanying dance was also suitably fearless. In interviews, the group said how difficult it was to master Keone Madrid's choreography, but they completely nailed it. A feast of energy and movement sees them switching effortlessly from speedy, almost martial arts-style whipping movements to slo-mo moves, interspersed with moments of cheekiness (dabs!) and *aegyo*. And they never let up on the perfect synchronicity. On top of all this, you just have to admire their stamina: watch the dance practice video on YouTube to catch the full intensity of the performance.

The third of the new releases, the more emotional 'Save Me', followed within a few weeks and had the vocal line to the fore. A more conventional

BTS lover's plea, it nevertheless grabs the attention with a superb synth beat of muted whistles and xylophones.

The music video was a one-shot take of the group dancing on the barren beach. It was the first time they had danced to the choreography of Norwegian-based team The Quick Style, who brought in some subtlety and contemporary dance moves while taking nothing away from the customary razor-sharp group dance. And, of course, BTS left us with a tease. As the video fades to black, a message is typed on screen. It reads 'BOY MEETS'. We wait for the next word, but that's it.

Only BTS could leave fans wondering like that! It was soon apparent that this trio of tracks would consolidate BTS's status as one of the top groups in Korea. On the day of its release, 'Fire' achieved the group's first chart 'all-kill', topping all the major real-time charts simultaneously, and BTS's performances of the song on *M Countdown*, *Music Bank* and *Inkigayo* brought them three more music-show trophies. Additionally, *Young Forever* went on to top the Korean album chart and stayed there for two consecutive weeks. In the USA, the BTS ripple gained momentum. *Young Forever* became their second consecutive album to make the Billboard 200, reaching as high as 106, while on the World Digital Songs chart they set a record never before achieved by a K-pop group: with 'Fire', 'Save Me' and 'Epilogue: Young Forever', they had three tracks in the chart at the same time.

In June 2016, Big Hit had something new planned for BTS on V Live. A preview episode of *Bon Voyage* showed the boys in the company boardroom discussing where they would like to go (Hawaii or rural South Korea) and who they would like to go with (J-Hope or Jimin). All this seems forgotten when they arrive back at the dorm – yes, we get to see the dorm at last! – to discover they're going to northern Europe and they're all going together. And so begins the V Live series *Bon Voyage*: eight forty-minute episodes (with extra 'behind camera' videos also available) following their ten-day backpacking trip across Norway, Sweden and Finland.

For boys who have spent at least four years doing little else but practising, performing and recording, this was a chance to have a holiday courtesy of Hitman Bang, but when they tour, everything is arranged for them by the company. Right from the start it is beautifully chaotic as panic and indecision reign in the dorm as they try to decide which clothes to pack. Suga is methodical as he counts his pairs of clean socks, Jung Kook plays the *maknae*, asking everyone else what they are taking, and Jimin just can't make up his mind what to pack.

Their first stop is Bergen in Norway. Thanks to RM's fluent English they negotiate their way from the airport to the city, only to discover Jimin has left his bag on the airport bus. It's surprising that the series wasn't called *The Lost Boys* because when they're not actually lost themselves they seem to be forever losing things – bags, iPads, tickets. When RM loses his passport, it is no longer funny; to the shock of the other members, he is forced to abandon the trip.

As their journey takes them on to Sweden and Finland, we see the others enjoying their time together as they sail down fjords, go on a bike ride, stay in an RV campervan, experience a sauna and cold lake dip, and visit Santa Park. This is BTS as normal guys in their twenties travelling together. They can't believe it, it's so relaxing, and J-Hope even discovers a phrase to keep the few fans they do encounter at bay: 'Sorry – important business!' On their last evening, as they sit by the lakeside reading the handwritten letters sent by Bang Si-hyuk and their manager Sejin to mark their forthcoming third anniversary, it does seem like the trip has made them value each other's company even more and appreciate what they have achieved. As Suga says in his closing comments, they are all like family now. In the summer, BTS flew out to Europe to top the bill at KCON in Paris and then to the States to the Newark and Los Angeles conventions. As Jeff Benjamin wrote in *Billboard*, 'If their headliner status didn't already indicate it, perhaps the charts can confirm that a new boy band is in town and ready to take over.' With the new tracks from *Young Forever*, plus 'Dope', 'I Need U' and 'Boyz with Fun', BTS now had a set full of sure-fire crowd-pleasers.

According to the organizers of the Newark KCON, which took place on 24 and 25 June, the 18,000-ticket BTS concert sold out faster than Bruce Springsteen. RM shared the MC duties on day one of the convention and the group closed the event on the second day. ARMY were reportedly the loudest fans ever heard at the venue and BTS even had the confidence to insert their own favourite, 'Cypher Pt. 3: Killer' from *Dark & Wild* into the set. That went down a storm, too. The next month they repeated the feat at the West Coast edition of KCON, which ran from 29 to 31 July. In the *LA Times*, August Brown wrote, 'BTS closed out the night with a reminder of why the group is one of K-pop's most lasting and influential acts ... The group bounded over the KCON stage with precision and verve, and took long, live turns to show off the members' rhyming dexterity in the thick of it all. K-pop has everything now, and Sunday's finale showed just how good a lot of it can be.'

In between the French and the two US KCON concerts came the great tradition known as *festa*, BTS and ARMY's annual celebration of their debut, now three years in the memory. It got off to a flying start with a free download of a new track, 'I Know', a tender duet recorded by RM and Jung Kook, before the fun kicked in with a specially choreographed version of favourite song 'Baepsae' and the family photo albums. These included some poses of the boys in their black tie and blazers or in uniforms complete with peaked caps, as well as Jin in a chef's outfit and a hilarious set of Suga and J-Hope goofing around in their orange 'SOPE' tracksuits (a video of the photoshoot can be found on YouTube).

The next video specially uploaded for *festa* stunned even dedicated ARMY. Titled 'J-Hope Dance Practice for 2015 Begins Concert', it was a sixty-second clip of J-Hope absolutely tearing up the dancefloor at Big Hit's studio and suddenly it was clear quite what the guy was capable of and how much he was holding back in the group dances – even in their most electric choreographies.

The summer ended as it had begun with BTS selling out huge venues in Japan for the last of their 2016 BTS Live The Most Beautiful Moment in Life On Stage: Epilogue concerts and competing in the second of the year's Idol Star Athletics Championships. Here they once again took the 4 × 100 metres relay (would they ever be defeated?) as J-Hope, Jimin, Jung Kook and Suga beat teams from BTOB and B.A.P, but they proved less successful in an archery competition. A Bangtan Bomb shows them looking good in their team tracksuit tops and shorts, Jimin now with blond hair, but they didn't really seem to be taking it seriously enough to win.

Young Forever – especially the three new songs – had taken BTS up yet another level. Somehow, these small company guys, writing much of their own music, were winning over not only their home country, but also their South-East Asian neighbours, as well as gaining thousands of fans in the Middle East, Australasia, South America, Europe and, whisper it quietly, they even had a foothold in the USA.

JUNG KOOK

MEMBER PROFILE

Name:	Jeon Jungkook
AKA:	Jung Kook, Kookie, JK, Nochu, Seagull, Golden Maknae, Bunny
Date of birth:	1 September 1997
Birthplace:	Busan, South Korea
Height:	1.78 metres (5'10")
Education:	Baekyang Middle School, Shingu Middle School, School of Performance Arts High School
Chinese zodiac:	Ox
Star sign:	Virgo
Instagram:	now deleted, previously @abcdefghi__lmnopqrstuvwxyv and @jungkook.97

SIXTEEN

JEON JUNGKOOK: THE GOLDEN MAKNAE

It was RM who came up with the name 'Golden Maknae' for Jung Kook, although chances are ARMY would have come up with it themselves before too long, for the baby of BTS is multi-talented, not just as a singer, dancer and gorgeous-looking band member, but also at practically anything else he turns his hand to. Barely a teenager when he started his journey to stardom, this baby has shown such maturity in coping with the adversity faced by the group and the stresses of idol life.

Having a special *maknae* is common in K-pop groups. The word refers to the youngest member and they are often the cutest and most playful, and receive the most affection from the others in the group. All this is true of Jung Kook – just see how BTS looked out for him in rookie stage performances or protected him during group interviews and TV shows in their early days. However, it soon became apparent that this *maknae* had something else, a real natural-born talent, and as BTS developed and grew in confidence, so did Jung Kook. Those who followed the group from debut had to take a breath and ask themselves just when he changed from being the cherished child to the jewel of the family.

Like Jimin, Jungkook grew up in the city of Busan. He lived with his mother, father and older brother, Jeon Jung-hun, so he had some experience of being the baby of the family. Indeed, his brother has shared many adorable pictures of his infant sibling online. It's probably fair to say that Jungkook didn't excel academically, but showed real talent in physical education, art and music, and in elementary school sport was particularly important to him. He took taekwondo lessons, eventually earning a black belt, played soccer and showed a particular aptitude for badminton. He used to dream of growing up to be a professional badminton player, and when his parents bought him his first computer his first games were e-sports.

Jungkook discovered music in middle school, especially the songs of the King of K-pop, G-Dragon, as the Big Bang vocalist's solo career went stratospheric with 'Heartbreaker'. The seventh grader began singing and was even inspired to try street dance, joining a local b-boy club. By 2011, he felt confident enough to audition for *Superstar K*, the biggest TV talent show in South Korea (think *The X Factor* or *American Idol*).

After queuing for hours along with thousands of other hopefuls at the Busan auditions, Jungkook was given his two-minute opportunity. With a slightly shapeless haircut and wearing a long-sleeved white T-shirt, he looked very sweet as he sang 2AM's 'This Song' and IU's 'Lost Child' (Jung Kook fans can find the performance online). His voice was breaking at the time and he says that was why he didn't progress beyond the qualifying round and make it on to TV, but he clearly had something, because following the audition he was contacted by no fewer than seven agencies who had seen his performance, including JYP, one of the Big Three.

What made him choose Big Hit? He saw RM in full rap mode and decided there and then. 'I thought RM was so cool, so I wanted to sign with them,' he told the *New Yang Nam Show* in 2017. Like the other trainees, he arrived alone in Seoul and took his place in the dorm. He was only thirteen years old, but he had to change schools, find his way around a new city, meet new friends and begin training to be an idol with much older trainees.

Jung Kook has admitted that the loud, sometimes boisterous schoolboy from Busan immediately became a quiet and shy trainee in Seoul. Members have recalled how he would wait until everyone was asleep before he took a shower and that he would avoid singing in front of them and cry if they pressed him. When Bang Si-hyuk told him there was no emotion in his dancing, it must have taken all of Jung Kook's strength not to pack up and go home.

Instead, the young teenager who had never been on a plane before went to America. Big Hit had booked him into an intense street-dance course at the famous dance academy Movement Lifestyle in LA. He found it tough, but learned a lot in just a month and still managed to buy a skateboard and master another new skill. By the end of 2012, Jung Kook had been revealed as the sixth and apparently final (not including the hidden V) member of BTS. The stage name Seagull, which is the official bird of the city of Busan and the nickname of its baseball team, was suggested, but Jungkook chose to stick with his own name (it has become clear over the years that, as a stage name, he prefers it to be stylized as Jung Kook rather than Jungkook).

Jung Kook's shyness was still an issue. Bang Si-hyuk admitted it was a gamble allowing him to debut, as many at Big Hit believed he wasn't ready, but the BTS team spirit kicked in. It must be remembered that he was still only fifteen. He has often spoken about how Jin looked after him, cooking for him and driving him to school, and Suga gave him fatherly advice such as his appalled reaction in *American Hustle Life* when Jung Kook looks forward to being able to get a tattoo (although JK doesn't have seemed to have taken that counsel to heart!). And their faith wasn't misplaced. As he grew in confidence, Jung Kook began to deliver. From 'Graduation Song', posted in February 2013 shortly after he had graduated from middle school, fans became aware of the *maknae*'s sweet voice, and after the debut they realized he was a sharp dancer as well. He still wasn't a live wire in interviews, but that could be overlooked for now.

As Jung Kook progressed through high school, he became a central figure in the group. He would now feature prominently in choreographies and his smooth, sometimes husky, vocals could be heard more and more in BTS tracks. Eventually, on *Wings*, Jung Kook would get his own song, 'Begin', written by RM, but with his personal input. He said he felt embarrassed to explain the lyrics to the other members as it tells of how he cried for them when their workload had become too much, but they are heartfelt sentiments and he sings it beautifully. Then, a month before *Love Yourself: Tear* was released, Jung Kook took the vocals for 'Euphoria: Theme of Love Yourself: Wonder', a track many ARMY were disappointed not to find on the album.

Over the intervening years, Jung Kook would post a collection of impressive cover songs – many of them in English. A self-proclaimed Belieber, he has recorded, to many fans' delight, Justin Bieber's 'Boyfriend', 'Nothing Like Us', 'Purpose' and '2U', but also Tori Kelly's 'Paper Hearts', Adam Levine's 'Lost Stars', Charlie Puth's 'We Don't Talk Anymore' (to which Puth tweeted 'Love this Jungcook') and enough others for YouTubers to create an imaginary covers album. In February 2018, he tweeted a cover of Park Won's 'All of My Life', where he played piano and sang stripped-down vocals. Within days it had over a million likes.

As Jung Kook's engaging and playful personality emerged in BTS video and TV appearances, he was invited to guest on various variety shows. In 2016 he appeared in *King of Mask Singer*, a TV series which pitches K-pop singers against each other while disguising their real identities. Jung Kook featured as Fencing Man, wearing a spectacular silver mask. Although he didn't win, his cover of Big Bang's 'If You' is a song ARMY still treasure.

BANGTAN BOMB

JUST WATCHING JUNGKOOK LIP SYNC SHOW

If you think Jung Kook is all about soulful sweet harmonies, just watch him rock out with V to Linkin Park's 'Given Up'. To an amused audience of Jimin and J-Hope, he gets the air guitar out and lip-syncs (including expletives) as if he was a fluent English speaking, nu-metal guitar hero. Even as a rock dude, he still looks pretty cute!

RM

JIN

SUGA

JUNG KOOK

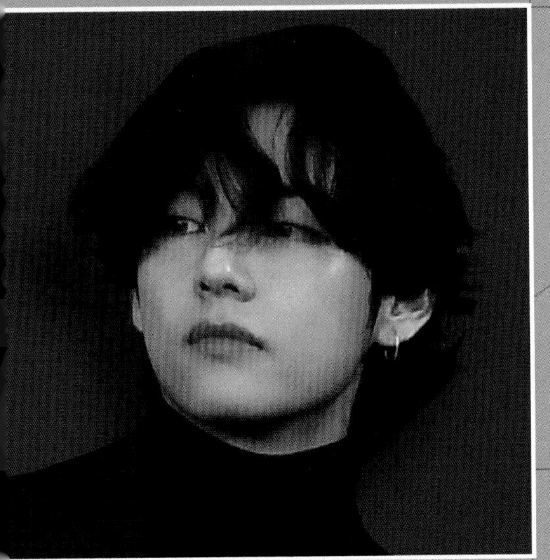

V

JIMIN

J-HOPE

TOP / RM addressing the United Nations and launching UNICEF's 'Generation Unlimited' youth campaign, New York, USA, September 2018.

BOTTOM / A suited BTS step onto the Grammy red carpet for the first time, Los Angeles, February 2019.

TOP / BTS back at the Grammys: astonishingly, they were overlooked for an award again, but they helped Lil Nas X to bring the 'Seoul Town Road' to the stage, Los Angeles, January 2020

BOTTOM / Looking smooth as they perform 'Butter' at the AMAs in November 2021. BTS took home the awards for Favorite Pop Duo or Group, Favorite Pop Song and Artist of the Year

TOP / Thankfully Jung Kook and J-Hope recovered from Covid-19 in time to join the rest of BTS in their iconic Louis Vuitton suits on the Grammys red carpet in April 2022.

BOTTOM / BTS's spy-themed performance of 'Butter' was the highlight of the show at the 2022 Grammys.

He would also feature in a series called *Celebrity Bromance*. Jung Kook was paired with Minwoo, a thirty-six-year-old first-generation K-pop star from the group Shinhwa. The older star's caring nature did much to help bring Jung Kook out of his shell and the scenes where they meet amid puppies in the dog café or when Jung Kook goes rock climbing to earn dinner are worth watching. Less successful was his appearance on *Flower Crew*, a travel-reality series. There was some controversy as some of the other participants were seen as being rude to Jung Kook and the voting process on which the show relied was skewed due to Jung Kook's popularity. He was even seen to mouth, 'Don't vote for me,' in embarrassment.

Meanwhile, his dorm mates had discovered their *maknae* had many other skills. The competitive youngster would invariably win the games they played, his drawing skills were more than impressive (it's genetic – check out his brother Jung-hun's drawings of BTS) and his sporting prowess, particularly in athletics, wrestling and archery, would inspire BTS triumphs in successive Idol Star Athletics Championships. He was living up to the Golden Maknae name his leader had given him.

That isn't the only nickname Jung Kook has picked up. As well as being affectionately called JK by fellow members and ARMY, you'll also catch him being called Nochu. This harks back to the *American Hustle Life* series when mentor Nate gave him a rap to copy, including the line 'Nochu ["Not you"], come thru'. Jung Kook copied it so well, Nate gave him the name and it stuck.

Other names he has been called include Muscle Pig (and more recently Jeon Cena after the US wrestler John Cena, now himself a BTS fan), a flattering epithet based on his strength and his biceps; Bunny, after his beguiling smile that shows off his front teeth; and International Playboy, which he introduced himself as in an early documentary *Go! BTS*, ironically because at the time he seemed unable to even look a girl in the eye! Finally, some fans talk of Jungshook, a reference to the bemused and bewildered face that he pulls in times of real confusion, such as when he was watching RM prepare for his UN speech. Such terms of endearment show how much members care for their youngest, but that doesn't stop them having fun at his expense. Jung Kook's sixteenth birthday arrived on 1 September 2013.

In a video on YouTube called 'BTS Surprise Birthday Party for Jung Kook!' we see the boys at a shoot for their trailer. During a break, Jung Kook reads his fan mail and tries to enjoy 'Kookie Day', but the dance manager starts to criticize his dancing, and the others, hiding their laughter, join in. Poor JK is confused and a little upset, but they keep the pretence going right up until a beaming Suga emerges with a cake, candles and a song.

Not that he always reciprocates with the respect expected by his *hyungs*. Jung Kook often pretends to be an evil *maknae*, teasing all the members with some excellent mimicry. Since debut, Jung Kook has grown taller than Jimin and doesn't he let him know it! 'Calling me short and stroking my head – I'm two years older than you!' poor Jimin has been heard to complain! It seems Jimin can forgive Jung Kook most things, though. He has said he reminds him of his younger brother and even when they're having fun there is a sense Jimin is looking out for Jung Kook.

Although he's also two years older, V is very much capable of acting like a kid, too, and Jung Kook has remarked how similar his and V's personalities are, saying, 'He's random. Our comedic chords match well.' Jung Kook and V also share a love of video games. In fact, Jung Kook is the real games addict of the group (look for the scar on his left cheek, a souvenir of a fight with his brother over a game controller). At the end of 2016, when the group moved to a four-bedroom dorm, Jung Kook won rock, paper, scissors to become the only member with his own room. He named it the golden closet and the other members always headed there when they were looking for a game. He particularly excels at *Overwatch* and is good enough to have impressed professional players with his skills and reaction speed.

When they upscaled again, he kept the name for his private recording studio. This is where he works on his covers, practises his piano playing, and it's also the home of Golden Closet Films (or G.C.F as it appears on YouTube), Jung Kook's film studio. Releases so far, directed and edited by Jung Kook, include short films of Jimin on a trip to Tokyo and of all the members having fun in Osaka, a behind the scenes of their journey to the American Music Awards, and a video shot in Helsinki while they pose for a photoshoot.

As Jung Kook was no longer the cute little brother, ARMY moved on from nicknames to titles. He was the 'King of Twitter' as the first person ever to have seven tweets that garnered 2 million likes. A 2021 selfie featuring his newly-dyed blond hair, a 2020 clip of him singing Lauv's 'Never Not' and a selfie captioned 'ARMY I miss you' are among his five entries in the top 20 tweets with most likes. They have also crowned him the 'King of Sold Out' after anything ARMY saw him touch sold out immediately. Demand immediately intensifies for identifiable T-shirts and clothes, amazingly even the modern *hanbok* he wore to the airport in 2019. And it is not just clothes; kombucha, sunglasses and fabric softener have felt the Jung Kook effect too.

At first, Jung Kook's solo ventures with BTS were limited to 'Begin' from the *Wings* album and 'Euphoria' which eventually appeared on *Love Yourself: Answer*. Fans delighted in the numerous covers he uploaded to SoundCloud, including Tori Kelly's 'Paper Hearts', Roy Kim's 'Only Then', Justin Bieber's 'Nothing Like Us' and David Guetta's '2U'. As part of *Love Yourself: Tear* he worked hard on writing and producing 'Magic Shop', a passionate fan song which he dedicated to ARMY. Then came Jung Kook's 'My Time' for *Map of the Soul: 7*, an acclaimed solo which went to number one on iTunes charts in the US, the Philippines, Saudi Arabia, Cambodia and Jordan.

'My Time', which Jung Kook wrote himself, revealed the difficulties of growing up in the BTS spotlight and a subsequent release further demonstrated his ability to write sincere songs using personal experience. The jazz-tinged ballad 'Still With You' was uploaded to SoundCloud during the 2020 *festa* (with an a capella version later appearing on *Proof*). He described wanting to write a Covid-lockdown song to show his feelings to ARMY. The idea had initially arisen while 'alone in my dark room', and he then worked on the lyrics and melody in his studio.

Jung Kook was doing pretty well in living up to the 'Golden Maknae' tag, revealing new talents with every comeback. On BTS's *BE* he was officially credited as the production co-ordinator and as a composer and songwriter for 'Stay' and 'Telepathy'. He was also named as the video director for the 'Life Goes On' MV, three years after his first G.C.F. production. The role found him behind the camera for the members' individual scenes and giving acting instructions for the group scenes in their pyjamas. He admitted he felt the pressure of the job, but worked alongside Lumpens, directors of over twenty-five BTS videos, and earned widespread praise for his efforts.

Those who follow JK closely are aware that he has always been keen on learning another talent: drumming. He had mentioned it occasionally, only to modestly dismiss his skills, promising to play in front of fans when he felt confident enough. When he finally did, it came as a complete surprise. Ahead of the 2021 Grammys, BTS took part in a fundraiser concert at the Academy. Midway through their 'Dynamite' performance, JK went and sat behind the drum set and played along while continuing to sing. ARMY reacted with awe: to both his blue hair and his percussion skills!

JK stans are always alert to his changing looks. They knew he had several ear piercings and a pierced lip – and he admitted to a (since-removed) eyebrow piercing too. And there was no doubting his growing collection of tattoos, either. Inking had always been a taboo in K-pop (hence Suga's earlier fatherly advice), but Jung Kook was willing to take on South Korea's conservative tastes. He displayed his first, the letters A-R-M-Y across the knuckles of his right hand, in September 2019, but the subsequent years saw him cover his arms with a variety of words and artworks. They include '0613', the BTS debut date; his birth flower, the tiger lily; two crisscrossing maxims that read 'Rather be dead than cool' and 'Make hay while the sun shines'; a snake and a design inspired by traditional Korean paintwork, *dancheong*. Many of his tattoos were done by one of Korea's most renowned tattoo artists, POLYC SJ, who in recent years has refreshed and covered up some of JK's earlier body art.

POLYC SJ was also responsible for designing and inking the group's '7' friendship tattoos (JK has his behind his left ear). They had talked over the idea at the monumental 2022 *festa* dinner in which their forthcoming break was announced. At the dinner, Jung Kook spoke from the heart about the decision. He said how everyone has a timeline that is right for them, that he felt the break should have come earlier and how they will return as even better people. His contribution was incredibly eloquently delivered and the group reacted immediately to how well he came across.

Suga remarked how grown-up their *maknae* was, while RM noted how well JK had 'summed up everything that I rattled on about for thirty minutes'.

Festa 2022 also saw JK continue to extend his solo repertoire, uploading a new song as a gift to ARMY. The self-composed 'My You' was a soft, acoustic-guitar-backed ballad containing both English and Korean lyrics that tugged at the heart strings. Admitting it was a sad song expressing how empty his life would be without his fans, JK sweetly explained he had tried to soften this by using beautiful words.

Earlier in the year, Jung Kook had released the single 'Stay Alive', an OS for the BTS webtoon *7Fates: Chakho*. The song was co-written and produced by Suga, who was so impressed with JK's first take on the moving ballad that he went straight ahead and used that version. With only the webtoon-based video to promote it, the song ranked number one on the Worldwide iTunes chart and took JK into the Billboard Hot 100 chart.

JUNG KOOK'S SPIDER OBSERVATION LOG

Who knew? Jung Kook is an expert on spiders. Here's the *maknae* showing off his knowledge of arachnology (and his man bun) when he discovers a tiny spider hanging from a web on the set of 'Black Swan'. We are treated to an explanation of how spiders fly, the dream in which he was chased by a giant spider and even a snippet of the *Spider-Man* theme. ARMY then had a great time picturing him as the superhero and expounding on why you never see JK and Spider-Man in the same room.

Now Jung Kook was a bona fide solo artist and, just after the 2022 *festa*, he enhanced his credentials with a collaboration. Back in 2016, and again the following year (with Jimin), JK had covered 'We Don't Talk Anymore', a song by one of his favourite singers, Charlie Puth. After the US singer famously replied with the endearingly misspelled 'love this Jungcook', the two stars kept in touch online. Now Jung Kook featured on his single 'Left and Right', a catchy and lively pop song about obsessing over a past relationship. The duo expertly harmonized in the song's chorus, with JK's smooth vocals complimenting Puth's higher register, and similarly exuded a great chemistry together in the humorous video.

JK's next solo endeavour displayed his talents to the world beyond the millions of BTS fans around the globe: in November 2022, he performed in the opening ceremony of the football World Cup in Qatar, watched by 60,000 people in the stadium and another 5 billion viewers worldwide. As a plethora of white-suited dancers filled the giant stage around him, Jung Kook stood out in his stylish all-black outfit to coolly and confidently deliver a new song, 'Dreamers'. It was a superb performance, especially as he had only had a day to learn much of the choreography. He later revealed that he had originally assumed he was performing with rest of BTS and had broken into a cold sweat when he discovered it was a solo endeavour.

'Dreamers' was the official 2022 World Cup song. An uplifting, inspirational anthem with a euphoric chorus, it was given a Middle Eastern vibe with Khaliji percussion, an Arabic refrain and additional vocals from the famous Qatari singer Fahad Al Kubaisi. The single was released on the day of the opening ceremony and was an immediate hit, reaching the top of iTunes charts in over 100 regions.

The opening ceremony performance was hailed as a great success, especially back home in South Korea. His growing international profile was a source of pride and he was credited as being a national treasure. Jung Kook was not one to bask in the adoration, though. In fact, his public appearances were few and far between. In February 2023, he also decided to delete his Instagram account, despite having over 50 million followers. 'I wasn't hacked,' he said casually on Weverse, 'I just never used it so I deleted it. Don't worry!'

If fans were concerned about seeing new photos of JK, they needn't have worried. The very next month saw Jung Kook announced as Calvin Klein's latest global ambassador. The subsequent Spring 2023 collection, which featured shots of JK wearing jeans with a selection of open denim jackets revealing a bare chest and sculpted abs, just about broke the internet.

For his photo folio project, Jung Kook said he felt shy and awkward and out of his comfort zone, but was determine to produce something ARMY would appreciate. *Me, Myself, & Jung Kook: Time Difference* did that and more. It featured Jung Kook as a vampire in a look he created himself. He threw himself into the fantasy concept, wearing satin and leather, frills and lace and even sporting a blood-stained mouth (with a lip-ring). It was mysterious and sensual and immediately the photos went viral. Job done, JK!

Weverse soon became his main channel of conversation with fans, including some marathon late-night livestreams. He joked and sang, played music recommended by ARMY, showed off his whisky collection, changed outfits, cooked and ate food and danced around his sofa, but most of all was just his charming self. One recurring question in the live chat was: when could fans expect to see his solo album released? Typically, he was laid back and honest in his response, replying that he hadn't really progressed at all. Indeed, he said he hadn't been doing much recently and that was what he liked best at the moment: not doing anything!

Many ARMY have grown up with JK. They have seen the slight, shy, cute-as-anything adolescent become a charismatic and muscle-packing, confident young man. It does often seem like he can turn his hand to anything: photography, ten-pin bowling, video directing, martial arts, gaming, songwriting, rapping (he has stood in for RM and Suga on stage), dancing, singing and, of course, looking like an Adonis. All credit to Big Hit for recognizing the potential in him, the Tannies for raising a little brother they can be proud of and, of course, to the Golden Maknae himself.

SEVENTEEN

DAESANG

In July 2016 BTS were still in Japan when the teaser pics went out for their second Japanese album. Released in September, *Youth* contained nine Japanese versions of their tracks, the single 'For You' and three new tracks. 'Introduction: Youth' is a rap intro and 'Good Day' a sweet vocal-line pop song, while 'Wishing on a Star' turned out to be a top favourite with ARMY around the world. A dreamy, mid-tempo song full of romantic echoes, the vocals are perfectly layered as it spells out the 'follow your dream whatever' message. *Youth* went straight to number one in the weekly and monthly Japanese charts, which was another first for BTS.

At the same time, something else was happening. Over nine days in early September, Big Hit uploaded a series of seven short (two- to three-minute) films to YouTube. Each film focused on a particular member, with Jung Kook's film titled *Begin*, Jimin's *Lie*, V's *Stigma*, Suga's *First Love*, RM's *Reflection*, J-Hope's *Mama* and Jin's *Awake*.

They are each introduced by a brief narration in English voiced by RM and feature a backing track with excerpts from a new song. The films are heavily stylized and repeat key images from previous BTS videos, including fire, petals, baths and Polaroid photographs – it's like they planned it all along! Dark and heavy with symbolism, they convey feelings of alienation, self-doubt, angst and despair. Each of the members has a serious acting role and they rise to the occasion, filling their scenes with emotion and depth. The mood is easy to comprehend, but the exact meaning of each of the stories is open to interpretation and has, as a result, filled many pages of ARMY blogs and fan sites.

In interviews, RM explained that the key to understanding the films and much of the new comeback album could be found in the German writer Hermann Hesse's coming-of-age novel *Demian*, first published in 1919. Bang Si-hyuk had given them the story of a boy on the cusp of manhood, who is presented with a choice between light and darkness, safety and danger, good and evil, and must discover his own path. In the novel, the main character questions accepted values and rebels against a system that is frustrating and repressive. For BTS, it was a pretty inspired choice. At the end of September 2016, Big Hit announced the date of the new album, *Wings*, and dropped a comeback trailer. Remember how the 'Save Me' video had signed off with the words 'BOY MEETS'? The trailer seemed to provide an answer as it was titled 'Boy Meets Evil'. Beginning with a quote from Hesse about shaking hands with the devil, it consists of J-Hope dancing to his own passionate rap.

J-Hope was the last of the rap line to get his own trailer/album opener, but his vocals are spot on – no swag, but rising and falling with intensity as he tells of temptation and of giving way to a love that is wrong but is too sweet to resist. Even more impressive is his dancing. Dressed in a long white shirt with ripped black jeans and new copper-coloured hair, J-Hope rips through a Dylan Mayoral-choreographed modern dance performance that is stunning in its expression and execution.

The concept photos soon followed. Matching all we had seen and heard in the past few weeks, the band moved away from their youthful, boyish image and instead embraced a more mature, sophisticated and elegant look. They wore crisp dress shirts and embroidered or floral jackets with plenty of velvet and satin. There were modern and vintage touches such as chokers and ruffled necklines, single feathers, cuffed jeans and flower appliqués. Although their hair was still multicoloured, it was more muted and chic, too.

The music video for the comeback was for a new track, 'Blood Sweat & Tears', released on 10 October. It was an ambitious work combining drama and dance as well as incorporating the symbolism and ideas of the short films. Continuing the theme of the concept photos, we are taken into an opulent world of high art as the guys enter a museum filled with classical statues and paintings. They are dressed in Saint Laurent and Dolce & Gabbana finery, and they look foppish, bohemian and absolutely stunning.

The dramatic section of the video gradually builds a feeling of innocence being left behind, of a yielding to temptation and of a falling. The group play out this narrative in various scenes leading up to Jin kissing the statue. All around are artworks reinforcing this story, including Herbert James Draper's painting of Icarus, Michelangelo's sculpture of the Virgin Mary holding the dead body of Jesus Christ, and *The Fall of the Rebel Angels* painting by Pieter Bruegel the Elder.

Yet this is a K-pop group. They are not 'supposed' to be delving into the world of art and philosophy any more than they were supposed to be questioning their education and career expectations in 'No More Dream'. Not content to write 'boy meets girl' lyrics, they are exploring ideas of what adulthood, and the choices it presents, means to them. It certainly provides food for thought for the viewer.

Except they also manage to distract many ARMY from such issues with their performance and choreography. This is by far the most deliberate attempt by the group to show a sexy and alluring side and, judging by the comments on YouTube, they completely smash it. The mood is created by heavy eyeliner, low necklines, chokers and soft lips while the dance retains the trademark razor-sharp moves but incorporates sensual glances, self-caresses and body movements. Add moments such as Jung Kook licking his finger or Jimin's naked-shoulder-revealing jacket flip and the video no doubt left millions around the world too stunned to intellectually engage.

While the video racked up more than 6 million views in under twenty-four hours, BTS were at the same time launching *Wings*, their second full-length album. Just as the record is about youth growing and flying, so it is about the group's individual members spreading their own wings. On this album every member gets their own solo track, which, with the exception of Jung Kook, is a song they wrote themselves. This is an extraordinary achievement, not only for the members themselves, but also for Big Hit, as groups controlled by the big three companies are rarely given such trust and freedom.

The fifteen tracks on *Wings* embrace a host of synth styles, including up-to-the-minute sounds of tropical house, moombahton and even neo-soul. It begins with the J-Hope rap 'Boy Meets Evil' used for the trailer, and 'Blood Sweat & Tears', which puts the spotlight on Jimin as he opens the track with a beautifully breathless, high-pitched vocal. To a luxuriously layered backing track of chimes, sirens and claps, the vocal line excels harmonically with the most infectious of hooks. Within the lyrics of this apparent love song, there is also something darker that alludes to the theme of the album. As RM explained in their concept launch, 'The harder a temptation is to resist, the more you think about it and vacillate. That uncertainty is part of the process of growing. ['Blood Sweat & Tears'] is a song that shows how one thinks, chooses and grows.'

BANGTAN BOMB

'BLOOD SWEAT & TEARS' MV REACTION BY BTS

If the symbol-searching and intellectual workout of the *Wings* short films and the 'Blood Sweat & Tears' music video leave you exhausted, then search out this Bangtan Bomb on YouTube. It shows the boys getting their first view of the music video. You won't find much to help you with the meaning, but there is plenty to smile about as they coo, cheer and whoop at each other's dance moves, acting and general sexiness.

The next section of *Wings* is taken up by the seven solo efforts of the group. These have the same titles as their short films. Jung Kook goes first with 'Begin', a slow R&B track that eases into a Bieberesque style as he recalls his arrival in Seoul at fifteen years old (in Korean age) and how his relationship with his 'brothers' in the group grew so strong. Next, Jimin takes the mic for his track, 'Lie', switching from sultry to emotional in a tour-de-force vocal accompanied by haunting orchestral strings, screeches, jarred instruments and eerie backing vocals. In contrast, to a classic instrumental beat, V's 'Stigma' plays out bass-heavy vocals, whispers and even near-screams in a sometimes spine-tingling, guilt-laden song of hurt.

'First Love' is classic Suga. An original and honest rap, he uses the tone of his spoken voice, rising from calm to impassioned to frame a hymn to his childhood piano. He later admitted crying while recording it. The rap line's contributions continue with RM's 'Reflection', a calm state-of-mind take on life's contradictions. Written while sitting in the very Ttukseom Park he raps about, it begins with his own phone recording of the sound of the passing subway.

J-Hope revealed that at a group meeting he announced that he intended to write a song about his mother and that it would be bright and 'Hope'-ful. True to his word, a jaunty, jazzy track backs his poem about mother and son love. The lyrics are beautiful in both their simplicity and detail, right down to the naming of the restaurants in which she worked, and the lovely gesture of including her voice saying 'Hello'.

Jin claims Suga originally thought a ballad-type song wouldn't fit the album, but the last soloist's track proved to be a favourite of all the group. A conventional slow number with an orchestral and piano backing, 'Awake' gorgeously showcases Jin's control and vocal range as he sings a song of heart-rending self-doubt and heart-warming self-motivation.

The group songs take over again with 'Lost', an upbeat track that throws the vocal line's voices against each other in deft contrast as they sing a message of hope. A partly RM-written coming-of-age track, it speaks of the difficulty of choosing your path in life and of believing in yourself to find the right way. This is followed by the traditional rappers' track, 'Cypher Pt. 4', which contains the usual statements addressed to their haters, but this time sounds confident and assertive (the 'I love myself' repetition especially), with none of the defensiveness and staged hip-hop arrogance that had flavoured some previous cyphers. The next track is 'Am I Wrong'. The first surprise is that it begins with a sample of a song by Grammy Award-winning blues singer Keb' Mo' from 1994. The second is that BTS make it their own, retaining the blues feel, but transforming it into a high-energy dance pop track with the hookiest of choruses. Talk about pushing the boundaries! The third of the tracks performed at promotions, '21st Century Girl' follows on nicely. Its driving beat, fun and relatively simple choreography and call-and-response lyrics make it an automatic crowd-pleaser. What's more, the lyrics show how BTS had progressed. The somewhat narrow male view of 'War of Hormone' has been replaced by a celebration of women for what and who they are. It's a heartening 'girl power' anthem that says 'love yourself' and, hey, it has the funkiest vibe, too.

And they keep coming: '2! 3! (Still Wishing for More Good Days)' was specifically written for ARMY. This first official fan anthem has a charming rap and vocal mix, a comforting message that we'll get through the hard times together, and a chant tailor-made for singalongs at concerts. The album concludes with 'Interlude: Wings', a poppy Jung Kook-led dance track that encapsulates the wings metaphor of embracing adulthood, facing the challenges and obstacles, but following the path you choose.

The album was released in four versions: *W*, *I*, *N* and *G*. They share the same black cover with a smoke pattern and the *Wings* logo of four differently shaded circles. The versions differ in the photo and lyric books included, as they follow the theme of the 'Blood Sweat & Tears' video and the short films by pairing up the members and leaving Jin as a lone figure. The photobook of *W* features glorious colour shots of Jin as well as group photos; *I* also has group pictures but features J-Hope and V; *N* focuses on Jimin and Suga; leaving *G* to RM and Jung Kook. They do, however, each come with a completely random Polaroid.

Their first comeback stage came on 13 October (Jimin's birthday) on Mnet's *M Countdown*, where they performed '21st Century Girl' in casual wear, followed by 'Am I Wrong' in different-coloured suit jackets, before appearing on a 'museum' set dressed in their sophisticated get-up for 'Blood

Sweat & Tears'. From the online reaction to the performances and songs, it was no surprise when the following weeks saw them pick up trophies on *Show Champion*, *M Countdown*, *Music Bank* (two weeks running), *Inkigayo* and *The Show Choice.*

BANGTAN BOMB

BTS 21ST CENTURY GIRL DANCE PRACTICE (HALLOWEEN VER.)

This is possibly the most error-strewn BTS dance practice ever, but go easy on them. It's Halloween and these boys love to dress up. It can't be easy doing the moves when you're costumed as a giant rabbit, a huge vegetable or a pantomime horse ... or a skeleton, Syaoran from *Cardcaptor Sakura*, Ryan the cartoon lion, or wearing full *hanbok* (traditional Korean clothing).

Wings was clearly BTS's most ambitious work yet: a collection of fifteen songs spanning music genres, composers, lyrical ideas and performers. They had been nervous about how it would be received, Jin revealing that he had had difficulty sleeping before the comeback, but from the day of release it was obvious it was going to be massively popular. Tracks from the album soon dominated the domestic charts, the album itself became the year's highest-selling title on the Gaon charts and within four days of release, 'Blood Sweat & Tears' had achieved the cherished 'all-kill', topping all eight Korean music charts. It was truly astounding. Around the world, BTS were making headlines, too. The single ranked number one on the iTunes charts in twenty-three countries, including Canada, Brazil, New Zealand, Singapore and Norway, as well as on the Chinese equivalent. It went straight to the top of the Billboard World Digital Song Sales chart. The album was hot internationally as well: BTS became the first Korean act to break into the UK album charts at number sixty-two, while in addition to the above-mentioned countries, Finland, Sweden, Ireland and the Netherlands all saw *Wings* making an impact on the charts.

North America had seen K-pop acts perform well before, but nothing compared to this. Canada had fallen for BTS big time. The album broke into the top twenty, while 'Blood Sweat & Tears' set a K-pop record at number eighty-six. Meanwhile, in the USA they were not only storming the album charts like no other Korean group ever before (reaching twenty-six on the Billboard 200 chart), but receiving critical acclaim, too. *Rolling Stone* named *Wings* 'one of the most conceptually and sonically ambitious pop albums of 2016', while another high-profile magazine, *Fuse*, listed it as the eighth-best album of 2016, applauding its 'fascinating concepts and wholly accessible productions that don't sound out of place on top forty radio'. Wow!

Once again BTS were determined to debut the performances of the new tracks to their fans. As November brought their third fan meeting at the massive Gocheok Sky Dome baseball stadium in Seoul, it presented the perfect opportunity. ARMY snapped up the 38,000 tickets for the two days in minutes and they were not disappointed as the group held question-and-answer sessions, performed old hits (including 'kindergarten' versions by J-Hope, Jin and V), Jimin made his rap debut alongside Suga, the boys showed off their new choreographies and gave their individual thanks to the fans. And no one who was there will ever forget V's tribute to his recently deceased grandmother (accompanied by Jung Kook's tears) or ARMY's goosebump-raising singing of '2! 3!', their new anthem.

Back in the summer, the group had shared a visit to Bomunsa temple on Seokmodo Island in South Korea. There, in common with many tourists, the guys had carved a prayer on a tile. On it they asked for *Wings* to be a great success. It was beginning to look like their prayers had been answered.

With award season about to begin, you could forgive them for thinking their dream of the ultimate prize, the *daesang*, might be around the corner. Good news or bad, they didn't have to hold their breath for long in order to find out. On 19 November 2016 they were back in the Gocheok Sky Dome for the Melon Music Awards. With EXO picking up the Artist of the Year award, many, including BTS, expected them to scoop up the best album *daesang*, too. So when *The Most Beautiful Moment in Life: Young Forever* was announced as the winner, the shocked look on the boys' faces was priceless. RM stood up, but the rest of the group remained seated, looking at each other with open eyes and gaping mouths. V walked to the stage, asking in disbelief, 'It's us? Us?' and RM had to compose himself before making his thank-you speech to ARMY, Big Hit and the members' families. At this point Jin was sobbing and J-Hope was forced to wipe away his own tears. The group hug before they left the stage was brimming with joy, relief and togetherness. They had worked so hard in the last three years and it meant so much to them to finally be recognized like this. A couple of weeks later, on 2 December, they not only attended the MAMA ceremony in Hong Kong, but completely owned the stage with their performance. From Jung Kook suspended in mid-air to J-Hope's solo 'Boy Meets Evil' dance, to his and a blindfolded Jimin's extraordinary mirrored dance, and the spellbinding group choreography of 'Blood Sweat & Tears', they left the fans in no doubt as to who the artist of the year was. And MAMA were ready to confirm the truth with just that award – their second *daesang* in as many weeks. Their emotional response was just as strong as at the MMAs, with RM struggling to start his speech and this time Jung Kook and Suga finding it impossible to fight back the tears.

In his acceptance speech, RM explained that they had been through so much since they debuted and that, although many had doubted they could make it, ARMY had believed in them and helped them fulfil their dreams. He ended with a wish: that in 2017 they might fly ever higher on their beautiful wings.

EIGHTEEN

ARMY: TEAMWORK MAKES THE DREAM WORK

BTS fans are as instrumental to the group's massive success as any of the members. They not only purchase the albums, download the tracks and buy up concert tickets in record time, but they provide a constant stream of love, support and encouragement to the boys. That's why, in almost every interview they do and every speech they make, BTS declare their affection for and gratitude to ARMY. Take what RM said when the band won the coveted *daesang* at the 2018 Seoul Music Awards: 'The reason at the end is always all of you. Thank you for being the reason we can do this work. We'll try to be even a small bit of help for you in your life. Thank you, ARMY!' He couldn't have made it clearer: BTS appreciate ARMY.

On 9 July 2013, a month after their debut, BTS announced that their official fan club would be called ARMY. It fitted well with the name Bulletproof Boy Scouts and, as noted earlier, had its own meaning: Adorable Representative MC for Youth. Just like the group themselves,

BTS's fans would speak out for their generation. Although there is an official fan club, you don't need to be a member to call yourself ARMY, because simply loving, supporting and following the group is enough.

BTS certainly make it easy to follow them. The top social artist awards won by BTS at the Billboard Music Awards every year from 2017 to 2021 confirm that no other group and their fans have the same level of connection. They are in regular contact on Twitter from their shared handle @BTS_twt, which the boys themselves tweet from; @BTS_bighit is the official account run by Big Hit Entertainment. Non-Korean speakers can also follow them on any one of the impressive fan-translation Twitter accounts, where Korean-speaking fans translate tweets and much more into English and other languages. They frequently broadcast live messages, skits or even whole concerts on Weverse (and previously V Live), and the BANGTANTV channel on YouTube uploads numerous videos of performances, dance practices, backstage footage and the sometimes silly and often hilarious Bangtan Bombs. Their group Instagram account, @bts.bighitofficial, is full of photos of the group, their Facebook page 'Bangtan.official' carries similar posts and since December 2021 the members have each had personal Instagram accounts (except Jung Kook, who deleted his in early 2023).

Once the only official forum for BTS fans was their fan café, which was largely conducted in Korean, but things began to change in February 2019. First BTS launched *Armypedia*. In a campaign running for a month, fans helped to amass a digital archive of the 2,080 days together as a group and fandom. The project involved fans finding QR codes both online and in real world locations that enabled them to access specific days and leave personal memories in the archive. Along with contributions from the members themselves, 540,000 fans participated in the project creating a priceless bond between ARMY and the group.

Soon after *Armypedia* came the app Weverse. Like the fan café, Weverse allowed fans to talk to each other but this time it was international and contained a built-in translator. It also featured messages from the members and other content such as the *Bring the Soul: Docu-Series* and *Learn Korean with BTS*. In just six months they had amassed nearly 4 million

Weverse followers. The final piece of the jigsaw came in September 2019 when BTS joined TikTok. ARMY knew there was fun to be had and a record 1 million followers signed up in around three hours. They were not disappointed as the boys dived in with the Chicken Noodle Soup challenge and the ON challenge.

It is difficult to estimate just how many ARMY there are. Some guesses exceed 100 million and they could be right. There are 59 million fan club members, the 'Butter' MV had 112 million views in 24 hours, with 'Dynamite' reaching 101 million, and 2022's Yet to Come in Busan concert livestreaming amassed 49 million viewers online. The official BTS profiles have 48 million followers on Twitter, 73 million on Instagram and 60 million on TikTok. It's safe to say you are never alone with ARMY.

BTS are understandably celebrated in their home country of South Korea, but their fandom transcends national boundaries. They set a record for the artist with a number one iTunes song in the most countries when 'Black Swan' topped the charts in 103 nations (an achievement now surpassed by the members' solo singles), have hundreds of fan clubs all around the globe and have sold out concerts in all the major continents of the world – according to Twitter, there's even someone claiming to be an Antarctica ARMY!

The really great thing about ARMY is that they are not a passive force; they are constantly finding new ways to support BTS. Hashtags to celebrate members' birthdays, to congratulate them and to send them get-well notes are common, but ARMY are capable of getting random messages trending too, such as #ThankYouJungkook, which appeared in January 2018 and was followed by similar hashtags for other members. They can be ingenious too. When BTS appeared on the TV show *You Quiz on the Block* in 2021, ARMY bought all the ad slots so there would not have to be any commercial breaks during the entire broadcast.

Other support is practical. Among many examples is RM's collaboration with Wale, which came about after fans got in touch with the US rapper, or the successful lobbying of radio station DJs, such as BBC Radio One's Adele Roberts, in order to persuade them to play BTS tracks. When BTS got caught in the rising tensions between South Korea and Japan in November 2019, ARMY started #ProjectBuy23, urging fans to buy BTS's 2016 song '2! 3!' to show their support for the band. It was soon heading for the top ten of iTunes charts in many countries around the world. ARMY are clever, too: they urged fans not to buy J-Hope's mixtape *Hope World* on its release date, having worked out that delaying by a day would result in a higher ranking in the Billboard charts.

ARMY are legendary for finding ways to support BTS through voting. Whether it's for TV music shows or national and international awards, fans' online votes help determine the winner and ARMY help to get every possible BTS vote out through reminders, hashtags and encouragement. Until 2021, the BBMAs' Top Social Artist award was determined solely by public voting and ARMY really came into their own. In 2021 ARMY cast tens of millions of online votes to ensure they won the award for the fifth year running. They also coordinate streaming of BTS music videos, helping the group establish new records for views on YouTube for virtually every new release.

Just like their idols, ARMY also look to see how they can help in the wider world. Instances of local ARMY groups arranging charity donations are numerous. They can be traditional rice donations to bring good luck to BTS concerts, or responses to emergencies in places like Nepal where local ARMY organized collection points to raise money and gather emergency supplies for flood victims. Often these gestures are in honour of individual BTS members. ARMY celebrated Jung Kook's twenty-first birthday by 'adopting' an endangered pygmy rabbit, and fans initiated a massive tree-planting project to mark RM's birthday in 2019. ARMY were also fully engaged in the BTS-spearheaded UNICEF campaign #ENDviolence, helping raise 1.6 billion KRW, or just over $1.4 million, and when BTS were forced to cancel concerts due to the coronavirus pandemic, ARMY encouraged each other to donate ticket refunds to relief funds and charities fighting the virus.

In June 2020, after receiving the news that BTS and Big Hit had donated a million US dollars to the Black Lives Matter campaign, ARMY set up #MatchAMillion and 35,000 donors raised the same sum in just 24 hours.

Away from the official fan clubs ARMY are always well represented on Instagram, YouTube, Twitter, Facebook, TikTok and Tumblr. There you'll find reviews, comments and theories, especially on the meaning of the videos, but also in-depth analysis of songs, clothes, hair and just about every aspect of each BTS member. The discussions are often the result of detailed research or diligent translation and they make for fascinating reading. Naturally, ARMY themselves like to get creative and there are some excellent drawings of the group on these sites. There are also lots of fanfiction sites, but beware, because these are not always of the highest quality and the content can be unsuitable or even upsetting for younger ARMY.

An exception to this was *Outcast*, a fanfic which appeared on Twitter in January 2018. This story, told by @flirtaus across a series of 'text messages', began with a fictional exchange between J-Hope and Suga over a missing person and developed to include all the members. It took the form of a five-night survival game where fans voted every night for their favourite resolution to the cliffhanger, with over 300,000 following the story.

Such is the commitment of BTS members and ARMY, there is always something new happening online. It might be a dance challenge – 'Run BTS' and 'Permission to Dance' are among the best – or as exciting as a spontaneous live conversation with a member on Weverse or Twitter. What's fantastic about this vibrant online community is that all ARMY get to take part and feel a connection to BTS. After all, only the very fortunate have the chance to attend the fan meets, *festa* gatherings or hi-touch sessions.

Those who have been lucky enough to witness a live BTS show experienced something very special. BTS live shows are astounding, with a degree of audience participation unheard of in the US or Europe. BTS put their heart and soul into their shows. Performances regularly exceed two hours as they run specially made videos, perform a carefully selected set of old favourites and new songs, take in changes of stage costume and engage with their audience. And it's the audience members that take the experience to a new level with chants, light sticks and banners.

The most common fan chant is one that calls out the names of the members. It's usually chanted at the beginning of songs or sometimes in instrumental breaks. It's important to chant the names in the correct order – 'Kim Namjoon! Kim Seokjin! Min Yoongi! Jung Hoseok! Park Jimin! Kim Taehyung! Jeon Jungkook!' – and just as important to finish with a shout of 'BTS!' Other chants take the form of echoes of words or phrases in the songs or responses to set phrases. There are fan chants for most of the songs with the exception of solo numbers, but the name of the member singing is often chanted during breaks. If you're lucky enough to have a ticket to a BTS concert, it's definitely worth checking out the chants on YouTube (the Mnet K-pop channel is a good place to start) beforehand and practising, although if you don't get a chance, the 'BTS!' chant is one that anyone can join in with. Anyone new to K-pop might be intrigued to see the thousands of dots of light emanating from the audience and even more amazed when they change colour simultaneously. The light stick is a K-pop must-have accessory. Each group has their own colour and BTS lay claim to silver-grey. The official BTS light stick is called an ARMY Bomb and has a spherical globe at the end of a short handle. The light can be set to remain on, to flash or to dim, and when at a concert a Bluetooth connection synchronizes the colour of the light with the stage lights. The effect is breathtaking.

One colour you will definitley see is purple. Ever since V's now-iconic speech in 2016 where he coined the word 'borahae', literally meaning 'I purple you', and more poetically meaning 'to love each other for a long time' (because purple is the last colour of the rainbow), ARMY have adopted the colour as representing BTS and ARMY's love for each other. BTS used the colour to represent their absent fans during their pandemic performances, and ARMY turned the cities of LA and Busan purple in honour of the group's performances in 2022.

ARMY across the globe come up with their own special ways of connecting with the group. They distribute banners, spell out messages with light sticks or even change lyrics to express their love for the group. These projects are often organized through local Twitter groups or on the day by dedicated ARMY, who hand out slogan cards or printed instructions on how to join in. One of the most iconic examples came on the second day of BTS's Wembley Stadium concerts in 2019. As the group prepared to perform their final song, ARMY surprised them with a seemingly spontaneous (but actually pre-planned) mass rendition of 'Young Forever', which reduced the members to tears.

BANGTAN BOMB

BTS '고민보다 GO' STAGE WITH ARMY ˜PERFECT VOICE˜

If you need proof of the special relationship ARMY have with BTS, just watch this bomb. As the boys record their comeback stage singing 'Go Go', ARMY are in full attendance. Wielding lightsticks and accompanying the song with well-drilled chants, they are a vital part of the show – and don't BTS just know it. Their words of gratitude from the stage show just how much they appreciate ARMY's dedication.

All these activities help strengthen the bond between ARMY and BTS at a live show, but there are certain songs that which unite the group and the fans. When '2! 3!', 'Spring Day', 'Mikrokosmos' or 'Epilogue: Young Forever' are played live it's the cue for ARMY to join in – and they often continue even after the music has finished! BTS and ARMY are inseparable; they inspire and support each other.

BTS have never forgotten their loyal and devoted fanbase. As they have become more successful, more and more songs have been dedicated to the fans or written with them in mind. The music video for 'Make it Right (feat. Lauv)' is a graphic example of the relationship between the group and ARMY, but other tracks such as 'Magic Shop', 'Home' and 'Mikrokosmos' are all inspired by the group's love for their fans. As ever, it is left to RM to beautifully encapsulate what it means. 'Wherever you are, wherever we are … BTS and ARMY is the same word, right?' he said in an interview with iHeart Radio in January 2020. 'It just sounds different, but I see the same word when we say BTS and ARMY.'

NINETEEN

WINGS OVER AMERICA

In their 2016 Christmas message on V Live, BTS harked back to 'A Typical Trainee's Christmas', the hardship song they had recorded four years previously. For a second it suddenly seemed to dawn on them how far they had come. And when they recalled the letters they had posted from Santa Claus Village in Finland, those who could remember what they wrote (the letters hadn't arrived yet!), revealed they had wished for a *daesang*. Now here they were six months later with two!

On 19 January 2017, despite taking home the most awards of the night at the Seoul Music Awards, including a *bonsang* (best album) for *Wings*, best music video for 'Blood Sweat & Tears' and best male dance performance, they missed out to EXO on the Awards' big one, the *daesang*. It had been a similar story at the Golden Disc Awards a few days earlier, but no matter. Nothing stays still in Bangtanland.

BTS were headline news now, with all the scoops that went along with the fame. In January, it was reported that BTS and Big Hit Entertainment had secretly donated a substantial sum to charities connected to the families of the 2014 Sewol Ferry Disaster. The ferry had sunk, killing over 300 people, most of them high-school students on their way to a field trip on Jeju island, a favourite destination for BTS. Each member had donated

₩10 million (around $8,500) and Big Hit had added some ₩30 million, bringing it to a total of ₩100 million ($85,000). Why the secret? It was simply that they hadn't donated in order to get publicity; it was just something they wanted to do.

Now it was time for a mini-comeback. The concept photos were a shift in mood from *Wings*. Altogether more relaxed, as multicoloured confetti fell, the group posed in front of a paint-splattered old building or were pictured in a bus shelter, silhouetted against blue sea and sky. They were happy, in colourful casual wear, and some of the group had been at the hair dye again, with Suga sporting blue streaks, RM a purple wash and Jimin fluffy candy-floss pink.

On 13 February they dropped a *Wings* repackage album called *You Never Walk Alone*, with four brand new tracks. In a sixty-minute preview show on V Live – much of it taken up by a hilarious game of Twister – they explained that the casual and younger look (J-Hope now had yellow-blond hair) was to reflect the new stories they were telling in this special continuation of *Wings*. The new tracks were all written by members of the group which, they said, were messages of consolation and hope. Just over an hour later, the music video for one of those tracks, 'Spring Day', was released. Once again they were pushing boundaries with the music as an indie rock style permeated the regular beats and EDM sound, while the vocal line filled the melody with incredible emotion.

The video, a beautifully filmed piece full of dreamy pastel colours and contrasting bright and muted light, includes a train journey, a mountain of clothes, Jimin carrying someone's sneakers and a hotel called Omelas, a reference to a short story by Ursula K. Le Guin, in which the happiness of the inhabitants of a city with that name depends on the perpetual misery of a single child. Naturally ARMY came up with lots of fascinating theories about what it all meant. When asked whether the song hinted at the Sewol Ferry tragedy, RM, who had written the lyrics with Suga, admitted he had read that suggestion, but said, 'Every viewer can have a different interpretation of the music or the music video, because it depends on their mind, so we wish to leave this open.'

'Spring Day' was an immediate 'all-kill', the number of downloads actually crashing the Melon site. It swept to number one in thirteen different countries' iTunes charts and hit number eight in the US iTunes chart, making BTS the first-ever K-pop band to break into the top ten. The appeal of 'Spring Day' now seems eternal. *Billboard* named it in the best K-pop song of the decade, it is the most-streamed song in Melon's chart history, and has been on Gaon's end of year chart for five consecutive years.

As the world was still digesting this latest offering, BTS put out another explosive track. In direct contrast to the previous week's hit, 'Not Today' was a riotous demonstration of power and energy. The music video focused on the choreography, although Big Hit also posted an eight-minute dance video, in which, supported by a fifty-strong, black-hoodie-clad dance army, BTS switch from elegant moves to lightning-fast jerks and jumps with military precision in another Keone Madrid masterpiece. A compelling and stirring uptempo dance fest, it cries out that we might lose in the future but not today; today we fight back.

You Never Walk Alone was released in two versions containing different sets of photos. The pink 'right' version has a photo of the paint-stained old building, while the green 'left' version has a picture of the empty bus shelter. Of course, the books were packed with sumptuous shots from the respective photoshoots and had the usual accompanying random photocards and posters.

In addition to the two released tracks there were two other new songs on the album. 'Interlude: Wings' had been given a remix, a dance break and a new J-Hope verse to become 'Outro: Wings', while the final track on the album is a completely new song. 'A Supplementary Story: You Never Walk Alone' spells out the message of this second part. A laid-back rap and vocal BTS-style track in which Suga and J-Hope even sing some of their rap lines, it offers a reassuring note after the harsh truths highlighted by many of the other songs. If we stick together, it says, we will be okay.

The 2017 BTS Live Trilogy Episode III: The Wings Tour began on 18 and 19 February with two shows at their new 'home', the Gocheok Sky Dome in Seoul. During the set, they broke so that each member could personally thank the fans for the *daesang* which, they stressed, they had won together. Suga poetically said how BTS were one wing and ARMY were another, so together they could fly; Jin joked how his handsomeness must be contagious, as over the years it had spread to the others; and RM talked of how he read ARMY's letters and felt they were walking together into the future. But it was J-Hope who set the tears flowing; he revealed it was his birthday (that much they already knew!) and said how privileged he was that his mother was there to hear his solo track, a song dedicated to her.

BANGTAN BOMB

BTS'S '봄날' WON @ MUSIC BANK (FEAT. 봄날 NEW DANCE BY JIN)

BTS only promoted 'Spring Day' for a week, but nevertheless managed to capture four music-show awards. This bomb shows backstage footage from the third of those victories, at *Music Bank*. The thanks to ARMY are heartfelt and fun, but the real attraction is in the second part of the bomb, where we see Jin's attempts to choreograph a 'Spring Day' dance to end the show. If you want to see what it looked like when they perform it for real, you'll find that elsewhere on YouTube.

In March, they took the tour to the Americas. First port of call: Chile. When they played Chile in 2015 they had sold seats for half of the Moviestar Arena. This time they would play to the whole arena and, when that sold out almost immediately, they hastily booked a second concert. The Beatlemania-type scenes at the airport on their arrival, outside their hotel in Santiago and at the arena, showed Chilean ARMY to be as passionate as any in the world.

The *New York Times* even wrote an article about how Chilean support for the Korean group surpassed support for groups such as One Direction. RM explained, 'We talk about our own turmoil and mental breakdowns as honestly as possible in the music … We believe Chilean fans tend to connect to those values, maybe a little deeper than fans in other countries.' On a diversion from the tour, BTS hit Mexico City to open the first ever KCON in Latin America and that was pretty wild, too. ARMY linked hands to form their own guard of honour at the airport and the band set the arena rocking with a set of hits, before playing KCON's Piñata Time game, in which they responded to tasks selected by an on-screen cartoon piñata, including blowing kisses at the audience and making a series of photoshoot poses for fans.

An estimated 8,000 ARMY were there to meet them at the airport in Brazil; in fact, so many fans turned up that the boys had to sneak out through a back door! Considering the Citibank Hall venue had a capacity of only 7,000, there were sure to be some disappointed fans, but those who made it to the concerts witnessed something really special. The group would later tell the Distractify website that the fans' synchronized dancing was a highlight of the tour: 'Hundreds of fans were dancing with us behind the seats like a flash mob,' they said. 'It was awesome!'

One particular moment lives on in BTS history. In RM's solo 'Reflection', he sings a recurring line about how he wishes he could love himself. Every time he did so on the first night in São Paulo, ARMY would reply in deafening tones: 'We love you!' The next night, revealing that he had heard ARMY's cries, he changed the lyrics to 'Yes, I do love myself'. In the BTS social media world, word travels fast. By the next concert and for the rest of the tour, it was a special moment that would be replayed between RM and ARMY again and again around the world. Thanks, Brazil!

In 2017 *Run BTS!* returned with some more choice episodes. 'High School Skit' (episode eleven) finds the guys drawing lots to determine their roles in a high-school drama, resulting in a nerdy V, emo J-Hope and a nice-but-dim RM competing to win the heart of a new female student, Min Yoonji, memorably played by Suga! Episode twenty-three is another must-see. BTS all love dogs so it's a special treat when they are each paired up with a canine friend. After each dog chooses a member, they spend time bonding before competing in a series of trials. It's just amazing to watch the chemistry and affection that develops between the boys and their dogs in such a short time.

BANGTAN BOMB

JUNG KOOK WENT TO HIGH SCHOOL WITH BTS FOR GRADUATION! – BTS (방탄소년단)

Awww! The *maknae* looks so cute in his graduation uniform as he picks up his high-school certificate. And if his solo track 'Begin' doesn't make his love for his fellow members abundantly clear, take a look at his excitement at them attending his ceremony – and his gleeful anticipation of the celebration meal of black bean noodles!

You also have to look up episode thirty-one in which they play games from old variety shows. Non-Korean viewers might find this confusing, but fast-forward to halfway through where they play the 'Half-asleep game' in which they have to sleep for thirty minutes and, on waking, remember a children's song, in this case 'The Cool Tomato Song'. We see them in their pyjamas, in deep sleep – Jung Kook doesn't really wake up even when he falls out of his inflatable bed! – and then they're woken and have to sing. It really is BTS gold.

BTS Gayo also returned with more games and challenges. They had a relay to draw pictures of K-pop songs, a K-pop quiz, and had to guess and sing children's songs. Track fifteen is the real highlight. Shot entirely in a hotel while in Chile on the *Wings* tour, the group are challenged to make their own music video. With RM as director, Jung Kook on camera and Jin as choreographer, they shoot an MV for 'Spine Breaker' in their rooms, the restaurant and even the elevator. The result is not exactly 'DNA', but it's a whole lot of fun in the making!

Having achieved their long-cherished dream of a *daesang*, BTS's new goal lay thousands of miles away. They wanted success in the US. They wanted Billboard chart glory and to fill stadiums like Beyoncé and Bieber. They were already on their way. They'd hit the Billboard 200, as well as the iTunes singles chart top ten, but further proof of American interest came before the tour when Wale and RM collaborated on the politically charged rap single 'Change'.

When their dates in Newark, New Jersey, on 23 March and Anaheim, California, on 1 April sold out in hours, it even took their tour promoters by surprise. Another night at each venue was quickly added and they squeezed a night in Chicago in between as they realized just how popular this K-pop act had become. All in all, 60,000 seats across the country were sold. 'We always hoped we could be popular in America, but we thought it was all a dream,' RM told the *Orange County Weekly* before the show in Anaheim. 'Even after we heard about Billboard, we didn't know that we could be a sold-out artist for five nights. So, it's like, "Ok, what's happening right now?" And everyone [in the group] thinks that they should learn English now!'

With the exception of RM, their English did not improve substantially, but they all made an effort to communicate with the fans. In Chicago, Jung Kook announced, 'We are far, far away, but we will always be together,' and RM took some pleasure in pointing out that he had practised that line 'a million times', but the lack of fluency certainly didn't stop them from developing a fabulous rapport with ARMY across the country.

'We actually were scared of performing in America as a solo act,' RM told the *Orange County Register*. 'But after we were on stage our fear disappeared. The fans are like friends. Singing along to all of the lyrics even through the raps.' American ARMY even developed their own way of demonstrating their affection. After the group finished the set, they accompanied their pleas for an encore by covering their light sticks and phone lights with coloured plastic bags, sometimes distributed in advance by fans, which created an incredible rainbow effect across the concert hall.

For those in the audience used to watching US acts perform, the performances were eye-opening. Not only was the bond between die-hard fans and the group unlike anything they had seen before, but the sheer energy and step-perfect synchronization over a draining two-hour show was incredible. No wonder hundreds of merely curious concert-goers left the venues as converted fans.

BTS left American shores to take the *Wings* tour to Asia to visit Thailand, Indonesia, the Philippines and Hong Kong – all to the same rapturous welcome. Just a few weeks later, on 21 May, they were back in the States, this time in Las Vegas, on the red, or rather magenta, carpet for the Billboard Music Awards. Their presence meant they were officially being noticed, even if many people didn't recognize them, as was made apparent when Jin received comments on Twitter about his good looks under the hashtag #ThirdOneFromTheLeft.

The BBMAs is one of the major music award ceremonies in the USA and a K-pop group had never been nominated for – let alone won – an award before, so BTS's bewilderment at winning the Top Social Artist award, a fan-voted honour which had been won by Justin Bieber for the previous six years, was understandable. Breaking all previous records, BTS had racked up a staggering 300 million online votes to take the award – many fans no doubt voting more than once.

Along with many others across the States, some US artists were beginning to realize what the BTS deal was all about. Halsey and The Chainsmokers were pictured with them at the awards, Suga revealed he had met rapper Drake, and V boasted that when Celine Dion had heard V was a long-time fan, she invited the group to her concert. Others declaring themselves fans included singer Camila Cabello, who tweeted, 'They r soooo sweet', and actors Ansel Elgort and Laura Marano.

Still on a high a few days later, BTS were able to thank some of ARMY in person when, on 26 May, they took the *Wings* tour to Sydney, Australia. It was their second visit Down Under, but it was apparent as soon as they touched down that their fan base had multiplied. Tickets had sold out within hours and the crowd at the Qudos Bank Arena was six times the size of their Red Bullet audience.

One member of the group has a special affection for Australia. When he was young, RM spent some time there with family and the first words he uttered on stage were, 'G'day mate!' Later, he reprised his Australian accent and closed the concert by saying, 'You know, I must say that you guys live in such a beautiful country. I went to the Opera House yesterday and I saw people sitting on the grass, and the sea and the wind – it was so, so legit. So if I can't live in Korea I want to live in Australia!' The Aussie fans savoured every second of the concert, reacting with hysterical screams to the solo stages, the latest hits and the 'rocket through the history of BTS' medley (© Jin). The Bangtan Boys had, if not conquered, then at least secured a foothold in yet another country.

On 29 May 2017, they made a triumphant return to Seoul, pausing for a press conference in which they posed in their magenta carpet suits with their BBMA trophy and spoke modestly about their incredible success in the US. Inevitably, the question of how far they would go to progress in America was raised, as it would be many times over the next year. Would they record a song in English? RM's reply was that they weren't planning to officially debut in the States, because they wanted to carry on doing what they did best. He said, 'We want to continue to rap in Korean and do things that only BTS can do, rather than switching gears to suit a new market.' Integrity had always been an essential characteristic of BTS; it was reassuring to ARMY everywhere that they were still not prepared to compromise.

TWENTY

IT'S YOUR ERA NOW

It seemed that fans in the US, UK and Australia would have to wait a while for an English-language BTS track, but the Japanese editions were proving to be a Big Hit masterstroke. 'Chi, Ase, Namida', the Japanese version of 'Blood Sweat & Tears', was released in May 2017 with a new music video, a vividly coloured and at times psychedelic alternative to the Korean original. The track immediately matched 'For You' by going to the top of Japan's Billboard Hot 100 and the Oricon charts. Not a bad start for the group on their new record label in Japan, the legendary hip-hop label Def Jam, now home to Justin Bieber and Kanye West among others.

Between the end of May and early July the boys played thirteen *Wings* concerts to around 145,000 fans across Japan. BTS were breaking new Japanese records for foreign group sales and their name was becoming familiar to more and more people there. They even made their first appearance on a Japanese variety show, *Sukkiri*, where they showed off their Japanese language skills and performed 'Chi, Ase, Namida'.

While on tour, they were also welcomed to the famous Koshien Stadium to watch the Hanshin Tigers play the Nippon-Han Fighters at baseball. Apart from J-Hope, who had his lucky '7', and Jimin with his birth date '13', the boys sported Tigers baseball shirts with their birth year as a number and Jung Kook was chosen to deliver the ceremonial first pitch in front of a packed stadium. The Golden Maknae proceeded to add baseball to his many talents as, to the delight of the watching members, he delivered a pretty decent throw. That's Jung Kook, some said: always pitch-perfect!

They might have been in Japan, but there was no way BTS were going to forget their *festa*. June 2017 marked their fourth anniversary and, just as on the previous three, they aimed to celebrate with their beloved ARMY. Celebrations got underway with a collection of pictures from the year in a Facebook photobook, Jung Kook and Jimin's now-cherished cover of Charlie Puth and Selena Gomez's 'We Don't Talk Anymore' and the YouTube release of two special 'choreography stages': the dance practice videos of 'Not Today', using a gymnasium rather than the usual dance studio to accommodate all the supporting dancers, and 'Like Pt. 2'. Then a surprise! They dropped a great new video of them filming themselves performing live in Sydney, so we see not only the group's view of ARMY in full voice, but also close-ups of them having a great time on stage and really playing up to the camera.

The traditional family photos provided the usual fun, including a hilarious update on their school uniforms-and-shades pic from 2014 (cue the 'haven't they grown up!' squeals).

The climax of the *festa* was their 'home party' back in Korea, when they held an intimate celebration at the Woori Art Hall in the Olympic Park in Seoul. The thousand tickets were sold only to those who had joined the fan club, although the show was also shown live on V Live.

After a genuinely funny filmed intro in which they re-enacted the 'Blood Sweat & Tears' video in their dorm, the guys teamed up according to their dorm rooms: team R&V (RM and V), team 3J (J-Hope, Jimin and Jung Kook) and team Sin (Jin and Suga). Throughout the show they played games, took part in quizzes on their roommates and gave team performances. Team R&V performed a self-composed song, '4 O'Clock', live for the first time; team 3J covered various urban dance choreographies; and team Sin's contribution was Jin rapping Suga's 'Intro: Never Mind' and Suga singing 'Awake'. Finally, after revealing particularly cute baby pictures of each of them, the audience was treated to a funny kindergarten medley of some of their hits.

In the summer of 2017 a second series of *Bon Voyage* appeared on the V Live channel and this time the trip was to their dream destination, Hawaii. The boys duly don their Hawaiian shirts and straw hats and, over eight episodes, we see them having fun together, playing hide-and-seek around the hotel, snorkelling and stargazing after watching an amazing sunset.

There are none of the Nordic trip's trials and tribulations, but they are forced to be self-sufficient when it comes to ordering their individual meals at Ken's House of Pancakes, although Jimin 'somehow' manages to attract help from a waitress, and, split into teams, they are tasked with finding their way to their lodge on Oahu. There the adrenaline-rush adventures really start as they take a helicopter ride over the active volcano – with Suga sitting right by the open door! – and swim in an underwater cage right next to a school of sharks.

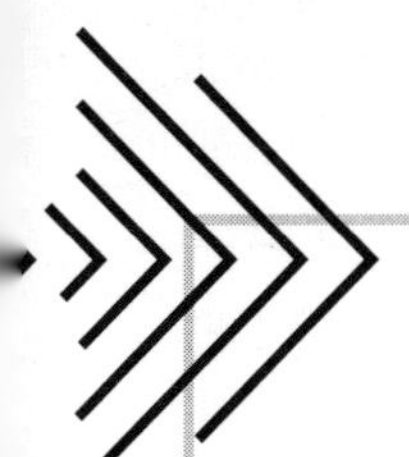

BANGTAN BOMB

613 BTS HOME PARTY PRACTICE – UNIT STAGE

A longer than usual Bangtan Bomb, this series of clips shows team 3J from the home party practising their moves for the *festa* extravaganza. While it can't help but make you smile to see them enjoying themselves, it also gives an insight into how hard they work at getting the choreography spot on – and just how much they love to dance, whether it's in the dance studio, backstage at the 2017 Billboard Music Awards or in J-Hope's hotel room (with Jimin practising in his dressing gown and a face pack!).

There's still fun to be had before they go back to idol life. They really enjoy tearing along the coastal road on quad bikes and, at a Polynesian-themed evening, J-Hope, Jimin and V are invited to the stage for some Bangtan Hawaiian dance, all in perfect synchronicity of course. The final episode sees them taking a boat ride. V is delighted when the skipper gives him the wheel, but as he piles on the speed, the others seem rather alarmed.

Fortunately, it all calms down for the finale. Each of them has written a letter to one of the others and, as they recall when they first met and reveal what they mean to each other, it's very emotional. The letter that really melts hearts is V's letter to Jimin, in which he describes how much his 95-line friend has helped him through the years. Most ARMY must watch the final dance party on the boat through tear-filled eyes.

While the *festa* had given BTS an opportunity to repay their fans for the love and support that had made them idols, soon they were able to repay a debt of a different kind when they were invited to participate in the twenty-fifth anniversary celebrations of Seo Taiji and Boys, the group that had launched the whole K-pop phenomenon. In 1992 their rap-rock track 'I Know' entered the Korean charts alongside the traditional *trot* numbers and ballads. It went on to the top of the charts and stayed there for seventeen weeks. Nothing would ever be the same again. Not only was their sound different, but they also sang challenging lyrics that reflected the frustrations of young people. Now who does that remind you of?

The Boys, Yang Hyun-suk and Lee Juno, had left in 1996 (Yang Hyun-suk starting major company YG Entertainment), but over the next two decades Seo Taiji had continued to push musical boundaries and now he was receiving his recognition as the godfather of K-pop, with an album, *Time Traveler*, featuring remakes of his songs and a special concert in Seoul. BTS were the honoured guests for both.

For the album, BTS revisited the 1995 classic 'Come Back Home'. A dark and gritty rap song, the original spoke of the pressures that made so many Korean teenagers run away from home, so it felt just right when BTS, in a style that harked back to 'No More Dream' and 'N.O', injected their own rap parts and some Bangtan lyrical magic, including a Jin falsetto opening, in an invigorating reworking of the song.

On 3 September 2017, in front of 35,000 fans at the Olympic Stadium, Taiji, often nicknamed the 'President of Culture' in South Korea, went through his impressive collection of hits. In place of the Boys were BTS, taking it in turns to serve as backup vocalists and dancers for their hero. At rehearsals they addressed him as 'Father', but the respect went both ways. In a break in the concert, Taiji acknowledged the achievements of BTS and pronounced them his successors by declaring, 'It's your era now.'

If this signified that BTS led the current generation of K-pop acts, then their summer change of logo and name reflected their position as a global force. They would still be BTS, but in English that would now stand for 'Beyond the Scene' – a new way of presenting themselves to the English-speaking world. At the same time, they issued new and complementary logos for BTS and for ARMY. These were pairs of simple but stylish quadrilaterals representing doors; the doors which youth pass through to adulthood. Both the group and ARMY were now ready for a new chapter in BTS's journey.

Back in May, at the 2017 Billboard Music Awards in the States, RM had announced in his acceptance speech: 'Please, ARMY, remember what we say: "Love myself, love yourself."' That phrase came to mind again three months later as the *Love Yourself* comeback got underway. It started with posters of each of the group, the first of which shocked ARMY by showing Jung Kook in a wheelchair. Each poster was accompanied by a short statement giving a downbeat and personal notion of love, such as, 'I lied, because there's no reason to love someone like me,' or, 'Don't come closer, it will only make you unhappy.' A further set of posters paired the members up in light and dark photos, although, as always, Jin was alone.

The four short videos (now available as a thirteen-minute highlight reel) that subsequently appeared, built on these images. As in previous films, they were loaded with symbolism and references to previous stories and, although these sparked an outpouring of online analysis from ARMY, they also contained a narrative that can simply be enjoyed. They feature each of the group looking like a boy next door (albeit a boy next door with a floppy fringe, stylish casual clothes and a to-die-for complexion) in a troubled romantic situation. Apart from J-Hope and Jimin, each is attracted to a different woman, but as the stories unfold, self-doubt, shyness, jealousy, frustration and even tragedy are shown to thwart the course of true love. And, for those who are still concerned, Jung Kook does get back on his feet – eventually.

The mini-album *Love Yourself: Her* was set to appear in four versions, *L*, *O*, *V* and *E*, and so four separate photo collections were released. There are no smoky eyes or remarkable hairstyles this time. The look is natural, the haircuts similar. Jimin, Jin, V and Jung Kook go for subtle colours and J-Hope gets most attention with a colour fans call 'pumpkin spice'.

In the photos for *L* and *O* the guys wear subdued colours and the shots are dreamy and relaxing, while those for *V* and *E* are more vibrant and they are in colourful casual sportswear. Meanwhile, the trailer featured a similarly dreamy Jimin (a yellow-blond Jimin!) solo in a setting that combined a dazzling white room with oceans and galaxies. In an article in *Vogue* magazine, Suga explained, 'It's about boys falling in love. There are four versions of love and we shot four different photos to show them. Though each one is different, the same feeling of love comes through in every shot. There's a sense of playfulness, of friends hanging out comfortably at home in their free time, and that kind of fluttering feeling.'

It was the colourful look (plus a lot of stonewash and Jimin's fabulous Gucci sequinned bomber jacket) that drove the dance-focused video for the lead track, 'DNA'. The boys are in an array of colours against a kaleidoscope of backgrounds that change from cheesy retro computer style to candy stripes, swirls, deep space, geometric patterns and neon.

Their choreography was stunning: controlled, at times intricate, and interspersed with a series of lightning fast moves. *Billboard* reported that when they performed it at the American Music Awards (AMAs) on 19 November the cameras couldn't keep pace with their footwork. Some claimed it was the most difficult set of steps yet and on a V Live appearance V joked, 'We mastered the difficult choreography after practising for more than four hours, but J-Hope finished it in ten minutes.'

In their press conferences and interviews it became clear that BTS viewed *Love Yourself: Her* as the beginning of a new era. RM referred to it as the 'second chapter' of the group and left a message on the fan café saying it would be a turning point for BTS. It was an extremely confident album and stylistically wide-ranging as they assimilated guest contributors alongside their usual producers. As billed, they portray the exhilarating, ecstatic but also uneasy feelings of young adults who fall in love, but they also use gender-neutral lyrics for the first time, acknowledge and even tease their fans, and include a track aimed directly at their own generation.

When the album was released on 18 September 2017, the opener was, of course, familiar from the teaser. It was the first time a vocalist had been trusted with the task and the privilege fell to Jimin. He delivers 'Serendipity', described as a 'chill-out-style urban song', with delicate ease, singing of a perfect predestined love. It is a theme that's carried over to the lead track 'DNA'. Jung Kook's catchy whistled opener is still lingering as the song begins in earnest with a unique acoustic guitar-based EDM track and a breakdown of the usual distinct rap and vocal lines.

At the Billboard Awards, The Chainsmokers had shared a photo of themselves with BTS with the caption, 'Love these dudes.' When the US duo played in Korea, BTS joined them on stage to perform 'Closer' and now a collaboration between the two groups appeared on the album. 'Best of Me' is classic electronic dance music: anthemic with a catchy chorus and totally uplifting.

The next track, 'Dimple', uses the tune of Allison Kaplan's 'Illegal' and the lyrics were written by the guy with the most talked-about dimples in BTS – RM – but he sits out as the vocal line, especially Jin, makes it sweet and sensual. This takes us on to 'Pied Piper', an ode to their fans – or is it? Tamar Herman wrote in *Billboard* that it was 'BTS's most subversive song of their career, thanks to its takedown of the very fan culture that has helped the act thrive'. Over the mellow disco number the group mercilessly tease ARMY everywhere by explaining what a terrible distraction they are from schoolwork and other important aspects of life, but, at the same time, openly relishing and celebrating their irresistibility.

'Skit: Billboard Music Awards Speech' isn't actually a skit; it's a recording of BTS's historic triumph at the previous year's BBMAs, from the winning announcement and the cheers of the fans to RM's acceptance speech and ending with feedback that takes us into 'MIC Drop'. Here the rap line returns in force with a song inspired by President Obama's 'OK, I'm done' mic drop at his final White House Correspondents' dinner. The pretend-apologetic bragging (sorry we aren't the failures you predicted) rap is an update on the old Bangtan sound enhanced by a chorus that hangs around in your head.

Have BTS forgotten their social conscience? Of course not. The next track, 'Go Go', proves that. It might have a trendy tropical-influenced soft disco sound, but the lyrics hit hard. In contrast to the music, the words are angry and defiant, condemning society for leaving a young generation bereft of ambition and expectations to seek thrills through a YOLO (you only live once), spend now, worry later lifestyle.

The album closes with 'Outro: Her', where, over a lush, laid-back instrumental, the rap line sounds so chilled they're virtually singing. There is no switching of the mic, just an extended verse for each of the three to display their own style and explain their notion of the uncertainties of being in love. And there, after thirty minutes of diverse BTS styles as the group forge new ideas, sounds and paths, the album ends.

The physical album treated buyers to two more 'hidden' tracks, which BTS felt didn't fit the 'love' concept but deserved inclusion. 'Skit: Hesitation and Fear' is one of their most revealing conversations and is worth reading in translation. You'll discover how scared they were that they might never debut, how they never took English or Japanese lessons seriously, and how anxious they are about coping with their success. The track 'Sea', mainly written and produced by RM, takes up some of these themes in an old-style BTS rap and vocal track based around the refrain 'Where there is hope, there are trials.' And that really is the end this time.

On 21 September 2017, BTS had their official comeback show with a live broadcast in which they performed 'MIC Drop', 'Go Go' and 'DNA' from the album, as well as 'I Need U' and 'No More Dream'. It featured the guys talking about the album along with some fun films of them at home and their recollections of the early days of BTS, including re-enactments of their auditions.

At home, *Love Yourself: Her* reached new heights. It debuted at number one in Korea on the Gaon album chart and became the biggest-selling physical album for sixteen years, every song from the album featured in the Melon chart top ten and it swept the board at the music shows. 'DNA' brought them another ten show awards, including their first triple crowns (three consecutive weeks) on *Music Bank* and *Inkigayo*.

BANGTAN BOMB

고민보다 GO (GO GO) DANCE PRACTICE (HALLOWEEN VER.)

This 2017 Halloween special where Snow White and the six dwarfs perform 'Go Go' is one of the most popular Bangtan Bombs ever with over 233 million views. That's no surprise because it's fabulously executed. From the moment the rock, paper, scissors game lands V in the dress, he steals the show with a magnificent deadpan performance, complete with poisoned apple, but his laughing dwarfs offer spot-on support.

BTS finished the comeback with another special broadcast. With Jin acting as MC, *BTS Countdown!* was a parody of *M Countdown*, with a chart show, music stages, a minidrama and game segments – but all starring BTS. It included a segment where they danced to 'Boy in Luv' using only the bottom half of their bodies, a slo-mo 'Fire' choreography and a punishment finale where the losing team – V, J-Hope and Jimin – had to dance at double speed to the song voted their best ever: 'DNA'. *Love Yourself: Her* was never going to flop. The million-plus pre-orders guaranteed that – but its success was perhaps even beyond their wildest hopes. On the day it was released the album immediately sailed to number one in the iTunes Top Albums Chart in over seventy countries. It reached number one in Japan in its second week, opened at number seven on the Billboard 200 and, for the first time ever, hit the UK Top 40 album chart, peaking at fourteen. Meanwhile, it was trending at number one on YouTube, an achievement unheard of for a K-pop group.

TWENTY-ONE

HEART AND SEOUL

With the comeback completed, BTS had a chance to spend time on some projects close to their hearts. Chief among these was a desire to support #ENDViolence, a campaign by the international children's charity UNICEF to stop children and teenagers having to live in fear of violence. Along with Big Hit, they sponsored the hashtag, giving nearly $350,000 to the campaign and pledging 3 per cent of sales income from all the physical albums in the *Love Yourself* series.

Next on the to-do list was a present for the city they had made their home, the South Korean capital, Seoul. To support the city's tourism department, they dropped a free track called 'With Seoul', a cheery orchestral pop hymn to the city sung by the vocal line. The video, which featured the whole group recording the song cut with the city's sights, was released on the official tourist website, which immediately crashed as fans attempted to watch it.

BTS also found time to get creative with their pens. No strangers to caricature versions of themselves, BTS had already seen the Hip Hip Monsters and the *We On* superheroes. Now Japanese messaging app Line gave them an opportunity to draw characters for an emoji sticker set. They came up with a set of seven adorable friends: the kind, parka-wearing alpaca, RJ (Jin); the eager-to-please puppy Chimmy (Jimin); a magic cookie named Shooky who is scared of milk (Suga); a dancing masked pony, Mang (J-Hope); the super-curious, heart-faced Tata (V); Cooky the wannabe tough-guy bunny (Jung Kook); and Koya, the thoughtful if sleepy koala (RM). They even came up with a character for ARMY, the friends' space robot protector named Van.

The characters were part of a fictional group called BT21 – inspired by Suga's suggestion that the characters should represent both BTS and the 21st century. The BT21 Universe is based on Tata visiting Earth and recruiting his friends to form a group to rival BTS. Over the following years, BT21 proved incredibly popular, with webtoons, merchandise, their own social media accounts and collaborations with Dunkin' Donuts, Hello Kitty, Monopoly, McDonalds, Dr. Martens and many others.

In November, they were off to the US again, because they had been asked to perform at the 2017 AMAs, which was a real coup – they were the first Korean group to receive such an invitation. Could they wow the US audience with 'DNA', singing in Korean? In their first major televised stateside performance? Actually, as they say in the US, they had them at hello.

Style authority *Vogue* declared that BTS 'shut down' the red carpet in their sleek black suits, courtesy of Saint Laurent designer Anthony Vaccarello. 'Standing together,' *Vogue* swooned, 'they reinforced their message of shared style with a personal twist. It won't be the last time we see it.' Before they even made the stage, the boys were caught on camera dancing in their seats and mouthing all the words to Demi Lovato's 'Sorry Not Sorry', but no one (except the thousands of ARMY around the world) knew what was about to unfold when The Chainsmokers introduced these seven incredible-looking guys in their 'DNA' outfits of jeans and assorted Gucci jackets.

The knife-like choreography was totally on point, the synchronization exact and they played to the audience, including viewers watching at home, perfectly. In short, their performance was immaculate, but even so the reaction stunned everyone. Led by a screaming ARMY contingent, the crowd, celebs included, gave them a standing ovation. 'I need a moment to recover from that performance,' said presenter Jared Leto immediately afterwards. He wasn't alone.

The post-event reaction was also incredible. Twitter caught fire with ARMY and brand-new fans raving about their performance in over 20 million tweets. 'All anyone cared about at the AMAs was South Korean boy band BTS', was the *Mashable* headline. And this on a night when Shawn Mendes, Selena Gomez and Christina Aguilera had also performed. BTS could have hung out with those guys had they attended the star-studded after-show party. Why weren't they there? Simply because they wanted to share their first offstage moment with their fans. In a live broadcast from their hotel room, they talked about their performance, how Suga had been so nervous his mic was shaking and how several stars – Jin is shushed when he mentions Zedd – had offered to collaborate with them.

One American, however, had beaten those stars to it. Legendary DJ and producer Steve Aoki had remixed 'MIC Drop' for the US market and the result was about to be unleashed. The remix transformed the song into a full-on rap track, as Aoki overlaid an EDM beat, introduced English-language verses and, for one version, brought in US rapper Desiigner. The track has a great music video, with the boys in both old-style BTS hip-hop black and white and their colourful new look. It features Aoki masterminding the track as BTS break free from an interrogation room and take on their black-hooded haters. Exciting stuff.

Having 'discovered' BTS, US television wanted more. ARMY packed the audience at *The Ellen DeGeneres Show*, with the host making comparisons to the reception the Beatles had received in America in the 1960s. With the help of an on-set interpreter, Ellen asked about the 'social conscience' messages of their songs and even dared ask if they had 'hooked up' with any ARMY. When they figured out what she meant, the completely shocked reaction of the guys was an answer in itself. On the show, they performed the new version of 'MIC Drop', which probably helped them become the first K-pop act to hit number one on the US iTunes charts.

Before the AMAs, they recorded a mini-concert for *Jimmy Kimmel Live!* – in front of a passionate crowd of around a thousand fans in Los

Angeles, they played 'Go Go', 'Save Me', 'I Need U', 'Fire' and 'MIC Drop (Remix)', which was played on the show itself (the full concert was uploaded to Kimmel's YouTube channel). In a short segment on the late-night show, Kimmel introduced BTS, explaining how many of their passionate ARMY had waited in line for the show. The clip then showed some of the fans' mothers being taken out of the queue and into the studio. They FaceTimed their so-jealous daughters as they met the boys. This trick was only appreciated by their girls when they were eventually taken to meet the group too!

More fun and games awaited them on *The Late Late Show with James Corden.* Before performing 'DNA', the group were persuaded to play Corden's game of 'Flinch', where they stood behind a plexiglass wall and tried not to flinch as Corden fired fruit at them from a high-pressure air cannon. Jin and J-Hope, described by RM as the biggest cowards of the group, went first and proved their leader right by freaking out (Jin) and collapsing hilariously (J-Hope). Although Jimin, Suga and RM, the last three to step up, acted pretty brave, they still recoiled, leaving the unflappable V and pretty cool Jung Kook as winners.

After returning to Korea, in December BTS themselves were given a present: a new dorm. Well, it was more a luxury apartment than a dorm, as they moved into Hannam The Hill, the most select and expensive block in Seoul. Although many idol groups choose to live apart when they become successful, BTS opted to stay together, although at least they each had their own room here. They remained living there until the lease ran out in 2021, when they finally moved into their own apartments. They had shared living space for a long time (RM and Suga had lived together for over 10 years) and at *festa* 2022 spent time reminiscing on the fun – and frustrations – they had shared in their dorms.

BTS brought an unforgettable year to a close when they stepped out at the Gocheok Sky Dome in Seoul for the final performances of a *Wings* world tour that had seen them play thirty-two concerts in ten different countries. It was a triumphant return, a thrilling three-hour-long love-in between BTS and ARMY which the *Korea Herald* described as 'tearful, beautiful and splendid'. This was not only the end of a long tour, but the finale of a trilogy that had begun back in 2014 at a time when many had still doubted them.

More than ever, New Year was a time for celebration. The recently released Japanese single, 'Crystal Snow', a beautiful and emotional ballad adorned with Jin's soulful high vocals, had not only reached number one in the Japanese charts, but had registered high on iTunes charts around the world. Meanwhile, back in the US, the group's profile remained high, with pre-recorded performances of 'MIC Drop' and 'DNA' appearing on the iconic TV show *Dick Clark's New Year's Rockin' Eve with Ryan Seacrest.*

As the awards season got underway, millions around the world followed BTS's progress and expectations were high. They would not be disappointed. They picked up *daesangs* at MAMA (Artist of the Year for two years running!), MMA (Song of the Year and Global Artist prizes), won their first Golden Disc Awards *daesang* for *Love Yourself: Her*, Seoul Music Awards *daesang* for Artist of the Year and, perhaps most impressively, became the first idol group to win the Korean Music Awards' Artist of the Year, a prestigious honour bestowed by critics and music professionals.

Early spring was a strange time and fans waited impatiently for news. Surely the next *Love Yourself* instalment was due? Were rumours of a global tour true? Would BTS be returning to the US for the Billboard Music Awards? Answers to these questions were not forthcoming, but on 2 March there was nonetheless something to get excited about in the form of J-Hope's mixtape, *Hope World.* This had been talked about for so long that ARMY had almost given up on it ever appearing, but it was worth the wait. A superb collection of upbeat, bouncy, but surprisingly introspective tracks that only BTS's very own ray of sunshine could supply, within hours of its release *Hope World* topped iTunes album charts in over sixty countries and J-Hope's music video for the lead song, 'Daydream', amassed 12 million YouTube views in its first twenty-four hours.

YouTube had long been an integral part of the BTS success story, so it was fitting that the new fly-on-the-wall documentary *Burn the Stage* was originally shown exclusively on the site. The series, taking a behind-the-scenes look at the group's 2017 *Wings* tour, makes for compelling viewing. As a group that have always been open and honest, they don't hold back, and allow the cameras to see their self-doubt, their fears and their arguments, as well as the elation, the fun, and the love and respect they have for each other.

It is not short of drama, with Jung Kook collapsing from heat exhaustion and a heated and emotional row between V and Jin over their onstage positioning, as well as fun moments like Jung Kook sneaking a chocolate ball into Jin's noodles and Jin thinking it's a mushroom. But what is most amazing is that all we have learned about BTS is true: they do work until they collapse, they do care for each other and they are involved in every aspect of their performance, from the music to the stage production. And if you think their words aren't heartfelt, these films show how much they appreciate the love and how they feel the burden of repaying the loyalty of ARMY.

The series played out to a flurry of BTS action. At the start of April, electronics company LG announced a new association with the group. So far, so dull. However, the accompanying photo caused ARMY to do a double-take. Yes, there were all seven boys with dark hair, for the first time ever! No wonder #BTSBlackHairParty was trending worldwide on Twitter. Two days later, a twelve-track Japanese album, *Face Yourself*, was released. It wasn't the album they were waiting for, but ARMY did at least have some new BTS music to enjoy. Along with Japanese versions of 'Blood Sweat & Tears', 'DNA' and 'MIC Drop', there were new intro and outro tracks and two previously unheard songs: 'Don't Leave Me' and 'Let Go'. 'Don't Leave Me' is a powerful and emotional EDM-based song that finally puts Jin centre-stage. He shows he deserves it by sending down some jaw-dropping soprano lines. 'Let Go', a sentimental ballad that swells and falls then rises again, is especially notable for Jimin's pretty perfect English singing. The album, of course, was a number-one hit in Japan, but BTS fans now had such an appetite for new material that it charted all around the world.

On 5 April BTS appeared in a video on DreamStillLives.com, a project to honour civil rights activist Dr Martin Luther King Jr, who had been assassinated exactly fifty years previously. The group were personally invited to contribute by the organizer, US soul legend Stevie Wonder, along with such famous faces as Barack and Michelle Obama, Mariah Carey, Meryl Streep and Elton John.

That same day saw the release of a nine-minute video titled 'Euphoria: Theme of Love Yourself: Wonder'. Did this herald the long-awaited album? Many thought it did. A dramatic introduction featured clips from previous videos set to classical composer Debussy's piece 'Clair de Lune'. Then there was a sudden change and Jung Kook's dreamy solo vocals rose over a bright synth-pop backing and an alternative scenario was played out where the boys, dressed in colourful but plain clothes, were having fun together once more. Finally, the end section found them all in white at the water's edge where V jumped from the pier in the 'On Stage: Prologue' video. Once again there were more questions than answers, but ARMY didn't mind. If you're up to some theorizing, it might help to know that the message in the final frame translates as: '*Hyung* is that all?'

Fans had two weeks to puzzle it all out before the new album was announced. To great surprise, it was to be called *Love Yourself: Tear* and not *Wonder* as many had assumed. The comeback trailer, 'Singularity', uploaded to YouTube on 6 May, featured V performing solo. The elegant RM-penned neo-soul track, with music from British producer Charlie J. Perry, was superbly complemented by a captivating video in which V dances alone or with backing dancers to lush backdrops or a recurring mask motif. It was just one member, but enough to convince ARMY that something momentous was about to drop.

The concept photos only served to heighten the excitement. Once again there would be four versions, this time spelling *Y*, *O*, *U* and *R*, although the pictures weren't released in that order. Seven boys in smart double-denim rocked the *R* version; dreamy black-and-white snaps made up the *O* shoot; the *Y* version showed the members posing against a blue sky in heightened colours; and the *U* version went for the unified white look seen at the end of the 'Euphoria' video. As people waited for the album to come out, the talk was all about the lead track, 'Fake Love', which they would perform for the first time at the BBMAs. BTS were once again nominated for the top social artist award and few bet against them taking it home.

For ARMY it seemed to take ages, but 18 May came around – eventually. The CD box was a reverse of *Love Yourself: Her* – just the title in white on a black background. It included the usual extensive photobook and photocards, but also a twenty-page mini-book of 'notes' with more diary-style stories from each of the members. The CD itself contained eleven new tracks, introduced by V's trailer 'Singularity'. The boys themselves were already in the US on release day, but the magic of V Live allowed them to broadcast their preview show to over 3 million viewers.

BTS promoted the album widely, but no interview was loved as much as Buzzfeed's YouTube video 'BTS Plays with Puppies While Answering Fan Questions'. Not a lot of information was gleaned but hey, puppies and Bangtan Boys: what's not to like? More informative, if a lot less cute, was RM's interview with *J-14* magazine's Liam McEwan. He neatly outlined the theme of *Love Yourself: Tear*, saying, 'Basically love is complex. There's sort of some sides that make us really feel bad or depressed. There could be tears, there could be sadness. So this time we wanted to focus on some of the parts of love that we want to run away from. So the name is *Tear*.'

The second and lead track, 'Fake Love', picks up this idea and is a breathless combination of epic beats, rap rock, lush vocals and serious harmonies tied together with the catchiest of choruses. Meanwhile the video utilizes many BTS trademark styles, bringing in contemporary dance and sharp, synchronized moves; amazing settings full of explosions, flames and floods; desperate running; and lingering shots. It was devoured by fans as soon as it dropped, #FakeLoveFRIDAY soon trended on Twitter and it racked up 4.8 million views in its first hour.

The album itself is a triumph of genre-hopping. The boys effortlessly move from the tender piano-accompanied ballad of 'The Truth Untold', written and produced by Steve Aoki of 'MIC Drop' fame, to the flutes and jazzy guitar of '134340', which takes the dwarf planet Pluto as a metaphor for lost love. The rap-fuelled 'Paradise', produced by Grammy-nominated MNEK, is another great BTS message song in which they reassure their generation that they can just enjoy the moment and ignore the burden of their dreams and ambitions, and the beautiful harmonies of 'Love Maze', with traces of BTS 2013-style rap, complete the first half of the album.

The second half seems to be gift-wrapped for ARMY. 'Magic Shop', written by Jung Kook (his first ever credit), offers fans strength and escape with BTS, and 'Airplane Pt. 2', a sequel to the popular track from J-Hope's mixtape, is a trippy feast with a fabulous Spanish feel (perhaps influenced by the success of 'Despacito'). The next two tracks, soon to be fan favourites, are 'Anpanman' (the name of a Japanese comic book superhero), four minutes of pure fun with great singalong and dance-along potential, and 'So What', the kind of uptempo anthemic dance track which brings ARMY and BTS together at concerts. Finally comes 'Outro: Tear', but there's no sweet-tongued ballad here, as the rap line spit out an angry and bitter break-up song as a defiant end to the album. However, the break-up had an extra meaning. In *Break The Silence: The Movie*, Suga revealed he had written the lyrics for the members. 'When I was writing the melody, at the time, we were deeply contemplating whether we should quit or not,' he said, adding, 'When I played the song for the members, we all cried together.'

As the group prepared for the Billboard Music Awards in Las Vegas, *Love Yourself: Tear* and 'Fake Love' stood at the top of iTunes charts in over sixty different countries. Around the world, in every time zone, fans watched them walk the magenta carpet in a live feed on Twitter. They appeared looking chilled and cool in seven different Gucci outfits, including RM in shades and Hawaiian shirt, Jin smart in a waistcoat and tie, and J-Hope in a piped school blazer and yellow T-shirt. They strolled across the carpet as if they owned the place.

They charmed the watching audience, sending a message to their fans in Korea and revealing their 'no tweeting when drunk' rule. They hung out backstage meeting old and making new celebrity friends, including Taylor Swift, Lil Pump, Pharrell Williams and John Legend, and, of course, they won the top social artist award – again. In his acceptance speech, RM dedicated the award to ARMY, saying, 'This time we had a chance to think about what "social" really means for us. And some of our fans told us that our music really changed their lives. And now we realize that our words truly carry weight thanks to you guys.'

A few days later, the guys were back on screen with a visit to their old friend Ellen DeGeneres. In front of another hyped-up audience, RM told Ellen that she was personally responsible for teaching the whole of South Korea the meaning of the word 'hook-up' after her presumptuous question in their previous meeting. When Ellen again asked if any band members had a girlfriend, most of the audience screamed, 'Pick me!' However, the 'fangirl' who jumped out at them on stage was a male stagehand in a wig, a prepared prank by the production team.

BANGTAN BOMB

'FAKE LOVE' LIVE PERFORMANCE @2018 BBMAS - BTS (방탄소년단)

In front of an already screaming audience at the BBMAs, the seven members perform 'Fake Love', their choreography, devised by Tokyo-based Rie Hata, creating a cascade of shapes, patterns, waves and synchronized movement ending in a perfectly timed and graceful group hug. The crowd went wild, celebrities from Tyra Banks and Rebel Wilson to the Backstreet Boys flocked to get pictures with them, and the internet nearly broke.

It was time once again to return to Seoul, but they wouldn't be home long as a new world tour was set for the autumn. First the tour would cross Canada and the USA, with the fourteen dates selling out instantly. Then, for the first time, they would tour Europe. ARMY across the continent had been pleading to see the boys perform live and now Big Hit had answered their prayers. Two concerts at London's O2 Arena, which sold out in mere minutes, would be followed by shows in Amsterdam, Berlin and Paris. Were the European ARMY ready for them? Oh yes!

On 27 May 2018, the weekly Billboard 200 charts were announced. *Love Yourself: Tear* was the number-one album in the USA and BTS were the first K-pop group ever to achieve that feat. Almost five years since their debut, they had accomplished the unthinkable: BTS had conquered the world.

TWENTY-TWO

ALL YOU NEED IS (SELF) LOVE

It was on this crest of a wave that the boys celebrated the fifth anniversary of their debut. *Festa* 2018 was one of the best ever. Treats included a Brit Rock Remix version of 'Spring Day', Jin's stirring solo cover of Yoon Do-hyun's 1994 classic 'In Front of the Post Office in Autumn', the rap line's 'Ddaeng', V and Jin singing 'It's Definitely You', their *Hwarang* duet, Jimin and Jung Kook dancing to Michael Jackson's 'Black or White' and a magnificent finale which saw the live debut of BT21, with each BTS member wearing their BT21 onesie outfit as they performed the fan favourite 'Anpanman'.

'Fake Love' was approaching 200 million views on YouTube and had just become the first K-pop track ever to break the Billboard Top 10 in the US. To celebrate, the boys returned to *The Late Late Show With James Corden*. Dressed in silk shirts and ripped skinny jeans, the boys gave a flawless performance, while Corden proved himself a true fan as he rushed to join the group embrace that ended the choreography.

When BTS played Seoul's Lotte Duty Free Family Concert in June, ARMY, ever vigilant, noticed that, apart from J-Hope, the whole group had changed their hair colour or style. V and Jin both now had blond hair,

Suga and Jimin had undercuts and RM's hair was a lighter brown. To the surprise and delight of his fans, Jung Kook, Mr '50 Shades of Brown', who hadn't significantly changed his hair colour for years, appeared sporting flaming pinky-red locks and looking divine.

There was a much bigger surprise just around the corner. On 16 July a new album was announced for release in August. *Love Yourself: Answer* was the final piece of the Love Yourself jigsaw – and featured seven brand-new tracks in a twenty-five-track compilation album containing songs from *Love Yourself: Her* and *Love Yourself: Tear*. Key tracks from these releases had been selected to form a narrative with the message that 'Loving yourself is true love'.

'Euphoria', which had been released earlier in the year via the 'Theme of Love Yourself: Wonder' video, began the album. A solo track by Jung Kook, with lyrics by RM, it has a future bass and tropical-house vibe and reverberates with the joys of new love. Next comes the first of three 'Trivia' tracks from the rap line: 'Trivia: Just Dance' by J-Hope is a funky, two-step track that could have taken its place in his *Hope World* mixtape. Using dance as a metaphor for the adrenaline rush of love-at-first-sight, its infectiously sunny mood is continued by the next three tracks, originally from *Love Yourself: Her* – Jimin's solo 'Serendipity' (this time a full-length version), 'DNA' and 'Dimple'.

RM's 'Trivia: Love', in which he deliberates the ending of a relationship over a bouncy but minimal instrumental changes the mood, and there is room for one more *Her* track, the rap line's outro 'Her' which explores the complexities, contradictions and pressures of love. Suga's jazzy 'Trivia: Seesaw', comparing the ups and downs of a relationship with being on a seesaw, is surprisingly funky and upbeat, and also features the rapper flexing his vocal skills – he sings, rather than raps, for much of the track. His 'someone just needs to quit the relationship' message, along with another former outro in the bitter break-up wake-up call, 'Tear', ushers in the final section of the main CD.

The four new tracks which complete the first disc confirm the group's maturity in terms of message and their music. They are superbly produced and performed and carry a clear message that not only complements and completes the whole *Love Yourself* narrative, but presents a philosophy that is confident and relevant to their young listeners: loving oneself is where true love begins. The first of these is Jin's 'Epiphany', an uplifting solo ballad sung with strength and sensitivity, it carries the core message that being able to love and accept yourself is the precursor to truly being able to love others. This is followed by 'I'm Fine', a euphoric EDM track whose defiant message of self-reliance answers 2016's 'Save Me'.

'IDOL' is the perfect celebration of this freedom, a project finale party bursting with pride, joy and self-affirmation. With unstoppable power the group take ownership of what they are and revel in it in a fun, chant-along dance number that maintains its intensity from start to finish. The rhythm that drives the song derives from the stripped-back, drum-heavy Gqom-style house music which originated in South Africa. BTS are clearly wearing their global credentials on their sleeve, but the song is also full of Korean instruments and influences such as the *chuimsae*, exclamations that are a feature of the traditional storytelling style of *pansori*.

The final track flips the album title to 'Answer: Love Myself' and provides an upbeat and soulful reflection of the *Love Yourself* process: 'the me of yesterday, the me of today, the me of tomorrow'. After the fun of the autotune gimmickry on 'IDOL', it's refreshing and uplifting to hear the true vocals delivering a classic BTS number with a lavish synth instrumental, rap verses and melodic two-part choruses.

The *Love Yourself* project had been a massive endeavour, fostering soul-searching and philosophical questioning. Amazingly, over the two and a half years, BTS had continued to produce superb pop songs outside the overriding theme. These were collected in a second disc which included 'Magic Shop', 'Go Go', 'Anpanman' and 'MIC Drop', remixes of 'DNA' and 'Fake Love', and the Steve Aoki 'MIC Drop' remix without the guest verse from Desiigner.

The album was an instant international success. It reached number one in South Korea, Japan and the US, and the top ten in charts around the world, from Mexico to Canada and from Finland to Australia. Many critics followed the lead of *Billboard* K-pop specialist Tamar Herman, who called the album, 'A masterful culmination of years of work and rife with meaning … undeniably a magnum opus from BTS that few other artists, boy bands or otherwise, ever can hope to achieve.'

'IDOL' was the obvious choice for a single and a video accompanied the release. A riot of colour and movement, it incorporated traditional Korean images such as the rabbit in the moon, the tiger and the yellow Gyeonghoeru Pavilion (a Seoul landmark) along with references to previous videos and drawings by the members, including Jimin and Jung Kook's dragons, Suga's BT21 character Shooky and Jin's whale. The boys, sporting the hair colours revealed at the concert in June (although RM now had silvery locks) wore chevrons, paisley and African patterned suits, and, again taking pride in their own culture, designer-styled traditional Korean *hanbok*. Similarly, the choreography drew influence from Africa as well as Korea (and is that a twerk, Jung Kook?) in a routine they agreed was their toughest yet.

The 'IDOL' video clocked up 49.5 million viewers overnight, making it the most-watched music video in its first twenty-four hours online. The track replicated the success of the album around the world, including securing a K-pop act's first ever Top 40 hit single in the UK, where it reached number twenty-one. Meanwhile, an alternative version of the song, featuring none other than US superstar Nicki Minaj as a guest rapper, appeared as a bonus track on the digital album.

A new video, featuring an insert of a colourfully suited Minaj dropped in early September, but those who didn't watch to the end might have missed another addition: various clips of members of the public trying out some of the dance moves appeared with the caption #IDOLCHALLENGE. The hashtag started when @sonia_oolo uploaded a video of a young boy performing some of the choreography. All around the world ARMY were soon joining in and J-Hope even posted his own – immaculate – effort while the band were filming their latest *Bon Voyage* in Malta. The vacation series once again produced some quality moments, including Suga teaching Jung Kook to drink Irish whiskey, the boys re-enacting V's K-drama *Hwarang* and the enduring strength of V and Jimin's relationship ('the friendship trip starts when Taehyung gets here,' says Jimin in anticipation of V's late arrival).

The *Love Yourself* concept had been a triumph for BTS, but for them it was more than an idea on which to base recordings. They meant it. In November 2017, they had launched the Love Myself campaign in support of UNICEF's #ENDviolence initiative, aimed at ending young people having to live in fear of violence. BTS and ARMY had promoted and donated to the massively successful project and as a result in September 2018 the group were invited to attend the United Nations to launch a new global youth initiative, Generation Unlimited.

BANGTAN BOMB

THE DAY WHEN '김연탄 (KIMYEONTAN)' CAME TO THE BROADCASTING STATION – BTS (방탄소년단)

Yeontan is a black and tan teacup Pomeranian – an unquestionably cute little puppy who is only a year old when this was shot. He is V's dog (which explains the Kim Yeontan name), but all the boys make such a fuss over their little friend when he visits them at a TV station, he's practically the eighth member. Little 'Tannie' is just as adorable as they are as he skips from one to the other for hugs and attention. How can they refuse? Unbounded cuteness ensues as they play catch with him, let him lick their face and carry him to the window to see the outside world.

RM was incredibly honoured to address the General Assembly and in a poetic and passionate six-minute speech he talked, in excellent English, about the issue of self-acceptance and self-confidence. He spoke from the heart about his upbringing and his struggle to find his true identity while growing up, saying that, with his fellow members and ARMY's support, he had 'come to love myself for who I am, for who I was, and for who I hope to become'. His wish, he continued, was that others all around the globe could do the same.

North America had completely fallen for BTS. The Love Yourself World Tour visited cities across the US and Canada through September. They appeared on *America's Got Talent*, even teaching judge Tyra Banks a few moves from 'IDOL', and performed live in Times Square in their now iconic coloured suits for *Good Morning America*. Most fun was had with Jimmy Fallon on *The Tonight Show* where they joined the host in the Fortnite Dance Challenge where they replicate dances from the game. They boys completely aced it, with J-Hope's Orange Justice and The Robot the pick of the dances. The American leg of the tour culminated at Citi Field in New York City, where BTS became the first-ever Korean act to stage a solo stadium concert in the US.

BTS may have physically left the continent, but they would not easily be forgotten. In LA in October digital billboards appeared saying just 'BTS'. Every twenty-four hours a new letter appeared. What became the 'Great BTS Billboard Hunt' eventually revealed 'and Steve Aoki'. The 'MIC Drop' producer's new single 'Waste It On Me' was in effect BTS's first all-English release. RM and Jung Kook (although Aoki wouldn't name names!) provided smooth and spot-on English vocals, with Jimin providing background harmonies, on a catchy EDM bop as they respond to a potential lover saying that love is a waste of time. Though the track didn't reach the heights of recent BTS singles it still charted around the world and reached number one in Malaysia and two in Singapore.

In Japan, 'Waste It On Me' climbed to number nineteen, but not for the first time South Korea-Japan relations were proving problematic. First, BTS had planned to release a new track, 'Bird', as their ninth Japanese single. However, it was replaced by a Japanese version of 'Airplane pt. 2' and 'Fake Love' when some Koreans protested against the lyricist, Yasushi Akimoto, a well-known Japanese songwriter, who had expressed controversial views on Japanese history. Then BTS's appearance on Japanese TV was cancelled when an old photo of Jimin was uncovered that showed him wearing a T-shirt that celebrated Korea's independence and liberation from Japanese rule. Soon, however, Japanese BTS fans were able to show their feelings by packing out the 50,000-capacity Tokyo Dome for the Love Yourself concert. At the end of the evening, Jimin spoke to the audience, saying that his 'heart hurts' at recent events and how proud he was of the Japanese fans' love for BTS.

Such upset would not be allowed to spoil a glorious year for BTS. At the major award ceremonies the boys shone. At the 2018 MMAs, in addition to receiving *daesangs* for the Artist of the Year and Album of the Year, BTS put on an incredible stage performance. Especially memorable was the intro to 'IDOL' which was accompanied by traditional instruments such as the *daegeum* (bamboo flute) while the group paid tribute to traditional Korean culture. Along with a cast of talented dancers, J-Hope performed the *samgomu* drum dance, Jimin performed a *buchaechum* fan dance (traditionally only performed by women), and Jung Kook performed a *talchum* mask dance.

Just two weeks later at the MAMAs in Hong Kong – where they picked up two more *daesangs* – BTS left a more modern impression. The opening of their performance of 'Airplane pt. 2' required Jung Kook to walk the long stage like a runway. He strutted, twirled and smouldered with breathtaking style. Social media was alight, and when someone on Twitter set a clip of it to Beyonce's 'Partition' it went viral, racking up 5 million views in a matter of hours.

TWENTY-THREE

A BTS UNIVERSE

As a group BTS were reaching unchartered heights. As well as dominating the Korean music awards, they had finished 2018 as the second-highest album seller (behind Eminem) in the USA, the video for 'DNA' became the first K-pop group MV ever to surpass the 600 million mark on YouTube, and they broke their own record by picking up five Japan Golden Disc Awards.

The winter had also seen many of them successfully furthering their solo careers too. RM had set things rolling with *mono.*, his first mixtape since 2015's *RM*. The introspective and soulful tracks were critically acclaimed and commercially successful – especially the single 'forever rain'. Then at the 2018 MGA (MBC Plus X Genie Music Awards), Jung Kook joined Charlie Puth to sing 'We Don't Talk Anymore', a duet ARMY had been pining for since JK covered the song in 2017.

Just minutes into 2019, Jimin made his first solo foray with 'Promise', a tender and uplifting love song set to an acoustic guitar, with lyrics penned by Jimin himself. The track racked up 8.5 million streams in just twenty-four hours: a new SoundCloud record. V followed in his friend's footsteps with his January release, composing, writing the lyrics and taking the cover photo for 'Scenery'. Suga, meanwhile, had contributed a chilled-out rap verse to Lee Sora's ballad 'Song Request'.

They were back together in February for the 2019 Grammy Awards in LA – their first visit to the prestigious awards. *Love Yourself: Tear*, nominated for Best Recording Package, was the first Korean album ever to be recognized by the Academy. It didn't win, but the boys sure made their mark, from their immaculate matching black tuxedos to their presentation of the Best R&B album to H.E.R. to the camera cutaways which showed them singing and dancing as Dolly Parton and Miley Cyrus sang 'Jolene'.

While the growing ranks of ARMY feasted on the footage of their idols among the elite of the music world, many had also been watching them in an alternative reality. The official webtoon *Save Me* was a comic series created by an artist named Lico and set in the BTS Universe (BU) which began in *The Most Beautiful Moment in Life* era. The sharply-drawn series follows the members in cartoon form in an exciting and sometimes emotional storyline that referenced BTS videos and notes of the past few years. It answers some of the riddles such as whether Jin is a time traveller, who V killed and if Suga survived the fire, but it set just as many new theories in motion. For those truly engrossed, an official book called *Notes 1* was published in Korean, Japanese and English in March 2019 in which the Bangtan Universe was explored through diary entries of the members' alternate-universe characters.

Back in the real world, Big Hit Entertainment had debuted their first new group since BTS. Tomorrow X Together, also known as TXT, are a five-member boy group with, at debut, an average age of seventeen. BTS were proud and supportive of their 'younger brothers' and passed on the lesson they had learned from Bang Si-hyuk: 'Always remember the importance of the team.' TXT certainly had a flying start when their debut, 'Crown', broke the record for the most viewed K-pop debut music video within twenty-four hours.

Once the excitement over TXT had subsided, BTS had their own news to share. A new album, *Map of the Soul: Persona*, would be released on 12 April 2019. The trailer, 'Persona' (which was also the album's opening track), a powerful rap backed by some screeching guitar, was a solo effort from RM. It laid out the theme of the seven-track release as the dilemma of identity and self-worth. The concept for the *Map of the Soul* album series is based on Swiss psychoanalyst Carl Jung's theories of the human psyche:

the 'persona' is the role we choose to play in life; the 'shadow' is the hidden, less-expressed side of our character; and the 'ego' is our conscious thoughts, memories, and emotions.

BANGTAN BOMB

JACKET SHOOTING IN THE BATHROOM – BTS (방탄소년단)

This scene will be familiar to plenty of ARMY: too many people in the bathroom at once, all trying to find a corner of the mirror to check their appearance. In this case the magnificent seven are not in a club bathroom, but posing for their *Map of the Soul: Persona* concept photos. We get to see the boys in full make-up and silky finery as well as some heart-warming interactions. If the comments are anything to go by, it is V's blue-haired gorgeousness which garners most attention, but it is also clear that J-Hope is doing some serious bias-wrecking here.

The album's concept photos were presented in versions showing photo-booth-style shots, the boys prettying themselves in pyjamas in a pink bathroom, posing with roses and looking like designer-clothed Greek gods as they seductively pose with fruit. While some ARMY discussed how it related to 'Persona' and their public identity, others just delighted in the pastel luxuriousness, discussed the new hair colours – RM in platinum, Suga in purple, Jin's subtle brown-green, Jimin 'the human grapefruit' in coral peachy pink and V in an amazing electric blue – or just swooning over Jung Kook's magnificent *aegyo* as he holds cookies to his cheeks.

Map of the Soul: Persona was very much a measure of where BTS had found themselves in Spring 2019. They were able to throw out self-reverential echoes of their debut album, call in heavyweight hitters of the pop world as collaborators and pick from a smorgasbord of modern pop styles. Halsey joined them for the lead track, 'Boy With Luv' (the title a nod to 2014's 'Boy in Luv'), a funky summer pop smash with a light touch and hooks that stayed caught, while Ed Sheeran, although not heard on 'Make It Right', co-wrote and produced the Western-style R&B number in which Jung Kook's falsetto stands out.

At their album press conference J-Hope talked of the track 'Mikrokosmos' as being 'about our interest and love for the world around us and the people around us'. The hushed lo-fi vocals of the song are contrasted by an anthemic feel and driving beat in another complex but smooth production. 'Home' narrows the focus to ARMY who are the home the band return to for strength when things get tough. The song mirrors lines from 'Magic Shop' as the rap parts blend perfectly with the soulful vocals.

The subunit track 'Jamais Vu' (featuring Jung Kook, Jin and J-Hope) talks of the pain felt despite making the same mistake in a relationship over and again, with sumptuous dovetailing vocals rising and falling in emotional intensity. Then, rounding off the album, the rap-heavy, raucous 'Dionysus' rants and raves with style and energy as the vocal line sing like a heavenly choir in the background. A beautiful chaos, it calls on the spirit of the Greek god of wine to inform their creative process, saying art is alcohol too, so drink it up.

Map of the Soul: Persona marked the start of a new era for BTS. They sounded more assured and indulged Western listeners with the Halsey and Ed Sheeran collaborations, but retained the BTS signature vocal mix, genre fusion, lyrical excellence and distinct individual contributions. For the first time, BTS found themselves with a number-one album in the UK as well as in New Zealand and Australia, while going straight to the top of the Billboard 200 made them the first band since The Beatles to have three number-one albums in less than a year. At home, it fared even better: by May it had become the best-selling South Korean album of all time.

The video for 'Boy With Luv' was released on YouTube on 12 April. It was a feel-good fantasy painted in cotton-candy colours and bathed in sunshine. Retro-styled with pastel sets depicting a movie theatre, a parking lot, a diner, a stage lit up by neon signs bearing the names of previous BTS hits, as well as a big yellow sofa (ft. Halsey), the video dispenses with plot and opts for dancing, smiles, the cutest of outfits and a nod to the classic Gene Kelly movie *Singin' in the Rain*. Guinness World Records were soon rewriting their entry for most viewed YouTube video in twenty-four hours – not just K-pop or MV but *any* video! It had nearly 75 million views, and within forty hours it had reached 100 million.

Their live comeback stage took place on the US TV show *Saturday Night Live*. In black suits and colourful shirts the seven members, accompanied by a live band, filled the show's tiny stage, but the choreography still shone. As complex as ever, it conveyed a chilled and playful feeling with leg flicks, skips, smiles and an overall sense of unity and friendship. Back home they began an intense two-week promotion of the song (whose Korean title translates as 'A Poem for the Small Things') on the music shows. They kept winning and winning, and a ninth consecutive triumph on *Show! Music Core* in June marked the song's twenty-first win overall – surpassing the twenty-first-century record set by Psy's 'Gangnam Style'. At the Billboard Music Awards in Las Vegas on 1 May, they performed live with Halsey for the first time. With a bigger vocal part than in the video version, Halsey fitted in perfectly, looking the part and nailing the choreography. Online, some fans were even calling her 'the eighth member' – high praise indeed.

On 4 May 2019 in Pasadena, California, BTS began the Love Yourself: Speak Yourself leg of their world tour. Despite playing stadiums bigger than they had ever played outside South Korea, the dates sold out as fast as the technology could manage. The group were soon adding more dates to the schedule in America, Brazil and Europe. The setlist was an updated version of the Love Yourself tour (a mix of *Love Yourself* singles and album tracks, fan favourites, and solo stages for each member) with a few songs from the new *Map of the Soul: Persona* album. Many fans were just as excited about the stage outfits; one of the most talked about fashion designers, Dior's Kim Jones, had created seven sets of clothing especially for the tour, with each member choosing the look they wanted. The result was a futuristic/utilitarian style with Dior's trademark shiny and lamé fabrics to the fore, which featured bomber jackets and cargo trousers with harnesses, buckles and specially designed industrial-style chains, which worked perfectly for the rap line's blistering 'Tear' before they were joined by the rest of the group for an explosive performance of 'MIC Drop'.

Despite playing to over 600,000 people across six shows in the US, hundreds of fans still camped out for days ahead of a free mini show for *Good Morning America*'s Summer Concert at New York's Central Park on 15 May. However, it was the following evening's *The Late Show with Stephen Colbert* which made headlines: BTS were performing in the very studio in which The Beatles had made their iconic 1964 US television debut on *The Ed Sullivan Show*. The similarities of a band taking America by storm with a legion of adoring fans was not lost on the producers; styled as The Beatles, with mop-top haircuts and 60s suits, they performed 'Boy With Luv'. Ed Sullivan had introduced The Beatles with nicknames, calling Paul McCartney 'the cute one'. Colbert followed suit, but called each member of BTS 'the cute one'. It was a hoot.

The tour moved onto São Paulo and then to London, where they played the iconic Wembley Stadium. 'This is the performance we've all been waiting for. We're going to do our best to write our history,' said J-Hope. Suga added, 'We still feel like we're walking through our dreams. We feel like we're pioneers.' Over 120,000 audience members attended the two sold-out shows, with 140,000 more watching a livestream. The members confessed they had grown up watching videos of the Live Aid concert at Wembley and, during the encore, paid tribute to Freddie Mercury, as Jin led the crowd in the Queen frontman's memorable 'ay-oh' chant. Two nights at Paris's Stade de France completed the European leg of the tour, with the first of these marked by a surprise guest appearance from Halsey.

BTS had a month break before the Japanese leg, but there was no let-up on the activity. Each week saw new BTS singles released in the run-up to the launch of a new mobile game called *BTS World* – a story-based simulation in which players manage the band's career and the individual lives of alternate-timeline members (not the BU alternate timeline, though!). The uptempo EDM 'Dreamglow' found Jin, Jimin and Jung Kook collaborating with Charli XCX; 'A Brand New Day', a breezy track featuring a Korean flute, teamed J-Hope and V with Swedish singer Zara Larsson and 'All Night' paired US emo-rapper Juice WRLD with RM and Suga in a '90s-style hip-hop track.

A full-length soundtrack album titled *BTS World: Original Soundtrack* accompanied the game's release and included another single, this time featuring the whole group. 'Heartbeat' is a hymn to ARMY and a celebration of mutual love. Tying in to the theme of the game, the slow-burning, anthemic pop song tells of the destiny that connects the group with their fans. The other seven tracks on the album were fun instrumental themes for each member's alternate life.

Less than a week later, BTS dropped another single and another ode to their co-dependence with ARMY. This time it took the form of a Japanese-language track called 'Lights'. A swirling, comforting power ballad, it features strong vocals from all the members – even the rap line. The accompanying video features the seven inside a movie theatre, where the scenes of loneliness and friendship not only play on the emotions but kept ARMY busy guessing at the deeper meaning.

By the time they arrived in Japan in early July, 'Lights' was the top track in the country and broke their own record ('Fake Love') for highest sales in a single day by a foreign artist in Japan. The massive crowds who filled the stadiums in Osaka and Shizuoka would not hear 'Lights' live, but were ecstatic to hear the Japanese versions of 'IDOL' and 'Boy With Luv', which had been released with the single.

BTS had worked non-stop for six years since their debut (not to mention their previous exertions as trainees). Their lives had been a constant parade of recordings, promotions and concerts. So although it came out of the blue, Big Hit Entertainment's announcement on Twitter that they would be taking an official break in August made perfect sense. They wrote that it would give the members an opportunity 'to recharge and prepare to present themselves anew as musicians and creators', and added: 'This will also provide them with a chance to enjoy the ordinary lives of young people in their 20s, albeit briefly.' It was virtually impossible to find anyone who said they didn't deserve it.

TWENTY-FOUR

SEVEN

What was a dedicated ARMY to do as BTS took their vacation in August 2019? First, they did what they always do: continued supporting the group by streaming their songs – including RM's recent guest spot on 'Seoul Town Road', a remix of Lil Nas X's 'Old Town Road'. Second, they looked after their idols, reminding everyone to give them space. And third, they made their own entertainment. They created all kinds of memes with one in particular going viral. This featured various clips – from Harry Potter to Spongebob to Peppa Pig – interrupted by V singing his 'crazy for myself' line from 'Home'. Well, whatever gets you through the long Bangtan-less hours!

Through August and September, the BTS members took it easy. They caught up with family and friends and headed off on short trips. They still kept in contact with ARMY though, posting photos – RM at an art exhibition, V's trip to Jeju island with his friends, Jimin in Paris, Jin and Suga on a fishing trip, Jung Kook celebrating his birthday and J-Hope on the way to LA – and recording vlogs to be released later in the year.

It was fascinating how the different members chose to spend their time. RM spoke of visiting over fifty museums and galleries, Jimin had got his driving licence and had been cruising all around and Jin rather ashamedly admitted he had played video games for sixteen hours on five consecutive days! J-Hope had been more productive. Out in LA he had recorded 'Chicken Noodle Soup' with Latina singer Becky G, a cover of a 2006 dance number by Webstar and Young B. The song, along with a colourful, energetic and infectious video, was released as the hiatus came to a close and was a big favourite with ARMY around the world, especially as the hilarious flapping elbow chicken dance went viral.

Their break ended with the members all coming together for a *Bon Voyage* trip to New Zealand. What is truly incredible is that these guys have known each other for ten years now and, having spent just a few weeks apart, reunite like brothers – truly pleased to see one another and perfectly comfortable in each other's company. As much fun as it is watching them sing cartoon themes and their own songs as they drive along in a campervan and an SUV or enjoying the outdoor activities of New Zealand, it is the beautiful interactions of the members which is the enduring highlight of the series.

Their first engagement following their rest and relaxation was a show in Saudi Arabia. They were officially invited to be the first-ever foreign artists to perform at the King Fahd International Stadium in Riyadh and on their arrival, the city's buildings were lit in purple to welcome them. The group modified some of their choreography out of respect for local culture, but fans were as vociferous and adoring as anywhere in the world, especially as they helped celebrate Jimin's birthday.

BTS had returned refreshed and triumphant and ARMY were once more having to keep up with the content. A remix of 'Make it Right' featuring US singer Lauv was released; over 2 million viewed the Love Yourself tour movie *Bring the Soul*; and thousands visited the 'House of BTS' pop-up store in Seoul, an interactive experience which allowed fans to pose with iconic sets from videos and photoshoots. And then there was TikTok…

Just days after they ended their vacation, Big Hit tweeted: '#BTS TikTok Channel Open!' ARMY, of course, responded. They helped BTS set a record after three and a half hours for the fastest an account hit a million followers and, by the end of the week, had taken the total to 100 million. Fans knew how much fun the boys could have with the app and were not disappointed. Almost immediately, they were joining in the Chicken Noodle

Soup challenge. Inspired by J-Hope's collaboration with Becky G, fans posted their own, sometimes hilarious, attempts at his arm-flapping dance.

BTS marked the grand finale of their tour in October with three nights at the Jamsil Olympic Stadium in Seoul. They were emotional and thrilling shows, finishing with 300 lit-up drones forming planets and the BTS and ARMY symbols above the stadium during the final song, 'Mikrokosmos'. 'This *Love Yourself, Speak Yourself* concept ends here, but the journey to search how to love ourselves will continue,' said RM in a beautifully fitting climax to an incredible era.

It wasn't completely over, though, as the awards season helped ARMY relive the group's achievements. BTS swept the board at the MTV Europe Awards, the Teen Choice Awards and V Live's V Heartbeat Awards and ARMY eagerly awaited the major ceremonies. First up was the MMAs. They had won plaudits with their performance the previous year, but this was even more spectacular with a set that included a Greek temple, Jin riding a huge Trojan Horse, a floating galaxy, aerial dancers, and a water tank (for Jung Kook's steamy solo stage). Their performance was a fabulous mini-concert of recent songs mixed in with tracks going right back to their debut, giving each member a chance to shine individually. If this wasn't enough for ARMY, BTS also became the first act ever to win all of the major awards as they collected the *daesangs* for Album of the Year, Record of the Year, Song of the Year and Artist of the Year.

Against this achievement it seemed astonishing that BTS were once again completely overlooked when the 2020 Grammy nominations were announced. Fortunately, the rival US awards, the AMAs, made no such oversight, honouring them with the Favorite Duo or Group Pop/Rock, Favorite Social Artist and Tour of the Year awards. Meanwhile, in Japan, BTS took the 2019 MAMAs by storm. They created history again as the first ever act to take home all four *daesangs* and became the first act to win four consecutive Artist of the Year awards. They closed the performance section with another staggering medley of old and new songs augmented with videos documenting some of the ups and downs of their career in their 'eternal journey'.

ARMY might have been overwhelmed by the MAMAs performance,

but the fact they said they were preparing for their next album certainly didn't escape notice. On 7 January, the announcement finally came that the new album *Map of the Soul: 7* would drop on 21 February. It nearly broke the internet as ARMY celebrated the news and turned '#7isComing' into a trending hashtag.

Things happened fast. The first phase began on 9 January when Suga's fierce rap 'Interlude: Shadow' dropped as a comeback trailer. Continuing the Jungian themes of *Persona*, it set the stall for the album as it explored the price of fame and the conflict between Suga and Yoongi, the star and the man. Another track, 'Black Swan', soon followed as the first single from the album. BTS were already treading new ground. They didn't appear in the 'art film' video; instead, the Slovenian MN Dance Company performed an elegant and poignant interpretive dance choreographed especially for the song. The track was orchestral with heavily autotuned and dramatic vocals leading some to call it 'trap-ballet' (and the album version was different to the one that appeared in the video). A quote from legendary dancer Martha Graham, 'A dancer dies twice – once when they stop dancing, and this first death is the more painful,' opens the video. This theme of the artist's attachment and dependence on their creative powers forms the inspiration for the lyrics as the group dive deep into the hidden aspect of their souls.

Between these two statements of intent, BTS launched a unique project called *CONNECT, BTS*: a global art series that spanned five cities and twenty-two artists. The initiative took BTS's vision of connectivity and solidarity into the realm of visual art through free exhibitions showing original work of great artists commissioned by the group themselves. These included a virtual journey through an imagined forest by Danish artist Jakob Kudsk Steensen, environmental artist Tomás Saraceno's solar-powered hot-air balloon and Antony Gormley's bridge installation in New York.

The lead-up to the album was interrupted at the end of January by the immovable Grammys. Though incomprehensibly overlooked for an award, they still attended the star-studded ceremony. On the red carpet *Elle* magazine reported that they 'upped the bar for all men's award show fashion' as they turned out in coordinated Bottega Veneta neutral-toned trench coats. V made a particular impression with casual viewers as many asked who the 'man in black' was. He endeared himself further when he grabbed the mic and said: 'I'm a little shy but I want to say I love you ARMY.' Inside, Alicia Keys sang of how 'we obsessed about BTS' in her special Grammy song and the group sent out another reminder to the judges of their talent as they took to the stage with Lil Nas X for his 'Old Town Road All Stars' performance, becoming the first K-pop group to perform at the prestigious ceremony.

While in LA it would be churlish not to look up their new best friend, James Corden. On his *Late Late Show* they debuted 'Black Swan', appearing in black suits and bare feet to dance an intense routine (by Brazilian choreographer Sergio Reis) in front of a backdrop of a mystical forest, with a waterfall and a floor made to look like a pool of water. They danced to the streaming version of the song, which retained the ominous feel of the 'art film' track but with a hard EDM beat and electric guitars.

BTS REACTS TO BTS DEBUT +5 DAYS - BTS (방탄소년단)

It was just five days after their debut and they were all younger than Jung Kook is now. Fresh-faced, earnest and shy, they line up for one of their first interviews. In this charming bomb, the boys look back on the footage themselves when they all wore shirts bearing their names – just until they are famous enough that people can tell them apart, explains RM. The BTS of 2020 react with just the right measure of embarrassment and pride. J-Hope might try to shoo his younger self off the screen, but they genuinely realize who they were and what they went through made them what they are today. They are not just putting out the 'love yourself' message; they are living it themselves...

If the two tracks released so far had led fans to think the album would be dark, then the next release, 'Outro: Ego' came as a surprise. A video that is infectious and full of colour and smiles (and gorgeous photos of Hoseok as a child) rings out with a joyous afro-beat-infused rap track. J-Hope's song, in the upbeat style of his solo work, finds him looking to his past struggles and the choices he made. It concludes with the optimistic realisation that he must understand and accept himself and choose his own fate.

Then it was time for concept photos. Pregnant with meaning, they reflected the themes of the album as they touched on the idea of acknowledging our unconscious selves. The first two sets presented a stark contrast. While the first found them by a deep abyss, dressed completely in white with small white feathers falling around them, in the second set they were kitted out in black with wings sitting by a dark lake. As fans debated the photos, the focus fell on Jimin and Jung Kook. While the sight of Jimin with bright blue hair caused many a sharp intake of breath, it was the pair of them in black corsets which really got everyone talking. The third set saw them looking cool, suave and suited at a lavish Renaissance-style feast, while the final photos, representing 'their true selves', were playful, boyish and full of smiles.

Map of the Soul: 7 was released on 21 February 2020 to rapturous acclaim from critics and fans. It was praised for its grand ambition, its effortless cross-genre compositions, heart-rending pitch-perfect vocals and spine-chilling melodies, and for its sophisticated lyrical approach: the search for truth, connecting the personal and the public and the refusal to patronise even younger listeners

The album features twenty tracks – five from *Map of the Soul: Persona,* fourteen new tracks (including the three that had already been released as teasers), and one digital-only bonus remix of lead single 'ON' featuring the Australian singer Sia. On top of the group songs, each of the members has a solo track and a subunit track, and there are rap line and vocal line songs too. It was truly a team effort, with each member contributing to the writing of at least one song. The title, *7*, referenced the seven members' journey through the seven years since their debut. At the album launch, Jin described the album as a 'confession' of their personal growth, including their highs and lows, while RM described his contribution to the songwriting as an emotional experience, reliving the past seven years.

This confessional and personal perspective is taken up by the first two of the album's yet-to-be-heard tracks. Firstly Jimin's solo track 'Filter' finds him reflecting on the different faces he presents to the world over a flowing Latin guitar accompaniment. Then Jung Kook's smooth R&B number 'My Time' likens his years growing up in BTS to living in a movie, always under the spotlight.

Then follow two group songs which progress the philosophy. 'Louder than bombs' – co-written with Allie X and Troye Sivan – brings many musical elements together in a ballad that surges and smothers with a wave of layered vocals and Jung Kook's incredible falsettos. It tells of facing pain and difficult times and overcoming it. To paraphrase J-Hope: 'Keep fighting. Don't be afraid of the dark.' The album's lead single, 'ON', comes next, with a similar theme. Inverting the title of their previous hit 'N.O', it is a swaggering anthem filled with brass and percussion, a defiant acceptance of pain and darkness as part of life that you will fight and win.

The rap line takes over for 'UGH!', a track reminiscent of the early cyphers and *festa*-favourite 'Ddaeng', as they spit fierce lines about people who hide their malicious anger behind anonymity over a trap beat. RM and Suga return to this theme later in the album, in a slightly more relaxed manner, as 'Respect' debates the word and concept. Confident, relaxed and nimble, they even throw in some *satoori* chat at the end – another nod to their early days.

The vocal line dominate the second half of the album with Jin, V, Jimin, and Jung Kook combining on '00:00 (Zero O'Clock)'. At times unbearably sad, then defiantly optimistic, the beautifully-sung track maintains the 'keep going, happiness is around the corner' theme. Then V's solo 'Inner Child' addresses his younger self in a touching account of self-discovery and change. It manages to be both intimate and anthemic as it reaches the chorus and was a track that ARMY immediately took to their hearts. Jin's upbeat and poppy 'Moon' takes up the album's other theme of the group's relationship with ARMY. He's called beautiful, he admits in the song, but it is the fans who have the real beauty. The love and sincerity in his delivery is striking as he explains how he will be the Moon to their Earth. In between these tracks lies the soul-warming duet 'Friends' sung by V and Jimin, with the pair once again finding comfort in many years of ups and downs and emerging with a stronger-than-ever bond.

'We are Bulletproof: The Eternal', the album's penultimate track, brings the shadow theme and the group's ties with ARMY together. Referencing the pre-debut 'We Are Bulletproof Pt. 1' and 'We Are Bulletproof Pt. 2' from their debut album (which 'The Eternal' samples), the song celebrates how they have overcome their hardships and grown stronger and united with their fans. Although a ballad that is tear-jerking in its emotional punch, it builds to a chorus that seems guaranteed to rouse fans at live shows – literally bringing the group and ARMY together.

It is left to the group's sunshine, the optimistic J-Hope, to complete the album with his 'Outro: Ego' which had served as a comeback trailer. With this uplifting and powerful message, BTS signed off on their most ambitious album yet – both musically and thematically. There was no doubt that it would be a commercial success (there were more than 4 million pre-orders) but the immense challenge was to justify the hype and hysteria that surrounded the release. It was one they had risen to with confidence and style.

TWENTY-FIVE

PANDEMIC

Map of the Soul: 7 was a global triumph – an instant commercial success unrivalled by any K-pop acts and one that put them in the highest echelon of pop artists. It went to number one in countries where they had already established a reputation, such as South Korea, Japan, the US, the UK and Australia, but also broke new ground, topping charts in Germany, Ireland and France and many other countries.

After a thirty-second trailer had crashed TikTok the day before, a video for 'ON' dropped on the same day as the album. Titled 'Kinetic Manifesto Film: Come Prima', it featured the boys by the Sepulveda Dam in Los Angeles performing a high-energy choreography accompanied by The Lab, winners of the US TV series *World of Dance* and the Blue Devils Drum and Bugle Corps. It was viewed 46.5 million times in the first twenty-four hours – a staggering figure, but one that hardly seems surprising for BTS!

Although they planned to return to South Korea to promote the album, BTS first took to late-night US television. On 24 February *The Tonight Show* dedicated an hour-long episode to the group. They rode on the New York subway with host Jimmy Fallon, made pastrami sandwiches at the famous Katz's Deli and, most stunning of all, they brought the whole dance ensemble from the video to a deserted Grand Central Station in New York for a jaw-dropping performance of 'ON'. The following evening saw them joining James Corden for 'Carpool Karaoke', a section of his *Late Late Show* that ARMY had been demanding they appear on for some time. They didn't disappoint. All seven of them squeezed into Corden's SUV and along with jokes and laughs, sang along to Bruno Mars and Cardi B's 'Finesse', Post Malone's 'Circles' and a few of their own songs, before joining James in his dance class.

The official music video for 'ON' dropped on 28 February 2020 and it was epic, looking more like a blockbuster movie trailer than a music video. It placed the boys in the wake of a battle and escaping a walled land. The allusions to dystopian movies such as *The Hunger Games*, *The Maze Runner*, *Divergent* and *Lord of the Flies* were clear, with other less obvious nods to *Bird Box* and *Game of Thrones*, and a lot of biblical references thrown in too – most obviously Noah's Ark. Once again BTS would break YouTube records: 1.5 million people watched the 'ON' premiere live, and there were 10 million views in just over an hour. While BTS online forums debated what it all could have meant, most agreed that Jimin's blue hair and Jung Kook's blue highlights were things of beauty.

Just a week later, to ARMY's complete surprise, BTS dropped an official MV for 'Black Swan' – and it was stunning. Shot in the deserted and opulent LA Theatre, the video offered a visual representation of the album's themes as the members change from black to white suits and interact with their shadows. The choreography, intense with incredible solo work (especially Jimin's), followed that performed on *The Late Late Show* – it was serious and breathtaking. ARMY wasted no time in getting the word out, with a million #BlackSwan tweets making it the biggest global hashtag on Twitter in a matter of hours.

BTS returned to South Korea to promote the album but landed in a country in deep alarm over the unfolding Covid-19 pandemic. They performed on *M Countdown* and *Inkigayo* with no studio audience and were forced to cancel their four shows at Seoul's Olympic Stadium. Suga, who grew up in the city of Daegu, the centre of the outbreak, donated 100 million won (US$83,000) to the Hope Bridge Korea Disaster Relief

Association and his generosity inspired many fans to donate their ticket refunds from the cancelled Seoul tour dates too.

BTS's epic performances on the award shows had promised something really special for their upcoming Map of the Soul world tour. The extravagant sets and the sheer quality of the new material, including possible solo stages for every member, had driven ARMY expectations to fever pitch. However, with the pandemic becoming more serious by the day, there was no option but to postpone the thirty-seven-date tour, which was due to begin the following month in Santa Clara, California.

Such was the uncertainty with which Covid-19 gripped the world, the tour remained temporarily 'postponed' for over a year. Live entertainment, with audiences necessarily in close contact, was a sector that was hit particularly hard. For groups such as BTS, who thrived on their connection with fans, being unable to perform was even more of a challenge. Anyone who has followed their history knows these boys – and their legions of fans – rise to a challenge. And so it was with Covid-19.

The Weverse series *Learn Korean with BTS*, which featured thirty weekly releases of three-minute episodes using clips from BTS reality shows, was already scheduled and began in March, but ARMY enjoyed a real treat at the end of March when the group appeared in James Corden's *HomeFest* special, which featured various global stars performing remotely. From their Seoul dance-practice room they performed a heart-warming 'Boy With Luv' that was super-casual, with V even dancing in slippers!

Through the tough months that followed, BTS members maintained their connection with ARMY through live broadcast, messages, online events and new music specifically designed to reflect the hardships of the pandemic. For fans confined to their home for most of the day, these were a lifesaver and they were boosted by impromptu interactions that now appeared regularly on V Live, YouTube Live, Twitter and Weverse.

The members appeared just to chat or to let fans know what they had been up to in quarantine. On Weverse, RM shared his wide-ranging book collection; Suga revealed his lyric notebooks and introduced his new passion for painting; Jimin held two surprise V Live sessions where he talked about movies he was enjoying (especially the 2009 blockbuster *3 Idiots*); J-Hope trended with his completely charming response to the TikTok six-second challenge and V set his own Stay At Home challenges on Twitter.

Big Hit also pitched in with their own BTS home entertainment by staging a free streaming event named Bang Bang Con (adding the Korean word 'bang', meaning 'room', to a shortening of the group's 'Bangtan'). Streamed for free on BTS's YouTube channel over two days in mid-April, the 'at-home BTS concert experience' featured eight concerts filmed between 2015 and 2018.

That weekend, some ARMY were still digesting RM's previous day's YouTube Live video log in which he revealed preparations for a new album and an intention to share the process with fans. Over the following months, group members posted regularly on the making of the album: they not only contributed to the writing and production of the songs, as usual, but also oversaw the concept photos, themes, design and music video, with each member taking charge of a different aspect.

The summer of 2020 continued to be ravaged by the pandemic, but BTS were never far away. Even ARMY were caught off-guard, though, when *D-2*, a second mixtape from Suga's alter-ego Agust D, dropped in May. Both it and 'Daechwita', the lead single from the album accompanied by a dramatic MV, were global chart hits and the talk of social media for some time.

June brought *festa* and, thankfully, Big Hit did not hold back. The usual family portraits included the satin pink outfits from 'Boy With Luv', while another set featured outfits from their solo performances on stage. Best of all was a third set that saw them go retro with 1960s-style black suits and ties matched with goofy coloured sunglasses (not forgetting Jung Kook with Elvis-style sideburns) – simultaneously fun and cool. It also featured photo-portraits and reminiscences from the *Map of the Soul* subunits, new choreography videos and a karaoke game, 'Map of the Song 7'.

In addition, the celebrations included an official animated MV for 'We Are Bulletproof: The Eternal', which plucked at the heartstrings as it took a nostalgic look back at the group's journey (with plenty of allusions to previous MVs to identify) and their bond with ARMY. However, for many, the most exciting was a special *festa* gift to ARMY. Fans had seen the title 'Still With You' on the *festa* schedule, but it was only at midnight on day five when it dropped on SoundCloud that they discovered it was the first-ever solo from Jung Kook. Produced by the singer with Pdogg, it was a delicious jazzy ballad with poignant and sincere lyrics telling of Jung Kook's feelings for ARMY. It is a track they still cherish.

BANGTAN BOMB

'MAP OF THE SONG: 7' BEHIND THE SCENES

BTS's *festa* 2020 karaoke game was brilliant. Divided into three units – Vminkook (Jimin, V and Jung Kook), Namjin (RM and Jin) and Sope (Suga and J-Hope) – they had to sing other member's songs to win a prize. The full video is available on YouTube too, but this is the chaotic, fun, hilarious version that shows off the chemistry between them to the full. Jimin, Jungkook and V going mad with the chance to rap, RM and Jin opening the door to see the *maknae* line causing mayhem, J-Hope's brilliant spontaneous dancing to Jung Kook's rendition of 'Moon' and so much more (usually involving Jimin).

As always, *festa* finished with a birthday party celebrating the anniversary of BTS's debut, but the fun hadn't finished. Somehow, they had to make up for ARMY missing out on the live events. The very next day was Bang Bang Con: The Live, with over 750,000 people from 107 regions across the globe streaming the live pay-per-view concert.

Despite having a Map of the Soul show ready for the tour, they put this aside for something specifically designed for fans in lockdown. Rather than an elaborate stadium concert, this was casual, light-hearted, warm and intimate, with viewers able to choose between six different camera angles, including one displaying a live chat, a virtual light stick and a world map showing the locations of watching fans.

Their 100-minute set was magical. It began with a nostalgic trip that included early tracks 'Dope', 'Boyz With Fun', 'Like' and the rarely seen 'Just One Day', including the much-loved chair choreography. A rotating stage then delivered the Map of the Soul subunits: ARMY at last getting to see Jin, Jung Kook and J-Hope perform 'Jamais Vu' as they took to a fabulous staircase set in matching outfits; then in a switch from monochrome to rainbow lighting and 1970s vibes, RM and Suga appeared in retro suits and tinted sunglasses, dazzling with their 'Respect' rap and choreography; finally Vmin (Jimin and V) stepped forward to perform 'Friends', comparing pinkies and holding hands and including a touching moment when, having finished the song, V alluded to the famous dumpling incident, saying: 'We're going to eat *mandu* [Korean dumplings] and not fight now, right?'

There was still time for a preview of the Map of the Soul tour with snippets of 'UGH!' and '00:00 (Zero O'Clock)', a full-length 'Black Swan' in a fairy-tale forest set and disco-style remix of 'Boy With Luv' to a backdrop of ARMY bombs. They finished with favourites 'Go Go', 'Anpanman' (accompanied by a giant flying ARMY bomb) and, of course, 'Spring Day', its comforting message more apt than ever.

It was everything ARMY could wish for, made extra special by the relaxed and friendly mood created by the members. Whether it was J-Hope distributing personalized bracelets to the other members, V jokingly accusing Jin of making up the compliments he received on the incoming ARMY messages, the group doing their own fan chant or saving a spot for ARMY in their final group hug, there was always love and friendship in the air.

This was the same spirit that had been evident when BTS had appeared on YouTube's 'Dear Class of 2020', a livestream event for graduating students of all levels whose ceremonies had been cancelled due to the pandemic. A whole host of stars from entertainment and sport had contributed messages or performances, but Beyoncé, Lady Gaga and BTS were the only celebrity speakers. Led by RM's words: 'You could be watching us from your bed or your living room alone, or with somebody. Wherever you are, you will all soon be breaking out of one world to soar into another,' all the members used the challenges they had faced to deliver inspiring message of patience, self-belief and the limitless opportunities that await. For many ARMY, though, it was Jimin's line that resonated most: 'Remember there is a person here in Korea, in the city of Seoul, who understands you.'

These qualities were never needed so much as in the days following the murder of George Floyd, an African-American man, by US police officers. BTS released a statement condemning racism and violence and supporting the Black Lives Matter movement. Along with Big Hit Entertainment, they donated US$1 million to the campaign – a sum that was matched by ARMY in less than a day.

In those times of uncertainty and anxiety, BTS seemed closer than ever to their ever-growing fandom. For many they were a reassuring voice and a connection to a bigger world. And they were a source of cheer – especially when new material was released. *Map of the Soul: 7 – The Journey*, BTS's first full-length Japanese album since 2018's *Face Yourself*, landed on 14 July. It contained Japanese versions of 'ON', 'Black Swan', 'Make It Right', and 'Dionysus', the 2019 Japanese single 'Lights', a new intro and outro and two new full-length songs.

The first of these was written as an original soundtrack for the Japanese drama series *Spiral Labyrinth – DNA Forensic Investigation*. 'Stay Gold' locked straight into the feelgood factor that BTS had promised to provide to their fans. A piano-based pop number with bouncing guitars and heavy drums, the instrumental was both comforting and uplifting. The lyrics followed suit, a declaration of love that demanded their object of affection carried on shining bright no matter what. With Jimin and Jung Kook's voices harmonizing and a chant-filled chorus, the tune takes off. It seemed to be just what the world needed in that moment.

The MV also reflected the harshness of the times and the sense of optimism that BTS sought. In the video each of the members are alone and seemingly trapped in secluded, dark and gloomy locations, but in their dreams (the choruses) they are together, enjoying simple pastimes and each other's company amid gently falling confetti in the soft golden light. As small glimpses of the light penetrate their dark confinement, they eventually join together in an earthly (ARMY-purple) paradise bathed in glorious sunshine. It has an ethereal atmosphere, but it is the resounding sense of joy that lives long after the song has ended.

Reaching 50 million views within five days, it soon became their most popular Japanese MV ever and topped iTunes charts in 82 regions, including the US, UK, Brazil, France and India. That was nearly double the record for any Japanese single (which was set by 'Lights'). The record did not last long, though. Within a month 'Your Eyes Tell', the other new full-length track on the album, had pushed the record to 92.

'Your Eyes Tell' had originally been written by Jung Kook for his as-yet-unreleased mixtape. It was the last version of the song submitted as an OST for the Japanese film *Kimino mega toikaketeiru* (which translates to 'Your Eyes Tell' and is a remake of the 2011 Korean film *Always*). The director was impressed enough to select it and to use it within the movie as well as over the end credits, as originally planned. It was BTS's first group OST, and the first time a foreign artist had written and performed an OST for a Japanese film.

It is a beautiful, utterly romantic ballad. The lyrics, which offset the thought of life without the one they love with an eternal belief that they will be together again, are heartbreaking, but underscored by an indefatigable optimism. The depth of emotion portrayed in the performance matches that of the lyrics with the stirring tones of the vocal line, including breathtaking high notes in the chorus, reinforced by the smooth, slow and sensitive lines delivered by the rap line. That Jung Kook had created such a captivating piece of music was an immediate source of pride for ARMY and for JK fans who had always believed in him.

BTS spent much of the early summer promoting the album in Japan, including debuting 'Stay Gold' on the famous show *CDTV Live! Live!* – kitted out in Dior suits, they sang sitting under a glowing tree in a white studio. But all this time, they had also secretly been working on something else. The first ARMY knew was in early August when, on a V Live broadcast, the members themselves announced that a new single – in English! – would be released later in the month. 'Dynamite' was coming, and it was explosive.

The teaser photos set the mood: vibrant and energetic with a retro vibe. The group seemed to be playing their own game, hiding their new hair colours from ARMY. RM took first prize for switching between brown and blond before revealing a return to the fan-favourite teal, which immediately prompted 'blue joon' to trend on Twitter; V kept his hair under a bucket hat before finally revealing a golden brown; while Jimin drew gasps around the world with his lavender-tinted locks. They don't call them teasers for nothing.

'Dynamite' was an antidote to the pandemic; a shot in the arm to put a smile on people's faces and a spring in their steps. It was written by British songwriting team Dave Stewart and Jessica Agombar, who had heard that the group were looking for an up-tempo and exciting English-language track. They hit the nail on the head with a disco-funk pop song – a twenty-first-century take on a Jacksons-style hit with lyrics that spoke of fun, confidence and hope.

The guitar bounces along, the groove never stops and the synth sprinkles glee like confetti. Singing the whole song in English was a new challenge, but the boys rise to the occasion. In harmony and solo, their vocals feed into and off one another. Uplifting, joyful, and with no intention but to provide cheer, it wore its heart on its sleeve.

The video pictured a retro American dream. Vibrant colours in glorious sunshine and cotton-wool clouds, an ice-cream van, a donut house, record store, basketball court, 1970s disco outfits and Michael Jackson dance references. All celebrated with a choreography that was simple and fun (even incorporating the TikTok 'hit the woah' move). They just wanted everyone up, on their feet and moving. YouTube records crumbled. The MV premiere was watched by over 3 million viewers, demolishing Blackpink's record; it amassed more than 10 million views in just 20 minutes and over 100 million in a day, making it the most viewed YouTube video in 24 hours.

BTS had always intentionally avoided releasing a full English-language single, but perhaps it was the Covid-19 situation, or the realization that to really crack the US market it was a necessity, that forced their hand. Either way, it worked. 'Dynamite' was a great summer single that cheered millions and charted in the top twenty in over thirty other countries around the world. It went straight to the top of the Billboard charts and soon returned for another week on top boosted by various remixes, including 'Poolside', 'Tropical', 'Bedroom', 'Midnight' and 'Slow Jam' versions. In all, it ended up spending thirteen weeks in the top ten, and thirty-two weeks on the Hot 100 chart.

In many ways 'Dynamite' wasn't a signature BTS song. It was a universal pop song, a summer bop. It could have been done by anyone – just not nearly as perfectly. But, in one move, just like that, BTS had taken another step to greatness. Certainly in America it was difficult to avoid them. They debuted the song at the 2020 MTV VMAs, performing remotely from Seoul, and collected the Best Group and Best Pop trophies as well as Best Choreography and Best K-Pop for 'ON'. In the following month they appeared on *The Today Show*, *America's Got Talent* and the (for this year, virtual) iHeart Radio Music Festival, before addressing an audience they had met before – the UN General Assembly.

As each of the members recounted their experience of the pandemic, they told of how their plans had been ripped apart and how their world was suddenly smaller and lonelier. And yet, they went on to deliver a message of hope and persistence, emphasizing the importance of knowing and loving yourself, connecting with family and friends and looking to the better times to come. 'Life goes on,' they said together. 'Let's live on.'

BTS had been true to their word of helping fans get through the weeks and then months of lockdown, illness and the effects of the pandemic, and they didn't let up. Their appearance on the iconic Tiny Desk series was particularly appreciated. Although unable to play in the familiar office in Washington, DC, they stayed true to the spirit of the show by performing with a stripped-back live band in the cramped space of a record store in Seoul. Dressed in oranges, reds and denim, they performed 'Dynamite', 'Save Me' and 'Spring Day', all comforting songs. The live band and the intimate surroundings brought out a unique vibe, with the clean vocals, spontaneous dancing, smiles and clear enjoyment all savoured by ARMY across the world.

It had been a long summer like no other. Like millions of ARMY on every continent, the day-to-day lives of the BTS members had radically changed almost overnight. For long periods they too had been confined to their homes and unable to meet friends or work. Nevertheless, they continued to hold true to what they said at the outset and reiterated at UN. They were patient, hopeful and determined to make lives better for those who looked to them.

TWENTY-SIX

ALONE AND TOGETHER

As autumn 2020 approached, the world was still in the grip of the pandemic. Many people were still in lockdown and any hopes of a let-up in the summer had been tempered by the clear threat of a second wave to come. There was no sign of the postponed Map of the Soul tour being rescheduled and the popular award shows and seasonal TV specials were set to be pre-recorded without a live audience. Undaunted by all this, BTS continued with their mission to connect with fans and do everything they could to help them through these troubled times.

The weekly V Live series *Run BTS!* was a highlight of the week for ARMY. All through the year the episodes (filmed many months in advance) of madcap competitions, pure silliness, occasional touching moments and most compellingly, the incredible chemistry between members, continued to delight. A particular favourite came in March with two episodes (97 and 98) of *Pyjama Party* where Chinese whispers somehow turned 'borahae' (V's 'I purple you') to 'ARMY', Jimin delighted with his sock sketches and they all brought ARMY to their knees with their now famous attempts at ASMR. The hundredth episode soon followed with a flower-arranging competition, but the series continued unabated until August.

Run BTS! took a short break while focus turned to their new eight-episode reality series, *BTS In the Soop*. They had been unable to film another *Bon Voyage* series due to the pandemic, so this was shot closer to home in the forest of Pyeongchang in South Korea (*soop* is Korean for 'forest'). There, the boys were left to recharge away from the stresses of the big city by gaming, cooking, playing with remote-control boats, fishing and of course music, which included spontaneously writing the theme tune for the series. As always there were plenty of laughs, but the lasting memories were from the quieter moments such as V floating along on his canoe singing the as-yet-unreleased 'Blue & Grey' (but in English), a touching one-to-one conversation between Suga and Jin, and late-night reminiscences from Jung Kook and V.

While *BTS In the Soop* showed the boys at leisure, the big screen showed BTS at work as *Break the Silence: The Movie* was released in cinemas in many of the countries not currently in lockdown. The movie gave fans a close-up view of the 2019 Love Yourself: Speak Yourself tour with footage from New York, Chicago, Brazil, London, France, Saudi Arabia, South Korea and Japan. This included fabulous scenes from Wembley Stadium and eye-opening backstage footage from the Saudi Arabia leg, but mostly it was a chance to delve deeper into the persona of each of the septet: how they deal with the rigors of touring, the love they receive and their own hardships, but also their sense of brotherhood, how they spend their free time and their ambitions for the future.

So much for the past. BTS were still out making their own history. In late September they also returned (while still in South Korea) to *The Tonight Show Starring Jimmy Fallon*, who dedicated a whole week to the group. Highlights included a new version of 'Dynamite' complete with a cappella accompaniment from the house band The Roots and Jimmy himself, the group in modern *hanbok* performing 'IDOL' after nightfall at Seoul's Gyeongbokgung Palace, a night of chatter and fun with Jimmy (including an entertaining 'Dance Your Feelings' game), and a very special version of 'Mikrokosmos', again performed in front of Gyeongbokgung.

Meanwhile, dedicated ARMY had picked up hints on Twitter and beyond that something else was going down. The dance track 'Savage Love (Laxed – Siren Beat)' had already been a summer hit for Jawsh 685 and Jason Derulo and had launched a dance challenge on TikTok. But on 2 October, a new remix dropped. It featured Suga and J-Hope rapping a new verse in Korean and a super-sweet chorus by Jung Kook, with the often-cherubic *maknae* stunning many by dropping the F-bomb amid his English lines. Boosted by BTS involvement, the song took off again, topping charts in more than sixty countries, including giving BTS their second number one on the Billboard Hot 100.

It was on this high that BTS held a two-day online concert, BTS Map of the Soul ON:E. Originally intended as an in-person and online concert to recompense ARMY for the postponed tour, new Covid-19 regulations in Korea led to them just being pay-per-view live online shows. This is BTS, though – they weren't 'just' anything. If Bang Bang Con: The Live was intimate, this was extravagant (reported production costs were eight times as large), with banks of watching screens full of chanting and dancing ARMY, a full live band, a plethora of magnificent dancers, costume changes and the most incredible stage settings enhanced by AR technology.

Then there was the performance. The two-and-a-half-hour-long, twenty-three-track set for both nights was built around *Map of the Soul: 7*. Each of the members performed their solo tracks, with the rap and vocal line subunits also delivering 'UGH!' and '00.00 (Zero O'Clock)'. But the show was also about their journey. The opening 'ON' transitioned to 'N.O' and 'Boy in Luv' was mirrored by 'Boy With Luv' with 'DNA', 'Dope' and 'No More Dream' acting as a finale.

The group put everything into a stunning performance, but it was their interactions and the words they chose when speaking directly to fans that brought tears. They knew what people were enduring and felt it and their final words – 'we are not seven with you' – and the promise to meet again never sounded so heartfelt. Almost a million people across 191 countries watched the concert live (and many more since) and none could have been disappointed.

Having finally performed the tracks from their last album, BTS set about promoting the new one. The pandemic had turned so much upside down that any plans the group might have had for album concepts were overshadowed by their wish to reflect the experience they had shared with

ARMY. The new album had been in production for most of the year, with the process regularly documented on YouTube. The members themselves had played a greater part than ever in the making of the album, with each of them given an area to manage: Jimin was project manager for music; RM was music director; V was the visual director; Suga and Jin were in charge of the album jacket; J-Hope was in charge of choreography; and Jung Kook was made director of the lead single's music video. In addition, they contributed to the production or writing of every track on the new album (with the exception of 'Dynamite').

The first teaser photo showed all the members in rock-band style. Surrounded by instruments, all of them sported dark hair and looked serious and moody. Then individual pics dropped with the members shot in rooms that they had curated to reflect their personalities and their interests. Jimin was surrounded by flowers, Jung Kook was in a room full of speakers and J-Hope created a playful and colourful space, though perhaps the greatest impression was created by Suga in his blue crushed-velvet suit sitting with his slider-clad feet on a mirror.

The themes of self-reflection and hope carried through to the album, named *BE* to reflect the state of both individual existence and potential. The first half of the album was clearly contemplative. The opening track and lead single 'Life Goes On' was calm and understated. The title directly echoed the words they had spoken at the UN, and the song partnered 'Dynamite' (the two tracks book-ending the album) with the lyrics exuding sympathy and support for carrying on through difficult times. Hip-hop wrapped in cotton wool, it was neither upbeat nor a ballad. Instead, it drew you in with a simple melody and an accompaniment of warm and comforting guitars with subtle vocals giving the song depth and emotion.

'Fly To My Room' continues the theme with a realistic portrait of a numbing and lonely life under lockdown matched by an escape conjured by will power and optimism. The piano backing and light beat create an infectious R&B vibe and a new subunit of J-Hope and Suga with V and Jimin combining to elevate the song. It is, however, 'Blue & Grey', the final track of the reflective trilogy, that gathered most acclaim as the album was digested. Written by V, whose own vocals are particularly strong on the song, its poignancy and poetry are written large in haunting harmonization. Backed by strings and piano, it hits an emotional note with lyrics describing how it feels to be at your lowest ebb when you struggle to see the end of the tunnel.

At this point the album changes tack, beginning with their first skit since *Love Yourself: Her*. The track records their reaction to the news that 'Dynamite' had given them their first-ever number one on the Billboard Hot 100 chart – and it was Jung Kook's birthday too! Such joy changes the mood and prepares us for some uplifting pop. First up is 'Telepathy', which Suga claimed to have written in thirty minutes and rejected, only for the others to demand its inclusion when they heard it during *In the Soop*. It's a fun, 1980s-style bop full of auto-tune-heavy vocals that tell how this is just a moment compared with the time they will have left to make music.

Three tracks destined to become fan favourites completed the album. J-Hope's 'Dis-ease' is a song originating in his love-hate relationship with his work that became an upbeat old-school hip-hop track on the uncertainty of the pandemic. ARMY had seen Jung Kook working on the penultimate track 'Stay' in a YouTube vlog in August, but few were ready for the funky and addictive EDM beat and the sincerity of the message of how much BTS missed their fans. It was left to the effervescent 'Dynamite' to close a short and sweet album that showed more than ever that BTS truly empathized and connected with their millions of fans.

'Life Goes On' led the promotion of the album. Jung Kook made his directorial debut with the video, which was deliberately low-key and homely – no big-budget scenery or exuberant choreography, just a portrait of twenty-somethings going about their ordinary lives. It felt comforting, intimate and poignant as it switched from colour to home video and to black-and-white footage of the group singing in an empty stadium.

Days after the album release, they also performed the song from the Seoul Olympic Stadium for the AMAs (where they picked up Best Pop/Rock Group and Top Social Artist awards) looking positively angelic dressed in identical white and black outfits. They looked altogether more casual on *Good Morning America* and *The Late Late Show with James Corden* where they picked up the look from the video and sang in super-soft pyjamas.

While some critics preferred BTS's previous albums for their bigger and bolder ambitions, both musically and lyrically, few failed to appreciate how accurately they had reflected the times they were living through. ARMY had no such qualms, appreciating the quality, heartfelt nature of the tracks and the comfort they offered. *BE* topped the charts across the world, including in the US, where it became their fifth album to top the Billboard 200. Though 'Life Goes On' failed to repeat the global success of 'Dynamite', it did become BTS's third Billboard 100 number one in three months, making it the first-ever Korean-language song to top the charts – a huge achievement. The USA had fallen completely in love with BTS.

BANGTAN BOMB

GRAMMY NOMINATION NIGHT

Jimin, RM and V sit on the sofa in their dorm and watch the live Grammy nominations on TV. With RM as translator, the tension rises. Will they finally get their just deserts on pop music's biggest stage? And will Jung Kook get his hair done in time for the announcement? Not so long ago a Grammy nomination seemed a faraway dream for a group who struggled to get a foothold in the US, but now they were on the brink of one of their biggest-ever achievements. Jimin's reaction says it all: 'Nothing else matters now. We got it.'

Their success in the US had been acknowledged in November with their first Grammy nomination (not counting the nod that *Love Yourself: Tear* received for Best Recording Package) and was further recognized when they were named *Time* magazine's 2020 Entertainer of the Year. In winning the prestigious award the magazine described them as 'not just the biggest K-pop act on the charts. They've become the biggest band in the world – full stop.' Not that Korea had forgotten them. They swept the board at the 2020 MAMAs with eight awards, won six more at the MMAs and picked up the first-ever 'Special International Music' trophy at the Japan Record Awards.

Such success was a real fillip for the members and ARMY, but there was one issue that prevented them from being completely happy. In November, Suga had surgery on a shoulder that had been an ongoing problem since an accident in his trainee days and had to miss the performances at the 2020 MAMA and MMA award ceremonies while he recuperated. He was clearly on the group's mind at the MAMAs, where they took to the Seoul World Cup Stadium to perform 'ON' with a full marching band and to a rainbow tunnel set for a Michael Jackson homage performance of 'Dynamite'. Taking the stage in all white for 'Life Goes On', they were joined by a hologram of Suga, but the best was saved for last. After guest host James Corden had announced they had won Album of the Year, Jimin took out his phone and Suga was on the line, waiting to give the acceptance speech.

On Christmas Day, BTS were at the 2020 *SBS Gayo Daejeon*. It was taking place in Daegu, the hometown of Suga and V and a place where they had always wanted to perform. Poor Suga was still unable to join them on stage, but again the members ensured he was not forgotten. When they performed 'Black Swan', Jung Kook and J-Hope covered his verses with dance, but for 'Life Goes On' and 'Dynamite' the cutest snowman appeared on set to lip-sync Suga's lines and the members played along, with RM even singing, 'Ladies and gentlemen, I got the snowman!'

The New Year brought good news. Suga was back. His return at the Golden Disc Awards even overshadowed Jung Kook's new blond hair. Although he was unable to join the performance, he was there in person at the acceptance and reduced ARMY to tears as he said, 'After not showing my face for about two months because of my surgery, I felt like I was slowly being forgotten. That's why I tried my best to return as soon as I could.' They would and could never forget him.

By the time BTS made their debut appearance on the *MTV Unplugged* series in February, they were seven again. Icons of rock and pop from Nirvana to Jay-Z to Paul McCartney had performed on the series, but BTS were undaunted. The thirty-minute show was a gem. In sets that took them from an arcade games room to a concrete conservatory full of plants and flowers to a retro-style lounge, they performed stripped-down versions of songs from *BE*, chatted about the pandemic, what the songs meant to them as well as their connection with ARMY. They even added a cover that took everyone by surprise: a beautiful rendition of Coldplay's 'Fix You'.

The group continued to be as visible as possible to fans. They appeared on the popular Korean variety show *You Quiz On The Block*, where they met superfan Kim Jung-hyun who had gone viral with her dance cover of 'MIC Drop', and were guests on a special *Let's BTS*, a talk show where the members interviewed each other. Meanwhile, ARMY looked excitedly towards the Grammys, the most prestigious music awards in the world. When they had been nominated for an award, there were high hopes that they would triumph. But it was not to be. Lady Gaga and Ariana Grande took the Best Pop Duo/Group Performance prize for 'Rain on Me' and ARMY had to be satisfied with an electrifying performance of 'Dynamite' from a Seoul skyscraper helipad with the lights of the city as a background.

It had been over a year since they had climbed onto the Grammy stage with Lil Nas X and it had been the craziest of years. They were unable to tour, had been confined to their homes for long periods, and yet they had performed two full-length online concerts, broken more world records, released two blockbuster albums and topped the US single charts three times. They had reached out to ARMY for mutual support and as a result had strengthened the already solid bond between them. The constraints of the pandemic still showed few signs of easing, but fans knew BTS would continue to be there for them.

TWENTY-SEVEN

THE WELCOME GENERATION

The journey of BTS was entwined in the story of Big Hit Entertainment. Back in 2013, BTS were a boy group given little chance of success as they were backed by a music company dwarfed by those that dominated the Korean music industry. As the group struggled to make headway in the charts, so the company struggled with finances, but working together they both defied the odds and eventually became giants in their field.

In March 2021, Bang Si-hyuk announced that Big Hit Entertainment was changing its name to Hybe. The company was looking to expand its operations beyond music, and now Big Hit Music, BTS's new label, came under the Hybe business umbrella. This announcement was soon followed by another: Hybe had bought Scooter Braun's Ithaca Holdings, meaning that BTS now sat at the table with Justin Bieber, J Balvin and Demi Lovato. Another step towards world domination!

So much for business news. Excitement on the stock market floor was no match for ARMY's anticipation when they heard about new BTS releases. First came a new Japanese song titled 'Film Out', which Jung Kook had written alongside Iyori Shimizu, the vocalist of Japanese rock group Back Number. A soulful, sentimental ballad, it tells of the difficulty of letting go and looking towards the future. It is beautifully sung and the MV reflected the sensitive tone with the members dressed in white and fading in and out of the group scene (with some ARMY spotting similarities to the 'Fake Love' MV). 'Film Out', which reached number two in Japan, was used as the closing theme for the Japanese movie *Signal*, and in June was included in a new album, *BTS, the Best*, a compilation of their Japanese-language tracks since 2017 (with the English 'Dynamite' as a bonus).

With summer approaching and the pandemic still not easing up in many parts of the world, Doctor BTS decided it was time to prescribe another dose of cheer and chose 'Butter', a track written by the experienced Canadian songwriter Jenna Andrews. Inspired by Michael Jackson's 'Smooth Criminal' (and suggested by Ron Perry, the CEO of Columbia Records), it was pure dance-pop. Led by a snare-drum beat and funky bass, a cool vibe permeates the verse, the raps swell with soft swag and the chorus is infectiously catchy. Like their other English-language single 'Dynamite', the lyrics are fun and positive rather than profound, but do include plenty of 1990s references. Just like butter, it was super-smooth.

The dance-focused MV saw the boys add moves to the mix. Smooth, fun or expressive – or all three at once – each member gets their solo dance time in the spotlight (or, in this case, elevator). And, in a special moment as RM raps out his acknowledgement to the fans, together their bodies spell out A-R-M-Y. From the retro black-and-white suits to the colourful 1990s basketball gear to the shorts and skirts, the outfits are super stylish. And not a hair is out of place: Jimin with slicked-back rainbow locks, Jung Kook's long, vibrant purple look and J-Hope's hair as yellow as butter itself.

The video premiere added nearly another million to the 3 million record set by 'Dynamite', and with 108.2 million views, it became the most viewed YouTube video in the first twenty-four hours. The single reached the top ten in more than forty countries around the world, including number one in India, Colombia, Hungary, Malaysia, Singapore and Vietnam and, of course, South Korea and Japan. Globally, it was the most streamed track in its first twenty-four hours on Spotify. And it continued BTS's run of success in the US. 'Butter' went straight to the top of the Billboard Hot 100 and stayed there for five weeks, beating the record for a song debuting at number one set by Aerosmith's 'I Don't Want to Miss a Thing' way back in 1999.

Already settled in charts and hearts for the summer, the now obligatory remixes gave it a further boost. There was a 'Sweeter Remix', a 'Cooler Remix' and, best of all, a 'Hotter Remix'. This jumping, house-tinged version of the track even had its own re-made video with the members off the leash and free to goof around, smile and wink at the camera. And it didn't stop there. Soon a '*noraebang* (karaoke) version' appeared where the members perform the song karaoke-style. The single even got a late-summer boost with a remix featuring self-styled 'Hot Girl Coach' and superstar rapper Megan Thee Stallion, who added her own verse to the song, which was accompanied by the same artwork as the original single, but this time in hot pink.

BANGTAN BOMB

'BUTTER' IN 노래방 BEHIND THE SCENES

Over ten minutes of grown men goofing around like they are at a kids' party? When it's BTS what's not to love? Their karaoke video of 'Butter' was fun, but the scenes as they made it are a real throwback to barmy Bangtan at their best. Jin is hilarious with his constantly changing shades, Jimin makes Suga sing the high notes with ear-shattering consequences and RM and Jung Kook are a top comedy duo.

Meanwhile, the fun continued with the two-day livestreamed 2021 Muster Sowoozoo, with hundreds of screens of real-life bomb-waving ARMY again making up the audience. As always, BTS packed in the content. There were fewer games and less silliness than usual but that meant more musical content. ARMY feasted on the first live performance of 'Dis-ease' as well as a Korean version of their Japanese track 'Wishing On A Star'; took in an OT7 freestyle dance to 'Chicken Noodle Soup' featuring the now-iconic Jin improvisation of 'popping, popping, popping, popping'; and adored the seven-member performance of Suga's 'Daechwita', where they each wore traditional Korean *hanbok* (with Jin and V sporting some questionable – but very funny – fake facial hair) and took turns to rap verses – V's look has gone down in ARMY history as 'Taechwita'.

'I've actually worked with BTS on their last record, and I've just written a song for their new record. And they're like super, super cool guys as well.' BTS news doesn't usually come from the US but when Ed Sheeran uttered those words on American radio show *Most Requested Live*, ARMY ears pricked up. Big Hit Music had already announced a CD release of 'Butter' that featured a new track and now we knew it was a Sheeran-penned (along with Jenna Andrews, Johnny McDaid of Snow Patrol and super-producer Steve Mac) sure-fire hit.

'Permission to Dance' continued the English-language, good-vibes theme. It was 'dedicated to anyone', Big Hit Music said, 'who is having a bad day or is discouraged in the face of reality'. The song had elements of 'Dynamite' and 'Butter', and if the piano, strings and handclaps made it feel lighter, it was just as infectious and danceable. Some fans and critics thought the song lacked character and failed to fully use the members' talents, but that didn't stop it being a global hit. A second consecutive number one proved India had fallen for the Bangtan sound, but the big story was still the US where it replaced 'Butter' at the top of the charts: BTS's fifth number-one hit in just over ten months.

The video was a sun-baked vision of a post-pandemic world. The Western setting brought out the cowboy outfits with denim, white tees, embroidered shirts, fringed jackets and cowboy hats. Jung Kook set hearts a flutter by bringing back his emo look, Suga went for cute blue-grey locks, J-Hope was cool in peroxide white while the jury seemed to be out on RM's choice of neon-yellow hair. Fittingly, the choreography incorporated Western line-dancing moves, but mainly it was designed to be easy enough for anyone to copy.

The video focused on inclusiveness, from the diversity of people in age and race to incorporating international sign language in the dance moves. There were also thank-yous to ARMY through the purple balloons, the key service workers who had been on the frontline during the pandemic and the group's backroom team, who joined the dance – with even Hybe chairman Bang and CEO Park Ji-won getting involved in the fun.

They promoted 'Permission to Dance' on a two-day takeover of *The Tonight Show Starring Jimmy Fallon*, where they performed in an empty shopping mall full of purple balloons, and on BBC Radio 1's *Live Lounge*, where they also continued the show's tradition of performing a cover. They chose to sing a version of Puff Daddy and Faith Evans' 1997 hit 'I'll Be Missing You'. It was a sensitive and superb cover, with Suga and J-Hope adding Korean raps to speak about how they missed their fans and looked forward to good times in the future. It was a heartfelt message, as they had just had to finally admit defeat and completely cancel the Map of the Soul Tour. The news was devastating for thousands of ARMY for whom the anticipation of the concerts was a beacon of hope at a bleak time, and it was also a serious setback for BTS members who were desperate to play in front of their fans.

In September 2021, they returned to a favourite venue to perform 'Permission to Dance': the United Nations General Assembly. South Korean President Moon Jae-in introduced them as 'probably the artist that is most loved by people around the world,' and noted that they have been designated as the 'special presidential envoy for future generations and culture'. For their part BTS spoke about young people's focus on environmental issues. Jin rejected the term 'Covid's lost generation', insisting that they are the 'welcome generation' who embrace change and keep forging ahead. Their recorded performance showed them popping up from behind the podium of the iconic building, dancing down the aisles and heading for the gardens, where they were joined by a troupe of dancers.

All summer BTS had kept the content coming, and they still had one more surprise to spring on ARMY. It was no secret that BTS loved Coldplay. J-Hope and RM had been to see them perform back in 2017, V regularly cited them among his favourites and, apart from BTS themselves, they were the most featured artist on Jin's Spotify playlist. Coldplay's Chris

Martin had made clear the feeling was mutual and had been delighted by BTS' 'Fix You' cover. A collaboration had often been rumoured, but no one expected 'My Universe', a track on Coldplay's forthcoming album, to feature South Korea's finest.

The idea of two massive groups from different countries and genres coming together fit the lyrics about love knowing no boundaries and triumphing over prejudice perfectly. Written by Coldplay with BTS's rap line adding their own Korean lyrics, the song was slice of quality electro-pop with a great anthemic chorus. The sci-fi video cleverly brought the two groups together, despite them being physically on opposite sides of the world, by casting Coldplay, BTS and fictional alien Supernova7 as rebel outfits coming together as holograms to break the evil Silencers' music ban.

Coldplay initially performed the song without BTS, although, to his credit, Chris Martin twice attempted to sing the Korean parts. However, for the 2021 Global Citizen Festival, which took place in Central Park in New York, BTS performed on screen in a video recorded in Seoul. On this occasion, Chris Martin introduced the song by saying: 'We collaborated with a band and we took their average age up about fifteen years, but it's been one of the most fun things we've ever done.' The coming together of two giants of pop was always going to be a commercial success and it made an impact on charts around the globe. It was their number one in the US Billboard Hot 100 that made the headlines, though – their sixth chart topper in just twenty-three months. Only The Beatles had amassed as many in a shorter time.

It was now two years since BTS had performed a live concert in front of their fans. Their virtual concerts had embraced the benefits of technology, utilized their back catalogue and big hits with some incredible set designs, but for a group who derived their energy from their fans it was hard to bear. To their credit they practised what they preached, remaining patient and waiting for the good times. To this end they devised a Permission to Dance on Stage show to be performed on two nights in October 2021 in Seoul, where newly-tightened pandemic restrictions meant it had to be online only, but also four dates in LA in November in front of real-life, chanting, lightstick-waving, dancing fans.

The huge Seoul Olympic Stadium (the site of their last in-person concert) with its 70,000 empty seats must have made it seem more like a rehearsal than a concert. With V having to sit out of the choreography due to a leg injury, it was doubly difficult, but they put on a great show regardless. In a test of stamina and a show of unity, all seven took part in every song; no subunits or solos to take a breath. They played the hits and fan favourites from every era, the sets – from the engulfing flames of 'Fire' to the mirror screens of 'Blue & Grey' to the giant furniture of 'Life Goes On' – were stunning, and the variety of costumes were spot-on. The emotion of the occasion built as the members delivered their 'ments' (the K-pop term for artists' short speeches to the audience) full of vulnerability, honesty and hope, and there could not have been many dry eyes among the 1.02 million ARMY watching from 191 different countries by the time they performed 'Spring Day' and 'Permission to Dance'.

For those with tickets to see the group in LA, a month must have seemed like a year. Especially as excitement intensified as the concert drew near. The preceding week saw BTS nominated for another Grammy: in 2022 they would once again be contenders in the Best Pop Duo/Group Performance category, but ARMY were infuriated that 'Butter', which had spent ten weeks at the top of the Billboard Hot 100 chart, had not been nominated in the Best Song category. As if to prove their point, just days later they won 'Favourite Pop Song' at the AMAs in LA, where they were also honoured as Artist of the Year for the first time and graced the ceremony by sharing a stage with Coldplay, performing 'My Universe' in front of a live audience!

After twenty-five long months, BTS and their fans were face to face once more as the group began their four-concert series at the packed SoFi Stadium. V's greeting, 'It's been a long, long time. Hello, ARMY!' was greeted by screams from every corner of the venue. Dressed in all-white, the group wasted no time in making an impression as, joined by a marching band, drummers and dancers, they went straight into an energetic rendition of 'ON', with red fireworks soon lighting up the stadium. BTS were back…

'Now we're charged back up thanks to you guys,' RM remarked during one concert, and Jung Kook added, 'Nothing can stop ARMY and BTS.'

These four nights proved their point. The LA setlist followed that of Seoul, with all seven members on stage for each song. It was full of their hits, ARMY favourites and songs from *Map of the Soul: 7* and *BE* that they had previously been unable to perform in front of a live audience. The members were clearly loving every minute; they fizzed with energy and moved effortlessly from ebullient dance hits to tender ballads and seemed closer than ever to one other as they joked their way through the night.

It was always going to be special, but it was more than that. On top of the performances, the chemistry and the emotion were great moments such as ARMY celebrating Jin's upcoming birthday, V performing in full *Squid Game* costume (with Jin appearing in pigtails as a nod to Young-hee, aka The Doll), and the whole septet touring the audience on mobile pods during 'Telepathy'. On day two, Megan Thee Stallion joined them for 'Butter', and Chris Martin took the stage for 'My Universe' during the final night's encore. At the end of the shows, the members took turns expressing what the concerts had meant to them. RM and V were reduced to tears and J-Hope and Jimin had to speak in Korean to precisely express their emotions. What was crystal clear was that however strong their feelings for ARMY, they were reciprocated 50,000 times over in the stadium.

The LA shows had been sandwiched between noteworthy appearances on *The Late Late Show with James Corden*. The first had been their first face-to-face meeting with the show's host for two years. And it was awkward. RM had wasted no time in remarking to Corden: 'You've been in some hot water with ARMY. Are you all right?' He was referencing the backlash to a weak joke that the man who liked being called Papa Mochi had made in which he implied that the BTS fanbase was just fifteen-year-old girls. Corden, who had received a barrage of complaints for the comment, was quick to apologize for the quip and double down on his admiration for the group by saying, 'I'm forty-three years old, and I consider myself to be one of the biggest BTS fans on planet Earth.'

BTS seemed happy with the resolution and the group returned after their triumphant LA concerts to perform 'Butter' as part of the show's thousandth-episode celebrations. Later in December, they were back yet again. In 2020, BTS had famously taken part in the show's 'Carpool

Karaoke' segment, but James Corden now had a new insert called 'Crosswalk Concert'. BTS's 'concert' took place outside the LA studio on a crossing on Beverly Boulevard. 'We just played for 50,000 people at SoFi Stadium, and now he wants us to play next to some gas station,' RM wisecracked. Nevertheless, when the pedestrian sign lit up, out they trotted in their 'Butter' outfits and performed in front of the waiting traffic. While they waited for the next light change, they swapped into their 'Permission to Dance' outfits and took their place mid-street for another quick performance.

Before their spell in California came to a close, BTS also found time to play one more time to a live audience with a short set at the 2021 Jingle Ball, where Ed Sheeran and Doja Cat were also on the bill. They also discovered that back home, they had won nine awards at the MAMAs, including winning all four *daesangs* for the third consecutive year. They had now collected the most awards of any artist in the prestigious show's history.

The American trip had capped an incredible year for BTS in which, despite all the restrictions and obstacles they faced, they had achieved so much. From a seminal speech at the United Nations, to three US number-one singles, appearing on *MTV Unplugged*, breaking so many records (twenty-three at that point) they entered the Guinness World Records 2022 Hall of Fame, becoming Louis Vuitton house ambassadors and even launching their own BTS Meal at McDonald's. Most of all they had consoled, entertained, been supported by and finally been reunited with ARMY. There was so much to look forward to in 2022 – but the future always has surprises in store…

TWENTY-EIGHT

NOT THE END

Over the course of the Covid-19 pandemic, BTS had worked tirelessly to engage with fans and produce content while at the same time enduring their own restrictions and stresses. They had achieved amazing success that had placed them among a small group of truly elite global celebrities. Such accomplishments had not come easy. Both physically and emotionally, it had taken its toll on all seven of the members. The time had come to relax and recharge in an 'extended period of rest'. It was to be the first time since their debut that they would be able to spend the holiday season with their families.

As with their last break in 2019, ARMY were understanding, especially as Big Hit Music had promised a new album in the pipeline and more live concerts, beginning with more Permission to Dance on Stage in Seoul in March. Understanding soon turned to concern on Boxing Day 2021, when it was revealed that RM, Jin and Suga had all contracted Covid-19 on their travels. Thankfully, all three had received their second vaccinations in August and their symptoms were not serious, so they followed the South Korean regulations and took care of themselves in quarantine.

As ever, fans were not short of BTS entertainment – there was now a second series of *In the Soop*, filmed in late summer 2021. This time the members – and Jung Kook's new Dobermann puppy, Bam – stayed in a villa in a mountain forest. Once again, there was plenty of cooking, gaming, sports, music and discussion. ARMY especially loved Jin and Jung Kook playing *Just Dance,* J-Hope getting scared at the abandoned house, watching the Olympics together and anything with Bam, but most of all it was fabulous to see the members' true personalities shine through without the stresses of work and fame.

Also in December, all seven members had shared their first posts on their new personal Instagram accounts. Their usernames were mostly logical, with Jin taking @jin, Suga @agustd, Jimin @j.m, and V @thv, but RM took @rkive (as in archive) and J-Hope went with @uarmyhope (a play on his 'you are my hope' catchphrase but with 'army' in there too – cute!). Jung Kook initially called his @abcdefghi__lmnopqrstuvwxyz but later changed it to @jungkook.97 before deleting the account in February 2023. To ARMY's delight, all seven were soon posting regularly and casual selfies, arty portraits and pics of V's dog Yeontan were soon amassing millions of likes.

By the middle of January, the quarantiners had recovered and the members had a get-together. Jung Kook posted a video that showed them tucking into strawberries that Jin had picked at his uncle's farm as well as various other snacks. Among these were *bungeoppang*, a Korean fish-shaped pastry (of RM's famous 'ain't no fish inside!' exclamation), which led to choruses of 'Baby Shark' and 'Super Tuna', the little ditty Jin had uploaded in December that – to his surprise – had gone viral.

A new BTS fantasy series, *7Fates: Chakho*, had also dropped and amassed 15 million views in just two days. A Korean folklore-inspired webtoon (also available on Wattpad as a webnovel), it told the story of seven men fighting supernatural creatures known as '*beom*' (the archaic word for tiger in Korean) in the cyberpunk metropolis of Sin-si. Each of the characters was based on a BTS member, although fictional and having different names, they looked like and shared many character traits with their Bangtan inspirations. For those more interested in the group's musical output, the OST was a powerful ballad called 'Stay Alive', written and produced by Suga and sung by Jung Kook. The MV featured all the members in a video that switched between real-life members and elements of the webtoon.

If it seemed things were looking up, ARMY soon received another knockback when it was announced that Jimin had not only tested positive for Covid but had also been rushed to hospital to receive surgery for acute appendicitis. No sooner had he been released from hospital than it was revealed that V had now also tested positive. The pandemic hadn't finished messing up lives yet and there were concerns for the three scheduled Permission to Dance on Stage: Seoul concerts in mid-March.

The concerts at the Olympic Stadium did get the go ahead, and both V and Jimin had recovered speedily. However, the long-awaited shows were not to be quite the celebration of Korean ARMY dreams. Covid was still a threat and the government had limited each show in the 70,000-capacity stadium to just 15,000 fans. In addition, as a precaution to avoid spreading the airborne virus, facemasks were required and any shouting, chanting or standing up during the show was prohibited. Instead, attendees were given clappers to generate noise.

'ARMY, since you can't scream, we will scream for you!' shouted J-Hope. It was clear from the outset that BTS were not going to let these limitations ruin their homecoming. They did their utmost to engage with fans and create sense of togetherness, even with the thousands watching on livestreams. The setlist remained similar, with 'Black Swan' taking the audience's breath away and the party vibe of the remixes of 'Boy With Luv' and 'Dynamite' enhanced by the appearance of their live band Ghost. The inclusion of 'Home' in the main set was particularly poignant. They were at pains to point out that 'Home' was wherever ARMY was, but at the same time stressing that Seoul meant something very special to them.

The very next day, at the Japan Gold Disc Awards, BTS picked up ten trophies, including 'Best Asian Artist' for the fourth consecutive year. Breaking their previous year's record of eight awards, they were confirmed as Japan's most successful foreign artists ever. Many ARMY doubted such success would greet them in the US, where they suspected the forthcoming Grammys would snub the group again. They were right.

BTS didn't win a Grammy at the MGM Grand Garden Arena in Las

Vegas, but most agreed they were unofficial winners both on the red carpet and on stage at the awards. On the carpet they posed in personalized tan, chocolate, white or slate-blue Louis Vuitton suits, with each member wearing a floral pin attached to their silk shirt: V took the prize with a giant floral bouquet brooch, but it was Jung Kook whose lip and other piercings and hand tattoos caught not just ARMY's but the world's attention, with the 'Guy in the Blue Suit', 'Guy in the Middle', and 'Piercing Guy' all trending on social media.

Jung Kook had got the all-clear to perform just in time, after testing positive for Covid upon arrival in the USA, but Jin, still recovering after surgery to his index finger, was to avoid strenuous choreography on doctor's orders. In a magnificent James Bond-style spy-themed performance, he played the man at the controls while the six mesmerized the crowd with their sharp black suits and even sharper dance moves. It was a performance played out with wit and style from the moment V, sitting in the audience, got the song going with a whisper in Olivia Rodrigo's ear and a flick of a card towards the stage. In the following days, BTS became one of the top searches on Google as ARMY recruits rocketed yet again.

There was no way what happened in Vegas was going to stay in Vegas. Especially as BTS practically took over the city for the following week. They had sold out the 200,000 plus tickets for the four shows at the Allegiant Stadium just through fan-club pre-sales and booked the MGM Grand Garden Arena (that year's Grammys venue) for a Live Play stream with a photo zone and live broadcasts from the soundcheck as well as the concerts, for ARMY who weren't lucky enough to get a ticket to the stadium. There were BTS-themed rooms in eleven different hotels in the city, a pop-up Korean café, a BTS water show at the famous Fountains of Bellagio and purple lighting nearly everywhere.

Thousands flocked to Vegas from all over the globe to see the last in the series of Permission to Dance on Stage concerts. Despite Jin having to perform some parts of the set while seated due to lingering pain in his finger, few were disappointed. 'I heard that Las Vegas is a city of miracles built in the desert,' proclaimed RM at the beginning of the show. 'It's a miracle that we are together like this today. If BTS and ARMYs are together, the desert becomes the sea.' This time, BTS had a massive audience in full voice and the two played off each other, never more so than when they added crowd pleasers 'Anpanman' and 'Go Go' to the encore set. At the end of the show, the watching fans were drained from chanting, screaming and pure exhilaration, but most still caught the message, '2022.06.10', and the tagline, 'We are bulletproof'.

Before then there was important business to attend to. Jimin released 'With You', a gorgeous ballad which saw him duet with former Wanna One singer Ha Sung-woon for the bittersweet romantic TV series *Our Blues* OST. And indeed, Suga produced, co-wrote and featured on Psy's new single 'That That'. But perhaps most importantly, the whole group went to the White House in Washington, DC to meet with President Biden. They were there to speak out about the more than 300 per cent rise in hate crimes against Asian-American people in the wake of the Covid-19 pandemic. President Biden sweetly played 'Butter' to make the group feel welcome and stressed his support of their messages of respect and understanding to all people.

Back home, details of the new album had been announced and it had provoked troubled thoughts among some ARMY. In recent years, talk of BTS's mandatory military enlistment had slowly intensified. Jin's deadline for enlisting arrived in December 2022, with the others' deadline dates looming by the end of the year in which they turn thirty. The members had no objections and although there had been some attempts from third parties to grant them exemption from service, none of these had been successful. And now Big Hit were releasing an anthology that spanned their career to date. Though nothing explicit had been said, it felt not so much the end of an era, but a sudden end.

Proof was released just days before the ninth anniversary of their debut. The three-disc album comprised forty-eight tracks, including singles, demo versions, songs selected by each member, and three brand-new tracks. In the pre-release 'Proof of Inspiration', a series of short videos, the members each shared how being part of BTS had enabled them to grow as musicians and find their own identity. They had each chosen two tracks (one subunit and one solo) for the album to express their feelings and their relationship with ARMY: V chose 'Singularity' and 'Zero O'Clock'; Jin 'Moon' and

'Jamais Vu'; Jimin 'Filter' and 'Friends'; Jung Kook 'Euphoria' and 'Dimple'; RM 'Intro: Persona' and 'Stay'; Suga 'Trivia: Seesaw' and 'Cypher Pt. 3: Killer'; and J-Hope 'Her' and 'Outro: Ego'.

The concept photos were also focused on the journey they had made as a group. The first set, titled 'Proof', featured the seven looking deadly serious and dressed all in black in front of a bullet-ridden vault. It brought back memories of the early days and reminded everyone of how they had survived the many 'shots' that had come their way. The second set, 'Door', was a complete contrast. They were all wearing pastel-coloured soft outfits against a chiffon curtain background and exuded an ethereal glow. As ever, theories abounded, but the metaphors for where they had come from and where they were now were clear to all.

The three discs of *Proof* follow the growth of the group in different ways. The first disc charts the journey through all of their singles; the second focuses on solos and subunits; and the third (which is not available to stream and is only included in the physical versions, with the exception of 'For Youth') is largely demo versions of previously released songs. Within these choices are a number of interesting tracks, including the album's very first track, 'Born Singer', a remaster of their pre-debut reworking of J. Cole's 'Born Sinner' (which had become a concert favourite); Jung Kook's a cappella rendition of 'Still with You', 'Boy in Luv' featuring its original bridge, Jimin joining Suga on 'Tony Montana' and Jin's all-English demo of 'Epiphany'.

Disc two kicked off with a brand-new track, 'Run BTS', on which RM, J-Hope, Jung Kook and Suga had all contributed to the songwriting. To a driving guitar and insistent beat, it was old-school BTS delivered by today's mature, confident version of the group, with lyrics looking back at the hardships they had faced over the years and their determination to overcome them. And among the demos on the third disc, there were two previously completely unheard tracks: 'Quotation Mark', a tender hip-hop number by RM, J-Hope and Jung Kook (very early BTS vibes), and 'Young Love', a hopelessly romantic RM and Jung Kook duet that could also have originated in the school trilogy era. The anthology ended with a new love song to ARMY, the epic 'For Youth'. From the opening sample of a stadium full of ARMYs singing 'Young Forever', through the allusions to favourite tracks, to V's final promise to be with them forever, it is a guaranteed tear-fest.

The new single, though, could be found at the end of the first disc. 'Yet To Come (The Most Beautiful Moment)' followed the rest of their singles, from 'No More Dream' to 'Butter'. A mid-tempo, hip-hop-tinged ballad, it beautifully conveyed an atmosphere and an all-encompassing message: for all our success, we are the same seven people we always were; we have had some amazing times, but there will be more in the future. It was a promise that, despite the looming threat of military enlistment, BTS would be back, eventually.

If the song acted as a pure comfort blanket for disconsolate ARMY, the video, filmed in a desert under a pure blue sky, reinforced the effect. The white-clad members are in a thoughtful (not sad or playful) mood, and the references to previous videos keep coming – from the rusty 'You Never Walk Alone' merry-go-round of 'Spring Day' to the winged statue from 'Blood Sweat & Tears' to the yellow school bus of 'No More Dream'.

For the first time since 'ON', BTS took to the music shows on Korean TV to promote the single. They registered nine wins, including taking maximum points for the fifth time on *M Countdown*. Meanwhile, the album and single were both dominating charts around the world, with reviewers and critics universally admiring how the anthology managed to avoid being just a greatest-hits collection and was instead a genuine record of the history of the group.

In the midst of all this, they had an emotional ninth-anniversary *festa* to undertake. It included the usual family portraits and photos, a song for ARMY (Jung Kook's deeply affecting 'My You') and 'Proof Live', a short livestream concert. Back in the desert, they performed 'Born Singer', 'Yet to Come (The Most Beautiful Moment)' with US artist Anderson .Paak on drums, and 'Young Forever'.

But 'The 2022 Real Dinner Party' on the final evening overshadowed all the other celebrations. Over dinner, the seven talked about getting friendship tattoos and reminisced about sharing a dorm now that they had all moved into their own apartments. Then things got serious. They revealed how the pandemic had wrecked their plans to end 'Phase 1' after the Map of the Soul world tour had been completed. Instead, as we saw, they worked hard to bring 'Dynamite', 'Life Goes On', 'Butter', 'Permission to Dance' and other content to the fans. Finally, they said it: in the immediate future, they were taking a break from group activities and concentrating on solo projects.

As each member spoke, some in tears, it was clear that it had been a difficult decision. However, they all were exhausted, felt pressured by group obligations and unable to move on with their lives. They expressed their nervousness over ARMY's reaction to the announcement, but they remained confident their bond was strong enough to endure.

On the stock market, Hybe shares plummeted. The word 'hiatus' had been used in an English (mis)translation, implying a long-term break, or even a split. This was quickly refuted with the proof that they were filming a new *Run BTS!* series and a promise that they would reunite in 2025, post-military. Some ARMY were even able to joke that, at five and a half hours between panic and resolution, it was the shortest hiatus ever!

ARMY were of course heartbroken, but also understanding and supportive. The group's messages on change and growth over recent years had not fallen on deaf ears and ARMY had also taken on board the importance of patience and optimism. Perhaps, for many, the news hadn't properly sunk in yet. After all, it didn't appear that much had changed. Within weeks, a collaboration with star producer Benny Blanco and legendary rapper Snoop Dogg had dropped. 'Bad Decision' was catchy and instantly danceable with a fun video that saw Blanco affectionately salute ARMY as he played a BTS superfan getting ready for a concert.

A new series of *Run BTS!* specials had also begun, with the group testing out their telepathic connection to each other with not completely successful but always entertaining results. Other specials released through the rest of year featured aerial yoga and a BTS Dalbang TV Special in which they each presented live shows, including Suga painting, J-Hope unboxing toys and V hosting his own 'Golf Show'. By the end of the year these and all the previous episodes (over 150 of them) had been uploaded onto YouTube.

The members were also still very present on social media. On Instagram they had begun showing the '7' friendship tattoos they had discussed getting at the *festa* 'Dinner Party'. So far RM had his above the ankle, J-Hope's was on his calf, Jimin's on his finger, Jung Kook behind his ear and Jin's on the side of his waist. Meanwhile, solo projects were also emerging. Jung Kook had joined Charlie Puth on his single 'Left and Right'; J-Hope released a solo album, *Jack In The Box*, linked up with Korean rapper Crush on the celebratory 'Rush Hour' and wowed crowds in his solo headline at Lollapalooza 2022 in Chicago; and V enjoyed a getaway with his Wooga Squad in an *In The Soop: Friendcation* spinoff.

And then they were back together again. On 15 October, the city of Busan was taken over by BTS just as Vegas was. The Lotte World Adventure theme park had BTS-themed attractions, pop-up booths and special events took place throughout the city, the museum had a BTS exhibition and the city was bathed in purple light. BTS were in town to perform a 'Yet to Come' concert in support of the city's campaign to host the World Expo in 2030.

If the Permission to Dance on Stage tours had been a catch-up with ARMY and 'Proof' charted BTS's journey so far, then 'Yet to Come' was a celebration of the present. The seven gave everything as they sang and danced their way through nineteen songs that displayed just how talented they were – right now. The setlist included the first live rendition of 'Run BTS', spine-tingling vocals and power rapping in performances of past and present subunit tracks, electrifying hit singles with killer choreography, 'Ma City' (Busan is the hometown of Jimin and Jung Kook) and, as a new addition to the ARMY-singalong encore set, 'For Youth'. As a concert it was exhilarating, and as an end of chapter concert it was a triumph. But what it was *not* was a farewell concert.

The message that began when Suga kept hold of the mic at the end of 'MIC Drop' instead of letting it fall as usual continued through the final ments: this was not the end. 'I believe what we've done so far is just a taste,' said Jimin, while Suga added, 'Let's grow old together.' The immediate future for each of the members was unclear, but they asked ARMY to believe in them. 'Our seven hearts are unified,' said RM. 'And if you trust us, whatever happens, we'll overcome it all.'

There had been considerable discussion about the members' military service, with many public figures advocating cancelling or reducing the time they would have to serve. However, the day after the Busan concert, Big Hit ended the debate by announcing that Jin was no longer deferring his enrolment. He would enlist when promotions for his debut solo single 'The Astronaut' were over, and the rest of the group would follow over the next year or so.

The wheels may have stopped for a while, but the engine kept humming. In November, BTS earned not the usual one, but three nominations for the 2023 Grammys. They would be considered for Best Pop Duo/Group Performance for the third year in a row for their Coldplay collaboration, 'My Universe', as well as Best Music Video for 'Yet to Come' and for Album of the Year as featured artists on Coldplay's *Music of the Spheres*. ARMY had learned not to hold their breath in anticipation, but at the more appreciative AMAs, they won Favorite Pop Duo or Group for the fourth consecutive year as well as taking the inaugural Favorite K-Pop Artist award.

Back at the MAMAs, the group picked up the awards for Album of the Year and Best Male Group as well as Worldwide Icon of the Year award and Worldwide Fan's Choice. Suga pipped J-Hope for Best Collaboration with 'That That' beating 'Rush Hour', but J-Hope won Most Popular Male Artist. Meanwhile, after releasing a choreography video for 'Run BTS', their dance challenge hit nearly 4 billion views. It was clear BTS were going nowhere.

On 12 December, eight days after his thirtieth birthday, Jin officially enlisted in the South Korean military. Exactly nine and a half years after their debut, BTS were no longer seven. The year 2025 seemed a long way off, but Big Hit did their best to reassure ARMY that they would be a group again. They are not the first Korean group to have a forced break due to military service, and many popular groups survive the career interval. Super Junior came back after a ten-year absence, 2PM reappeared in 2021, even the scandal-rocked Big Bang made a successful return in 2022, and both EXO and SHINee have scheduled 2023 comebacks. On an international level, meanwhile, groups such as the Jonas Brothers, Take That, Fall Out Boy and My Chemical Romance have all made massive comebacks after a hiatus.

Some groups find their popularity has diminished in their absence and struggle to make a fresh impact. There should be few such worries for BTS: they are a group like no other. In an interview with *Vogue Spain* RM talked directly on the subject, saying, 'Many bands disband and fall apart but I hope that's not what happens with BTS. I just love music, love my job, love my members and I love myself.' When we look back at their career it seems that everything BTS have been through and achieved has prepared them for this time and the days ahead.

As teenage trainees they faced hardships such as homesickness, hunger and fatigue that even the military will find hard to match. They were required to learn languages, songs and complex choreography, and rapidly get up to speed on any area they found difficult. They adapted to public interviews, live performances and increasing fan interest. And they fought against the odds, battling to succeed against groups backed by the bigger, wealthier companies.

BTS also had, and still have, a reason to survive as a group. They have given a voice to a generation that is so often ignored. They speak of opportunity, equality, self-respect and the future of the planet and have inspired thousands to fight for social justice. The connection they have formed with fans throughout the world is unprecedented. Since the months before their debut, the BTS members have been frank and open in their regular communications with fans. They treat them like friends, having fun and being unafraid to confront problems. That is why the bond is strong and the love between BTS and ARMY will endure.

BTS are also at the height of their popularity. Estimates vary wildly, but it is safe to say there are well over 50 million fans worldwide and the number is still growing. None of the groups mentioned above had such a following before their break. In 2022, they broke records for most followers for a music group on Instagram, TikTok and Twitter, they have more number-one hits on the Billboard 100 chart than any other artist over the last ten years, and they were the first artist in iTunes history to have eight songs reach number one in 100 countries. They are admired the world over and that amount of love takes a long time to dissipate.

Each of the member's solo work finds the same incredible response.

There can be little doubt that they will continue to develop as solo artists now they have the time and space to grow. This does not detract from their commitment to BTS as a group. They have an amazing camaraderie. They are a band of brothers who have stood by each other in good times and bad. They talk through any disagreements, face challenges and setbacks as a unit and always emerge stronger than ever.

What BTS have achieved is beyond anyone's wildest dreams. They have produced the most incredible music, shown they are consummate performers on stage and screen and even in front of empty stadiums. They are loved on every continent in the world – the kind of popularity only enjoyed by a select few like Elvis, The Beatles and Michael Jackson. Once innocent young boys, they have all grown to be switched-on, intelligent and sensitive men. And they have been a constant source of entertainment, inspiration, comfort and succour to millions of fans.

There will be disappointment, sadness and even tears at the group's absence, but BTS are not going anywhere. They have promised to reunite as soon as possible and there is no doubt that their fabulous solo output will sustain ARMY until then. The story has not finished. The future begins now – and it is full of hope.

'No matter what happens, everything will be fine. I don't know what's going to happen, but I just want us to do our jobs and be with our fans for as long as we can. Nothing else would really matter.' – Suga

GLOSSARY

K-pop has its own distinct culture and vocabulary, so you might find some of the words and concepts unfamiliar. The following is a reference to some of the Korean and K-pop-specific words used in the book.

4D: A K-pop description of someone who is quirky or eccentric. Intended as a compliment.

Aegyo: A display of cuteness through facial expressions or body language.

Ahjae joke: A terrible joke or pun, a 'dad joke'.

All-kill: When a song simultaneously goes to number one in a number of charts, usually immediately after release.

ARMY: The official name given to BTS fans, standing for 'Adorable Representative MC for Youth'.

Bias: A personal favourite of a group.

Bias wrecker: A group member who does something (good) to question or change your bias.

Big Three: Historically, the three biggest, most successful and dominant entertainment companies in K-pop: YG Entertainment, SM Entertainment and JYP Entertainment.

Bonsang: A prize given to up to twelve different acts at an award ceremony (less prestigious than a *daesang*).

Chocolate abs: Defined abdominal muscles that resemble the subdivided parts of a chocolate bar – also known as a six-pack.

Comeback: When an artist releases a new single, mini-album or album and promotes them with TV broadcasts or performances.

Daebak: A word to describe a great success or something awesome, or an exclamation similar to 'wow!'

Daesang: The prestigious 'Grand Prize' at a Music Awards, awarded for artist, song or album of the year.

Debut: An act's first performance (usually on TV). The official launch of an act is a crucial opportunity to make an impression on the watching public.

Fandom: Short for 'fan domain', it includes everything that goes on in the fan community, from fan clubs to online forums.

Festa: A festival or celebration.

Gayo: Any kind of pop music.

Hallyu: Refers to 'The Korean Wave', a growing interest in South Korean culture that has spread worldwide in the twenty-first century.

Hwaiting!: An exclamation of support and encouragement similar to sports fans' cries of 'Come on!' – it translates as 'Fighting!'

Hyung: A Korean mark of respect spoken by a man to an older brother or close older male friend. It can stand alongside or be used in conjunction with the name, such as 'Namjoon-hyung'.

Idol: An artist in mainstream and commercial K-pop.

Line: A word used to link together group members or friends. Often used with a year (e.g. 95 line) to group individuals born in that year or with a group designation such as 'rap line' or 'vocal line'.

Maknae: The youngest member of a family; as such they are allowed to be silly or mischievous and are expected to be cute. In K-pop, this applies to the youngest member of a group.

Ment: The short speeches that happen when the members of a K-pop group stop performing to address the audience, usually at the beginning and end of a concert.

Mini-album: An album containing four to six songs.

MV: Abbreviation for 'Music Video', usually uploaded on YouTube.

Noona: The name a man gives to an older female.

Rookie: A group who has debuted but is still in their first – or sometimes, second – year.

Satoori: Korean word for 'regional dialect'.

Selca: A selfie.

Single album: Like an EP with a lead song and one or two other songs.

Stan: A passionate fan. Also used as a verb, as in 'You should stan Jimin.'

Teaser: Photos, messages and short videos put out before the release of a single, album or concert.

Trainee: A young performer signed to an entertainment company in order to train in dance, singing and other performing arts with a view to becoming an idol.

Underground: Non-commercial-focused acts who work outside the mainstream. Comparable with the English music term 'indie'.

Visual: The group member who is considered the most beautiful or a member who is included in the group primarily because of their looks.

ACKNOWLEDGEMENTS

This is now the third edition of *BTS: Icons of K-pop*. I don't think any of us who originally worked on the book telling the story of a successful pop group realized quite how far their journey would take them. I would like to thank Louise Dixon at Michael O'Mara Books for initiating the project, Nora Besley whose interest in BTS first prompted the idea and Lisa Hughes for reading drafts and suggesting improvements in every edition. It is, however, Becca Wright at Michael O'Mara Books who has driven the book from the very start. Without her invaluable editorial advice and indispensable knowledge and understanding of BTS and K-pop, it would have been a lesser work and a considerably more difficult endeavour.

PICTURE CREDITS

Page 1: Han Myung-Gu / WireImage / Getty Images (both)

Page 2: Paul Zimmerman / Getty Images (top); John Shearer / Getty Images (bottom)

Page 3: RB / Bauer-Griffin / GC Images / Getty Images (top); John Salangsang / BFA / REX / Shutterstock (bottom)

Page 4–5: Steve Granitz / WireImage / Getty Images

Page 6: The Asahi Shimbun via Getty Images (top); Steve Granitz / WireImage / Getty Images (bottom)

Page 7: Kevin Winter / Getty Images for The Recording Academy (top); Kevin Winter / Getty Images for MRC (bottom)

Page 8: Axelle Bauer-Griffin / FilmMagic / Getty Images (top); Cliff Lipson / CBS via Getty Images (bottom)